ANALYSIS
AND EXILE

For Stephen Jonathan Christian Heller

ANALYSIS
AND EXILE
BOYHOOD, LOSS AND THE
LESSONS OF ANNA FREUD

VIVIAN HELLER

First published in 2022 by Confer Books, an imprint of Confer Ltd

www.confer.uk.com

Registered office:
Brody House, Strype Street, London E1 7LQ

1 3 5 7 9 10 8 6 4 2

This is a work of nonfiction. Some names and identifying details may have been changed or omitted to protect the privacy of individuals.
"The Fate of the Drives in School Compositions", translated by Inge Schneier Hoffman, from A WAY OF LOOKING AT THINGS: SELECTED PAPERS 1930 TO 1980 by Erik H. Erikson, edited by Stephen Schlein, Ph.D. Copyright© 1987 by Erik H. Erikson. Used by permission of W. W. Norton & Company, Inc. Every effort has been made to trace the copyright holders and obtain permission to reproduce this material. If you have any queries or any information relating to text, images or rights holders, please contact the publisher.

British Library Cataloguing in Publication Data
A catalogue record for this book is available from the British Library.

ISBN: 978-1-913494-36-0 (paperback)
ISBN: 978-1-913494-37-7 (ebook)

Typeset by Bespoke Publishing Ltd.
Printed in the UK by Ashford Colour Press.

CONTENTS

PHOTOGRAPHS   vi
ACKNOWLEDGMENTS   vii
CHARACTERS   ix

PART 1

1. Early Sorrow *Vienna, 1920s*   3

2. Visitations, Habitats *Vienna, 1929–30*   21

3. The Hietzing School *Vienna, 1927–32*   35

4. Lessons in Self-defense *Vienna, 1929–31*   55

5. The Real Berlin *Berlin, 1929*   69

6. The Zobeltitz Plan *Vienna, 1931–2*   89

7. Sex and Politics *Berlin, Italy, Vienna, 1933–7*   111

8. Graduation *Vienna, 1938*   135

PART 2

9. Experiments in Living *England, 1938–40*   153

10. Kindly Come Along with Me *England, 1940*   163

11. The Isle of Man, *1940*   179

12. Sea Legs, *1940*   193

13. The New World *Canada, 1940–1*   203

14. Camp N *Canada, 1941*   233

EPILOGUE   247
AUTHOR'S NOTE   251
EXPLANATORY NOTES   255
SOURCES   265
INDEX   268

PHOTOGRAPHS

Plates

1. The Heller candy selection, a page from the catalogue. Private collection.
2. Margaret Steiner, standing 2nd from left, and Hans Heller, standing 2nd from right, 1924. Courtesy of Peter O'Connor.
3. Peter Heller as a boy. Peter Heller Album, Courtesy of the Sigmund Freud Museum, Vienna.
4. Photograph of the Burlingham children and Anna Freud with Wolf, c. 1930. © Freud Museum London.
5. Hietzing School Children's Party, Peter Heller Album, Courtesy of Freud Museum, Vienna.
6. Hietzing Faculty Portrait with Erik Erikson, seated far left and Peter Blos, seated 3rd from left. Peter Heller Album, Courtesy of Freud Museum, Vienna.
7. Children of the Burlingham-Rosenfeld (Hietzing) School at play in front of the schoolhouse. Peter Heller Album, Courtesy of the Sigmund Freud Museum, Vienna.
8. Children of the Burlingham-Rosenfeld (Hietzing) School in front of the schoolhouse, May 1929. Peter Heller Album, Courtesy of the Sigmund Freud Museum, Vienna.
9. Prisoner of War Camp, Camp N, Sherbrooke, Canada. Library and Archives Canada PA 114463.
10. Peter Heller as a young man. Private collection.

ACKNOWLEDGMENTS

Many thanks to Christina Wipf Perry and Liz Wilson of Confer Books Ltd, for bringing this project to fulfillment and thanks to Emily Wootton and to Viv Church for their valuable assistance. Thanks to Monica Pessler and Daniela Finzi of the Sigmund Freud Museum Vienna, for making it possible for me to rediscover the album of images that my father donated in 1992. Thanks to Bryony Davies of the Freud Museum London for her kind help. Special thanks to Hermann Teifer and to the Leo Baeck Institute of New York, where the writings and papers of my father and grandfather have found an honored resting place.

Thanks to Daniel Myerson, master story-teller, for always telling me exactly what he thinks and for showing me what it means to have faith. Thanks to Maura Spiegel, for the depth of her insights and her boundless support.

Thanks to the Vassar College Library for making it possible for me to pursue my research; to Nick Midgely, for sharing his important work on Anna Freud; to the late Erich Koch, for telling me parts of my father's story that I had never heard before; to Ernest Steiner, for letting me sit in the garden where my father and his schoolmates used to play.

Thanks also to Ann Burack-Weiss, Mindy Fullilove, Simone Fortin, Jim Gilbert, John Kavanaugh, Craig Irvine, and Jack Saul for their excellent advice; to Hilary Kliros, for setting me on the right path; to Karen Starr, for helping me to follow it; to Rochelle Gurstein, for being an early supporter of this project; to Jane Sobel, who has taught me so much; to Paul Lazar, for his enthusiasm and encouragement; to Ethan Taubes for our ongoing conversation about the world that our fathers came from.

Thanks to Marc and Christine Heller, for their generosity, even in the hardest time. Thanks to Joan Heller for being with me every step of the way and for her courageous spirit. Thanks to Eve Heller Tscherkassky for remembering so many of our stories and for reclaiming lost territory. Thanks to Justin Humphreys, for helping to preserve the history of our family.

Acknowledgments

Thanks to my husband, Kenji Fujita, for giving me the idea of writing this book and embracing the consequences, and to my children, Naomi and David Ulysses Fujita, for the blessings they bring to me every day of my life.

CHARACTERS

Part I

Peter Heller, a little boy subject to *pavor nocturnus* (night terrors).

Hans Heller, enlightened industrialist, father of Peter Heller.

Margaret Steiner, "Mem," artist, mother of Peter Heller.

Jenni Steiner, mother of Mem, center of a Viennese salon.

Leopold Steiner, father of Mem, General Secretary of the Skoda Works.

Inge Schön Heller, lover and second wife of Hans Heller.

Max Fellerer, Mem's architect lover, who designed a summer house
for her.

Karl Frank, member of the anti-Nazi underground.

Käthe Leichter, tutor to Mem and member of a radical
left-wing organization.

Anna Freud, among her many accomplishments, founder of a
progressive school.

Eva ("Muschi") Rosenfeld. After the tragic death of her daughter Madi,
she opened her house to an experiment in education.

Dorothy Burlingham, youngest daughter of Louis Comfort Tiffany,
who came to Vienna to be treated by Sigmund Freud.

Erik Erikson (also known as Homburger), teacher at the Hietzing
School, later world-renowned psychologist.

Peter Blos, teacher and director of the Hietzing School, later analyst.

Bob, Mabbie, Tinky and Mikey Burlingham, children of
Dorothy Burlingham.

Victor Rosenfeld, son of Eva and Valentin ("Valti") Rosenfeld. A friend present throughout Peter's childhood and youth.

Sigurd and Basti Beer, Elizabeth and Mario Iona, Walti Aichorn, Ingho Wimmer, Ernstl Halberstadt (later analyst Ernest Freud), students at the Hietzing School.

Sylvia, Peter's girlfriend in his Gymnasium days.

Tommi Wolf, younger cousin of Peter Heller.

Victor Opalski, brother-in-law of Inge.

Part 2

Eclectic group of deportees from Austria and Germany, ranging from Cambridge intellectuals to professional wrestlers.

PART I

1.

Early Sorrow

Vienna, 1920s

I.

WHEN my father was a little boy in Vienna, he told Anna Freud this dream:

He is walking on the rim of the white gravel path that leads around the oval pond in the upper part of the Belvedere Gardens. The birds are singing, the sun is out; his hands are in his pockets, he's whistling to himself. Suddenly he becomes aware of a distant rumbling that seems to be coming from the lower part of the garden. He looks down the path and doesn't see anything at first. Then a blue–black machine with a brilliant array of handles and shafts comes into sight; it is flattening the gravel, making it level and smooth. The machine is heading straight towards him; he tries to get up off the path onto the soft green grass, but even though it's only a matter of a few inches, he can't lift his feet. The machine comes closer and closer, finally catching him up and pressing him with its huge rods and shafts. He calls out for help as loud as he can, but no one comes to rescue him. There is nothing he can do; the machine grinds him up.

Night after night, this dream kept coming back, so that he was afraid to fall asleep. But sleep always caught up with him in the end, no matter how hard he tried to resist. Sometimes he woke up in the kitchen, face-down on the stone floor; other times, he woke up in a bath of ice-cold water. He knew that he had been screaming because his voice was hoarse. Sometimes there were bruises on his arms and legs.

Anna Freud told my father that she knew something about dreams, and that by putting their heads together, they could probably make his dream go away. And so a conversation began that lasted for the next four years, and that played itself back to him for the rest of his life.

In the preface to his case history, which he published when he was 63 years old, my father wrote that he was brought up in a "left-wing liberal, capitalist avant-garde style." Culture had taken the place of religion in his family; he remembered being brought to Seders at his grandfather's house, but these occasions had felt a little like funerals, awkward and embarrassing.

At the time of his dream, his father Hans was taking his doctorate in economics and running the family business. Heller Candy was as famous in Vienna as Nestlé or Schrafft's; the factory took up several city blocks, with a giant smokestack, a vast courtyard, labyrinthine interiors, and an underground storage vault known by the workers as "the Catacombs." The candies that poured out of the factory's gates were miniature works of art. Simple sugar took on a lavish variety of forms – pink grapefruit slices, translucent pears, pink–gold peaches, garnet-red raspberries, purple grapes; brown–gold walnuts, stamped with the company crown; light-gold honeycombs, with their own bees; black licorice mountain flowers; pastel-colored chocolates in the shape of seashells, butterflies, and swords; dark chocolate in the shape of pianos, flutes, and violins; liqueur-filled chocolate bottles, with labels that said "Amaretto" or "Kirsch" or "Cointreau": chocolate walking sticks, chocolate mushrooms, chocolate stags, chocolate dwarves, chocolate mountain huts, chocolate dredls and chocolate Christmas stars (*see* Plate 1).

Imbued with the socialist ethos of "Red Vienna," Hans prided himself on being an enlightened industrialist. Within Vienna, his workers had access to the Heller Swimming Pool, the Heller Sports Club, the Heller Dance Group, the Heller Fussball (Football) Team. Outside of the city, in the town of Prein, there was a peaceful and secluded spa resort that was open to "*Heller Leute*" (Heller people) throughout the year.

But although he was committed to maintaining the high standards of the firm, Hans didn't want to see himself as a businessman. He avoided socializing with people in the trade; he made his elegant house on the Karolinengasse into a meeting place for artists, poets, musicians, intellectuals – American composer George Antheil, comedian Max Pallenberg, actress Sybille Binder, etc. etc. When he wasn't entertaining his talented friends, many of whom depended on his financial support, he was spending long nights at his desk, writing a novel entitled *Ein Mann Sucht Heimat* (*A Man Searches for a Homeland*), which he eventually published under a pseudonym and which never brought him much acclaim.

A tall, imposing man with delicate nerves, he had married his childhood sweetheart after four years of service as a lieutenant in the First World War. Her name was Margaret Steiner, but she went by Kletta, Menga, Greta, Gretl, Memka, and Mem – no one name satisfied her entirely. Mem, a kind of childish name, is what everybody who knew her well called her. Like Hans, she was an assimilated Jew who came from a background of high culture and money. Her father, Leopold Steiner, was General Secretary of the Skoda Works, the leading Austro-Hungarian conglomerate in armaments and heavy industry. Her mother, Jenni Steiner, led a literary salon that included the philosopher–writer Popper-Lynkeus and the young literary critic Georg Lukacs. Raised in the lap of luxury, Mem wanted to break away from what she saw as bourgeois hypocrisy. But although in this regard she and Hans were in sympathy, other elements soon began to pull them apart. A photograph taken of Hans and Mem in 1924, four years after their son, Peter, was born, when Hans was 28 and Mem was 25, provides a glimpse into their life together (*see* Plate 2).

The three women have just stepped out of a costume ball, with Mem standing in the center, in traditional Austrian peasant dress. She turns her head to the side, staring off into space, restless and disconsolate. The wreath of leaves that crowns her head only draws attention to the mixture of refusal and desire that sets her apart from everyone else. Hans stands behind her, in a tuxedo, tailored shirt, and white cravat, taking on the camera with an amused smile. But there is also a quizzical expression in his eyes, as though he is waiting, a little impatiently, for someone to make him more comfortable. The man to his right and the woman to his left are enjoying a moment of flirtation; the pleasure that they steal so easily offsets the distance between my grandparents.

When Hans was serving in the First World War, he had written long, passionate letters to Mem and she had fallen in love with him. But after a few years of marriage, during which she had sparkled in society, the young man who had written to her so beautifully seemed like a stranger to her, remote, overbearing, and impotent. She discovered that he was seeking out other women, including a close friend of hers who tried to commit suicide when Hans broke off the relationship. Mem helped her friend get back on her feet, but she also made a pact with her: if either of them ever wanted to end her life, the other would assist in her suicide.

During the same period, Mem had a miscarriage. She wasn't prepared for how devastated she felt. While she was losing their child, Hans was off on a business trip. She had never felt so completely alone.

In his memoirs, Hans admitted that when he came back home, he had only the vaguest understanding of what Mem had just gone through. He had been off in Denmark, enjoying himself. "I took my first flight on a commercial plane, went to the famous seafood restaurant WIVEL and ordered delicacies that were unavailable in Austria and enjoyed a little flirtation with a Danish actress." When he came back, he felt sorry for his wife, but he couldn't understand why her mood was so dark. From what he understood, these things happened all the time. Why was she so terribly upset? They were both young and healthy, after all. When the doctor allowed it, they would simply try again.

Only in retrospect was Hans able to understand how blind he had been to Mem's grief. "I must have been a selfish, primitive young man when it came to understanding traumatic events as opposed to theorizing about the human psyche or interpreting literature," he confessed. But even here, he seems to be posing, like a man apologizing in front of a mirror.

Eventually Mem started to go out again and, for some reason, wherever she went, she found herself crossing paths with a tall, blond, Aryan architect by the name of Max Fellerer. When she was with him, she was able to laugh and enjoy herself. She started to go out in the hope of running into him.

One night at a party, she was sitting next to Fellerer on a couch and she found herself nestling under his arm. When she got up to leave, he got up too. Without exchanging any words, they went to his apartment. On that first night, after they had made love, she realized that she couldn't go back to Hans again. Hans had never fully understood her as a woman in all these years; Fellerer had understood her in a single night.

When she finally gathered the courage to tell Hans, she burst into tears. "I don't want to hurt you, but our marriage is done," she told him. "I've met someone else."

At first Hans flew into a rage, but then he became resigned. "If you really feel this way, there's nothing I can do. I won't try to stop you – but I hope you understand that nothing is going to make me give up Peter."

Mem eventually moved to Berlin to pursue her dream of becoming a screenwriter. She told herself that she had no way of supporting her four-year-old son, that, in the long run, it would be better for him to be raised by his well-positioned father. In return for custody, Hans agreed to send her money for as long as she remained unmarried. She and Hans claimed that they were still good friends and that they would always love each other, rejecting the idea that marriage was a form of ownership. But despite their enlightened views, there was a great deal of bitterness on both sides. Mem felt that Hans was incapable of real emotion; Hans blamed Mem for undercutting his masculinity.

At the time of the dream, Peter was eight or nine years old and Mem and Hans were separated but still not divorced. Although Mem had long since moved out, Peter still hoped that she would get tired of her little apartment in Berlin and come home. She had told him again and again how close she felt to him, closer than she felt to anyone else. As it was, she came back to see him every few months, though these fervently anticipated visits were never long enough. But who was she really?

II.

By the time she was 16 years old, Mem was already engaged to Hans. They were childhood sweethearts and they had made a vow that when the war was over, they would get married. But they were also believers in free love, and while Hans was serving in Italy, Mem was gathering experiences.

Suitors came to the stately house on the Wattmangasse and she would receive them in one of her many satin negligees. "Have you brought me a gift?" she would demand. "No? Then go away! And don't give me that hangdog look!" Or, "Do you think I'm running a flower shop here? Next time, bring me something interesting or don't bring anything at all!"

Apart from various young men, tutors came to the house to give her lessons in Latin and art and history. One of the tutors was a young woman by the name of Käthe Leichter. She was a member of the Viennese Youth Movement, a radical left-wing organization, and in the years that followed, she became the most important socialist feminist in Austria.

But, like everyone else, she needed money, and for a time she supported herself by tutoring students from wealthy families.

Her new student made such an impression on her that she wrote about her in her diary. She remembered walking into the magnificent salon of the Steiner house and finding Mem sprawled on a couch, nibbling on caviar when all Käthe could afford was cornbread with turnip marmalade. Her pupil was striking, if not conventionally beautiful. "She had the same eyes – enormous green–grey eyes with long eye lashes – as her equally enticing mother, and she had black hair," she records. "She was completely impudent, spoiled and wild, and she was raised in an atmosphere of excess and laxness that made me as critical of the milieu as the product."

In the beginning, the idealistic Käthe thought that maybe she should walk away, that she was violating her own principles by working in an environment like this. But there was something about her pupil that made her stay. "Soon I was overcome by the originality, the directness of thinking, the fluent mode of expression, the swift and certain power of judgment of this little girl, " she admits.

And again, "When, half an hour later, after we had gone through a little art history, she explained to me what she saw in a painting of the holy Saint del Piombo or in the Primavera of Botticelli, and I stood overwhelmed by the new impressions that flooded my educated awareness before these images, I was once again intrigued and reconciled."

While Käthe taught her pupil about history and art, Mem tried to instruct her earnest teacher about more down-to-earth things. "Ideas are very good, but what about men? If you don't have sex, you are merely sublimating your desires. If you deny it, you're fooling yourself!"

One afternoon, after their lessons were done, they decided to go out to get ice cream. But before they left, Mem pulled her tutor aside. "You've taught me so much. I will repay you now by teaching you how to put on a hat." And they stood in front of the mirror for a long time, getting Käthe's hat to sit properly before going out.

In the ice-cream parlor, the lesson continued. "Now I'll teach you how to flirt."

"But I don't like flirting! Why should grown-up people play such stupid games? I think that men and women should be open and honest with each other."

"Nonsense. You don't believe in it because you don't know how. Here, stare at that boy at the table over there. Just stare at him – there, now he's looking at you. Now smile a little, just a little, and turn your head away. Very good. Look at that! In another second, he'll find some excuse to come over to our table. Just you watch. Think of it as a social experiment."

While Mem taught Käthe how to flirt, for her part Käthe encouraged Mem to make something of herself. They became close friends and took summer vacations together in the Austrian Tyrol. When Mem became unhappy in her marriage, Käthe urged her to go to Berlin and realize her dream of making films. Why should someone with a talent like hers confine herself to being the dazzling center of a salon? Let her walk away from affluence and complacency. Let her make something of herself.

Disillusioned with Hans, disgusted by bourgeois life, overflowing with plots, stories, ideas, Mem chose to go away and pursue her ambitions – but she agonized over whether she had done the right thing for the rest of her life. As for Käthe, she eventually fell in love and had two sons. When the war came, she saw to it that her sons got out of Austria before it was too late, but she lingered over the arrangements for too long and was interned in Ravensbrück, where she eventually died. According to feminist historian Gerda Lerner, she succeeded in reconciling the various aspects of her life: "In Käthe Leichter's life there was no divide between theory and ... [action]; she combined her work as a journalist and organizer with her duties as mother and wife, her political leadership role with her research work as a social scientist."

Of course, Mem was different. She wasn't as fearless as Käthe; in fact, she was afraid of many things. She was afraid of becoming mediocre, of losing her power over men, of the ease of wealth, of the hardships of poverty, of being too dependent, of ending up alone, but, above all, of everything that deadened her imagination, her creativity. If she was going to be a screen writer, there was no question that she had to live in Berlin, the capital of European film. But what if Peter started forgetting her? There was no way to silence this fear, which grew louder over the years.

III.

While his mother struggled to find her way, Peter had his sessions with Anna Freud, which followed the same pattern every day. The chauffeur would pick him up from the Evangelical Elementary School in his father's

Italian sports car and drop him off at 19 Berggasse. Walking up the worn marble steps to the second floor, he would run his hand from knob to knob of the iron railing, counting to himself. When he finally got to the door, he peered through the little glass spy hole, trying to see if the door-keeper was peering back at him. In the waiting area, he kept his eyes on Sigmund Freud's door and now and then he caught a glimpse of him, thin and bent, with a balding head and a grey beard, sitting at an enormous desk crowded with ancient figurines. Everyone said that Sigmund Freud was a very great man, but when Peter actually crossed paths with him, he would simply say, in a faint, mumbling voice, as though he had a piece of unchewed food in his mouth, "Is this really the Heller boy? My, how you've grown," exactly as any other grown-up would.

In Anna's office, there weren't any figurines, only a portrait of Sigmund Freud that followed Peter with its eyes. The portrait couldn't see him when he lay down on the couch, which made up for the fact that he couldn't see Anna, even though he was often tempted to twist around and check whether she was really listening to him. Since he wasn't allowed to look at her, he looked instead at Wolfi, a coal-black German shepherd with sharp yellow teeth, that lay on a tattered rug with his head between his paws. He was afraid of Wolfi the first few times, but after that he mainly felt sorry for him, trapped indoors all day, without any hope of going outside.

Sometimes just the clicking of Anna's needles made Peter want to jump off the couch, run around the room, and knock her lace-covered tables down. If only Wolfi would leap up and bark like mad! He knew just how to get him to do it, but it wasn't allowed.

As time went on, Peter learned ways of distracting himself without Anna noticing. If he squinted, for example, he could make out the titles of her books, even though the glass-covered bookshelf was halfway across the room. Once she let him take down a book and leaf through it, even though, strictly speaking, it was against her rules. It was by the philosopher Nietzsche: she had his complete works, which took up two entire shelves.

"I want to be a great writer," he told her. "My father says that a great writer must have read everything." He rattled off the titles of some of the books that Hans had read to him, hoping that she would notice how advanced they were. No answer – just the snoring of Wolfi on his rug and the clicking of her knitting needles. Was she even listening? He was nothing to her, just another one of her customers. Why had he ever thought that she was beautiful, with her drab clothes and her hair pulled back in a bun? She was only really interested in hearing about shameful things, things that normal people, like his nursemaid Thesi, considered piggish and disgusting, like his habit of spying on men in the public toilet.

He didn't know why he had to come here every day. Wasn't it just a waste of time? She didn't even think it was that important to be great. She said that it was more important to develop into a real human being, whatever that meant. How could a grown person not care about being great? Didn't it bother her that she was going to die? Her own father had written that there was no such thing as God, which meant that when you died, you just evaporated into space and your atoms scattered across the universe. The only way not to disappear was to be great, like Goethe, or Shakespeare, or Karl May, who had written at least 100 adventure books. If you couldn't be immortal like Zeus, at least you could be immortal in words, like the creator of Faust or the author of *Winnetou*.

Sometimes he hated the sound of her voice, so reasonable and steady and matter of fact. Other times he wondered what would happen if he broke all of her rules, fell down on his knees and hugged her legs.

She told him to draw pictures of his dreams, even though drawing really wasn't what he did the best. She liked looking at his drawings, no matter how sloppy they were, and would ask him what every squiggle meant.

One of Peter's childhood drawings

11

He made his drawings more and more elaborate, so that he could stretch out the time of sitting right next to her on the couch. She didn't use perfume, the way his mother did, but she smelled nice anyway.

Still, he wished that she would pay less attention to his drawings and more attention to his stories, because, as his father said, a writer needs an audience. She didn't want to use all their time hearing him read his stories out loud; she said that it was more useful for him to lie on the couch and say whatever came into his head. He could still tell her his stories, but they came out sounding more like dreams, and he often forgot important details when he was telling them to her, only remembering them later, when the driver was speeding him back home. Finally, she told him that if he brought his stories to her, she would read them in the evening, when her sessions were done. He pictured her sitting in her red velvet armchair late at night, with Wolfi lying at her feet and his pages in her hands. He gave her a ten-page novella that he had finished before he started coming to her, all about a factory owner who starts out wanting to kill himself and ends up deciding to stay alive after he starts a revolution in the factory. She liked the story so much that she typed it up for him, and she typed up all his stories after that, keeping them in a special drawer along with her own papers, so that they wouldn't get lost.

In a way, Anna was like a mother to him, or maybe a cross between a mother and a scientist. She never hugged him or kissed him the way his mother did, and she wouldn't let him hug or kiss her (although it was alright for him to talk about wanting to). But she knew things about him that not even Mem knew, things that he had never planned on telling anyone, like what happened to his body when he got excited, or the fact that he sometimes wet his bed.

He felt guilty about liking her so much, especially because she really didn't approve of Mem. She was never happy when Mem came to visit him; she thought that it would be better for him if Mem stayed away. But Mem's visits, which were never long enough, were his favorite times in the world. As a grown man, he still remembered them vividly, describing one in a thinly fictionalized story:

Boredom blows itself up in you like a balloon. The nanny takes her charge to task. She says to the child, "An intelligent boy does not get bored." And to his father, she says "Certainly Herr Heller the boy longs for the lady of the house, his mother, but he misuses his misery to shirk his responsibilities."

In the vacation with his mother, everything is different. They wade in high reeds until they are close to huge grey birds; they find mushrooms in the darkening woods. They pick berries in the clearings. They are in high spirits. They find, for example, a scooter in the shop of a bent little man who calls the scooter "Pezickel" and they laugh so hard that they can scarcely bring the purchase to an end. They have their secret words whose meaning can't be explained to anyone. She speaks about "difficult grown-up things" with him and he understands everything. She also tells him fantastic stories like the one of the railroad manikin. All this is shot through with the premonition of departure, which is at the same time a remembrance of former farewells.

In the same story, he will describe a departure scene that repeated itself as relentlessly as his Belvedere dream:

On the platform white steam hisses from a valve of the black machine.

"Chocolates, cigarettes!" She still runs to the bookstand which makes him anxious. Finally she is back again.

"We're both grown-ups now," she says. "This time it doesn't bother us so much."

"Not half a year? Only three months?" On the great clock of the railroad hall the hand leaps ahead."Go now," he says. He is afraid she might miss her train.

Men with light brown suitcases. A crying little girl holds her handkerchief in her fist.

"You go too," she says, "and don't turn around." Along the broad squares of the platform he must not, just as in olden days when he was still little, tread into the cracks, otherwise she won't come again for a long time. A baggage cart drives toward him. Attention. Now I stepped on the crack or doesn't that count?

"She's gone," he says to the chauffeur. "Home please."

The house always felt bleak and cold in the days after his mother left. If only he could follow her to Berlin! He begged Hans to let him go by himself on the train, and Hans didn't say no, but then Hans talked to Anna, who said that it would be a very bad idea.

When he told Mem what Anna had said, she wasn't at all surprised. She knew very well that Anna disapproved of her, which was probably quite flattering to Hans. In a conversation that Peter recorded as a grown man, Mem revealed that, at some point, she had been in direct contact with Anna Freud. She had been told that she should refrain from being too physical with her own son, a piece of advice that infuriated her. When one listens to the recording, one can hear the pauses, the trembling in her voice:

> I was struggling in the arena of life – with affairs and love and confusion – when this dry, didactic "scientist" woman turned up: a person ignorant of the world and the exuberantly blossoming and sacred chaos of life. For to live means to have a child, man, lover. What can such a person know of life! She should first feel in her whole body what it is like to want a man. I was a woman: she wasn't. With the profound hatred of the spinster – which is at the bottom nothing but envy – she had the impudence to offer me impertinent remarks that I will not be able to forget as long as I live. And I, poor, confused person, felt compelled to allow her to say such things to me. "Children," she told me, "are not there for the purpose of giving pleasure to their parents." By her I had to be enlightened about my duties. Ah – if I were to meet her after my death, I would hit her straight in the face. Surely, I am unjust. Still: I was right. They took away my son because I had no money – and I had all the … complications with men – and then the good contact, the soul connection between us was destroyed by this alien person, this employee of Hans – and to him, as her client, she was of course by far more polite and considerate.

Although he had no way of understanding these feelings when he was a boy, Peter knew that Mem would have been quite happy if he stopped seeing Anna. But Hans was now in charge of him, and Hans felt that Anna was getting somewhere with him. Peter was glad that he didn't have to decide, because he was becoming very attached to Anna. Even though he told her all kinds of disgusting things, she didn't think that he was a pig. And she said that his stories were very well written and quite sophisticated for a boy who was only nine years old.

One evening, in the midst of reading to him, Hans broke off. "There's something I need to explain to you," he said, in a serious voice.

"Why can't we go on reading?" Peter said, reaching for the book.

"Your mother and I will always be good friends," Hans went on, holding the book away from him. "But you should stop waiting for her to move back in with us."

Peter turned his face to the wall, tracing the pattern of leaves on his wallpaper until he reached the stain that looked like a panther with scraggly fur. Hans didn't say anything more; all Peter could hear was the ticking of his cuckoo clock. When he turned back to Hans, he seemed small, as though he was looking at him through the wrong end of a telescope. He wished that Hans would put his glasses back on; his eyes reminded him of soft-boiled eggs and he hated the embroidered handkerchief that his father was wiping his glasses with – he hated the big "HH" and the little Heller crown, the mark of a tradition he would have to carry on. "Why did you have to stop reading?" he complained, pulling his blanket over his head.

A few days later, Anna told him all about eggs and sperms, and what a man's penis was for, and what husbands and wives did together when they were ready to have a child.

"I'm sure that Mem and Hans never did anything like that," Peter said.

"How do you think it happened?" she asked him.

"In a doctor's office," he shrugged. "With the doctor telling them what to do." It was hard to lie still after that, so he drew instead, covering several pieces of paper with lop-sided circles and squiggly lines.

"Do you wish I hadn't told you?" she asked, when the hour was finally over.

"No," he said, jumping off the couch in relief. "It was quite worthwhile."

On the way home, he stared out of the windows of the car, looking at the couples walking along the Ringstrasse, some hand in hand, others arm in arm, others walking a few feet apart. Could it really be true? He shook his head. He was never going to get married, that was for sure. He couldn't believe that Mem, who was always so elegant and clean, would do something as dirty and disgusting as that.

His father's new girlfriend, Inge, was starting to spend nights at their house, spreading herself out on Mem's place on the bed. He could sometimes hear her and Hans laughing together behind the closed French doors. They weren't married, so what were they doing in there? Inge wasn't nearly as intelligent as Mem; she didn't read much, and she talked about silly, empty-headed things. He liked it when she kissed him on the lips, but he didn't like it when she talked baby-talk to him and made him sit on her lap.

Anna felt it was very clear that Peter wasn't happy at the Evangelical Elementary School. He didn't get along with the students there: they spoke in a lower-class dialect that he could barely understand, and they were constantly drawing him into fights by calling him names like "filthy Jew" or "rich Jewish pig." He was obviously an intelligent boy, but his mind was being coarsened and dulled. Why not enroll him in the school that she had helped to form, a school that would not only engage his mind in a positive way but reinforce his therapy?

The school was located in Hietzing, on the Wattmangasse, in a comfortable, middle-class neighborhood. Unlike the Evangelical School, it had no high metal fence; it had a low picket fence instead. The students spoke the same refined German that Peter spoke at home, and many of them had lost a parent to death or divorce. Classes were held in a narrow, two-storey house that smelled of freshly cut wood and that wasn't visible from the street, nestled in the backyard of Eva Rosenfeld, one of Anna's closest and most trusted friends.

Life at the Hietzing School seemed amazingly relaxed to Peter after the grinding discipline of the Evangelical School. There were only two hours of classes in the mornings, and the students sat at work tables rather than desks. There was never a problem about going outside; as a matter of fact, students were allowed to climb out of a window on the second floor into the gnarled branches of a walnut tree, lingering in this "balcony" or sliding to the ground. After lunch, there was a period of free work during which students turned to projects they had chosen themselves. A few of the children did free work all afternoon, but most of them went off to analysis, either with Anna or with other analysts who were part of the Freudian circle.

Anna had always believed in the importance of developing a pedagogy that would correspond to the principles of psychoanalysis. Eva Rosenfeld, who was under analysis with Sigmund Freud, not only provided her with the physical setting that she needed to realize this goal but devoted her days and nights to helping her see it through.

Eva's sprawling household was completely intertwined with the school; there were at least four or five students boarding upstairs with her at any given time. Music classes were held in her parlor, with Eva taking part, organizing musical events. When anyone was hurt, or hungry, or upset, they came to Eva first. Bustling, attentive, and capable, she could always be counted on.

And yet, although the Rosenfeld house was always full of life, there was a sadness there, just below the surface. Two of Eva's sons had died of dysentery at the end of the First World War, leaving her with her daughter, Madi, and her son, Victor, a lean, tousle-headed boy who was roughly Peter's age. In 1927, when Madi was 15 years old, she fell to her death while climbing the Backenstein, a mountain overlooking the Alpine lake of Grundlsee.

Some said that Eva helped to create the school as an answer to her grief, while others said it would have happened without her. There is no denying that the foundations of the school were sunk into the same flowerbeds that Eva and Madi had planted together when Madi was a little girl. After Madi died, Eva was never without young boarders in her house, including little Ernstl Halberstadt, Anna's nephew, whose mother had died when he was five years old. Tending to the needs of others, Eva was able to forget herself and to keep Madi's memory intact. "I let myself die so that Madi could live," she said when she was an old woman, perhaps somewhat morbidly but definitely still in the style of someone who had been involved with the Freuds.

Apart from contributing hugely to the running of the school, Eva brought a sense of family to it. For her, the school was a community defined in opposition to the authoritarian, anti-Semitic world outside, a community in which competitiveness and meanness had no place. No matter how irrational the world became, the school would be an island of humanity. "As Jews, we were always outsiders," she said. The community within the school became everything.

By becoming the mother of the school, Eva was able to endure her grief. Yet despite all she did for everyone, there was a touch of iciness in her that nothing could melt and that only the children with the keenest feeling for maternal unhappiness could detect, Peter being one of them.

Although the school was rooted in Eva's Austrian–Jewish life, it was financed by a blue-blooded WASP. Dorothy Burlingham, the youngest daughter of Louis Comfort Tiffany, had come to Vienna with her four children in search of emotional stability. Married to a New York surgeon who suffered from manic depression, she and her children lived in constant fear of his psychotic breaks. Seeking treatment for herself and for her oldest son, she had entered into analysis, first with Theodor Reik and then with Sigmund Freud. Before long, she was forging a friendship with Anna Freud that was to draw many other lives into its orbit.

All four Burlingham children attended the school: Bob, 14, Mabbie, 12, Tinky, 10, and Mikey, 8 years old. For Peter, the Burlinghams were perfect in every way, and he wanted desperately to be accepted by them. As he wrote later, "I admired, worshipped, and loved the fair, fine, sensitive, attractive patrician children in their effortless grace, their carelessness, their American sense of humanity, even in their lack of zest or commitment." Their way of being was wild and seemingly uncivilized, yet they were unfailingly elegant, and even noble, in his eyes.

The entire family was magical to him. Tinky, who was one year older than him, was the most magical of all. Slender and fair, with a mischievous smile, she became his childhood love. Peter was enthralled by Tinky's boyish looks, her imagination, and her elusiveness.

Anna and Eva had been very close before the Burlinghams appeared on the scene. Anna cherished her relationship with Eva as one in which she was understood, not merely as an analyst but as a human being. It was Anna who rushed to Eva's side when she received the news that Madi died. At Eva's request, she had gone into Madi's room and gathered together all of her things. And yet it was Dorothy Burlingham who provided Anna with a second family, and a way of leading a life that was separate from her father. "The Professor," as she always insisted on calling him, was a figure of absolute authority for Dorothy, but Anna was her partner in life. Whether or not they were lovers, no one knows, but the life-altering intensity of their friendship was evident to everyone. Finding herself in the path of that intensity, the self-denying Eva stepped aside.

These were the three founders of the school. Without them, the school would never have come into being. Taken together, they provided a substitute for the mother that Peter was in the long process of losing.

2.

Visitations, Habitats

Vienna, 1929–30

A ND so Peter sits at a low table covered with blocks of wood, bottles of ink, clumps of moss, branches of trees. At his elbow sits a boy with curly brown hair and a long, pointed face that resembles a satiric mask. In a few years, Victor, known as Vicki within the school, will transform himself into Victor Ross, taking on the manners of a British gentleman and becoming the lord of a magnificent Cornwall estate, to the envy of Peter, who will never manage to earn as much money as Victor will. But for now, Victor is a middle-class Viennese boy, restless, clever, acutely conscious of social rank, surrounded, as he is, by children of privilege, some of whom have moved into his mother's house. He and Peter are whittling branches into spears, competing to see who can finish the job in the least amount of time.

Across the table from them sits Ernstl W. Freud, who is carving a face into a bar of soap. If only the teachers had supplied him with a real walrus's tusk, so that the image that he is carving would never dissolve! (What would his grandfather Sigmund have to say about this?) Elfin and pale, with transparent skin and a silvery voice, he seems to be made of air. His future occupation as a specialist in prenatal psychology will be strangely compatible with his looks, which won't alter much over the years. For now, he is absorbed in his bit of soap, staying out of the competition across the table.

A sensitive-looking man stands at the opposite end of the table, bending over the woodcut that he has just stamped onto a piece of brown paper. This young man, whose name is Erik Homburger, is guiding the class with a light hand. Before he began to teach at the school, he was trying to make his way as an artist, but then he fell into a depression and lost his conviction in his work. The playfulness of the artist is still evident in everything he does; the world-famous analyst, Erik Homburger Erikson, hasn't yet declared himself.

"Why do we have to learn about the Eskimos?" the precocious Peter asks.

"Because they have a lot to teach us," Erikson says.

"But there are no Eskimos in Europe," Vicki points out.

"That doesn't mean that we can't learn from them."

"What exactly *can* we learn from them?" Peter demands.

"How to survive."

"But we don't live in a land of snow," Peter presses. "We live in Austria."

Into the room walks Peter Blos, strikingly handsome, neatly dressed, and not in the least bit bohemian. He has gone from tutoring the Burlingham children privately to directing the school that has essentially been created for them. A student of biology and animal behavior, he has thrown himself into pedagogy, reading deeply in Dewey and implementing the notion of project-based work. But for all his progressive ideas, and his belief in experiential learning, he retains a Germanic sense of discipline.

"What a *Schlamperei!*" Blos remarks, surveying the litter on the table.

"They'll tidy up when they're finished," Erikson says, his cheeks turning red. He knows that the Director is only teasing him; after all, he and Blos are close friends. It was Blos who got him this job, persuading Anna Freud to hire him, not because he had any experience working with children but because, as he put it to her, he was a person of "rare ability." Erikson knows how devoted Blos is to him, but he blushes nonetheless. These blushes of his endear him to the younger children, or "*die Kleinen*," as they are called, but they are afraid of Peter Blos, who is known for being strict.

Just then a boy bursts through the door, pulling off his cap and hurling it at the coat stand in the corner.

"Where have you been all this time, Basti?" Erik asks.

"I was eating my lunch, dear *Spiegelei* (Sunnyside up)," Basti says, using his nickname for Erik, which is inspired by the way his eyes bulge out. Peter and Vicki laugh appreciatively; Basti sits down next to them, grabbing Peter's half-finished stick and waving it in the air.

"Behave yourself, Basti," Blos says warningly.

"Alright, I'll give your little sword back to you, *Eierdidiwasserkopf* (moron-egghead)," Basti says.

But as soon as Blos leaves, Basti does everything he can to exasperate Erikson, with Vicki and Peter acting as co-conspirators. Although he lives in a castle outside of town where his parents run a music school, Basti can be as wily and foul-mouthed as a street urchin, which earns him the respect of the other boys.

Month after month, "the little ones" try to build igloos out of clay, cutting sloped cubes that represent blocks of ice. Covering their hands with ink, they make woodcuts of Arctic foxes, seals, walruses, ptarmigans. They build umiaks and kayaks by stretching cloth over sticks and boiled meat bones, testing them in the stream at the edge of Eva's garden. They learn how the Eskimos traveled great distances that they measured out by the number of sleeps, and they memorize all the Eskimo words for "white" and "snow."

Entering into the world of the Eskimos, with their ingenious dwellings, their waterproof parkas, their marvelous boots, the children are shielded from the changes happening in their own city. Here the fabric of life is rapidly coming apart. Red Vienna is breaking down, Fascism is on the rise, and the economy is about to collapse. Hatred of the Jews, a given of Austrian life, is more apparent than ever. But the vision that guides the school is defiantly Utopian, and the freedom granted there makes it seem like a paradise. The two main teachers, Erikson and Blos, are full of ideas and energy. Eventually they'll have to free themselves from Anna Freud, Dorothy Burlingham, and Eva Rosenfeld, a trio they privately refer to as "The Three Fates." But for the moment, they are devoted to the task of running a school that corresponds to the ideals of psychoanalysis, a school in which even troubled children can grow into "real" people.

When Peter goes home, there is agitation; his father's hot temper when he refuses to do what he says; the wild parties that happen at his house every week; Inge's tantrums when Hans won't give her the money to buy new clothes.

To make life even more chaotic, Hans and Inge decide to redo the house in Bauhaus style with the help of their friend, the designer Franz Singer. The rooms are all decorated in black and red squares, with tables of black glass and white fluorescent lights. Their soft, velvet-covered sofas disappear: in their place stand huge box-shaped couches covered with scratchy black cloth. They threaten to redo Peter's room as well; he begs them to allow him to keep his wallpaper, with its special stains and blossoming wreathes, and also his metal cot, which he can still fit into, if he sleeps curled up.

His pleas are ignored: one day his room is painted in a palette of "modern" colors, topped by a ceiling of lemon-yellow. His cot is replaced with a red-lacquered folding bed, and there is no way of getting it back. A party is held to show off the ruined apartment, and the guests tramp in and out of Peter's room.

"Well, how do you like it?" Franz Singer says, turning to the man next to him.

"I'm sick of Bauhaus," says the other man. He is the guest of honor, Adolf Loos.

The two of them start arguing by Peter's bed, with other guests forming a circle around them. If only he could run away to be with his mother in Berlin.

He envies the students who live at the school; he wishes that he could stay at Eva Rosenfeld's, along with Vicki, Ernstl, and the others. Vicki says he's lucky, and that he lives like a prince, but even though he can see the Belvedere Castle from his front step, there are things about the Karolinengasse that Vicki doesn't know. The house is dead when he comes home from school; Thesi and the cook are usually the only ones there. When they sit gossiping in the kitchen, he has nothing to do; he spends hours in his room by himself. On some nights, he sees a little girl in a fluttering white shirt who holds her arms out to him. Is she a ghost? What does she want from him? When he stamps and shouts, she disappears, but he never knows when she'll come back again.

The Burlinghams move into the apartment above the Freuds on the Berggasse and the school is invited to a reception there. Bob treats the little ones to an American delicacy – cornflakes, sugar, and milk. Vicki points out that the apartment isn't elegant at all. It has many rooms, but only the simplest furnishings. "The Tiffany lamps are nice," he admits, "but Tinky's grandfather probably gave them to Dorothy for free."

Tinky is wearing a white blouse, a red and blue plaid skirt, and an Indian headdress with white and orange feathers. How fantastically smashing she is! Peter wants desperately to be part of the Burlingham household; he doesn't care so much about the Rosenfeld house anymore.

Everything about the Burlinghams is magical, and he wants that magic to rub off on him. If he lived here, he could see Tinky whenever he liked; no one could say that he was running after her. He's a little afraid of Tinky's mother, with her leathery skin, faraway eyes, and craggy face. But he discovers that she can be kind, and that she looks more stern than she really is.

When he's near Tinky, he doesn't care that Mem is in Berlin or that Inge has practically moved into their house. All he cares about is Tinky, with her bobbed, straw-colored hair, her up-turned nose, and her mischievous smile. How is it that her eyes can be so wide and bright one moment and so sly and narrow the next? He has never met anyone like her before – she seems to have floated straight out of a fairy-tale. She likes nothing better than to make fun of him, so that when he is around her, his feelings are often hurt. But when he reads his stories and poems to her, she listens to every word.

He doesn't want to talk about Tinky with Anna, but he can't stop himself from writing her initials on his drawings. Anna says that Tinky is helping him to get over his sadness about Mem, but he doesn't agree with her. How could Tinky be helping *him*? He constantly tries to find excuses for touching her, but at the last moment she moves just beyond his reach.

Christmas is coming and the tables are piled up with home-made presents and ornaments. The older children are putting together a Christmas journal, and everyone is invited to contribute, except for him.

Why can't he be in the Christmas journal? It's completely unfair. He writes better than any of the little ones, including Victor, who is pretty good. Anna says that he shouldn't care so much about being important and great; he should concentrate on being a complete human being instead. Why is everyone ganging up on him? If he gets his hands on the journal, he'll tear it up.

The school (there are 20 students in all) goes on a Christmas vacation in the mountain resort of Breitenstein. Peter is very excited about the trip. He happens to be an excellent skier, and he wants Tinky to notice it. But after his first time down, he feels dizzy and hot, and the whiteness of the snow hurts his eyes. He rolls on the ground and laughs and cries; nothing makes any sense to him. Why are his skis leaning against the mountain hut with their curved tips pointing up at the sky? Why is Tinky perched on that mound of glittering ice like a small yellow bird that is about to take off? Vicki asks him why he is making such a fool of himself, but he is too carried away to answer, drawing letters in the snow – "T" for Tinky, "P" for Peter, "L" for love, "H" for hate. Vicki goes off in disgust, but then he stands at a distance, with his arms folded across his chest. He knows that Vicki is judging him, and he feels a little disgusted himself, but nonetheless, he writes feverishly in the snow, praying that Tinky will see how he is suffering for her.

"Come inside everyone!" Eva calls out. "The Christmas entertainment is about to begin." The Christmas tree is all lit up and the older children are about to enact a nativity scene, with Tinky playing the part of the infant Christ. Peter gets a chair in the very front, afraid that he won't be able to see Tinky from the back. But Eva sits down next to him, discovers that his forehead is burning, and whisks him away to his room to rest.

"Basti is going to take my chair," he complains, as she tucks the featherbed in around his feet.

"You can't go down again. You're sick."

"It isn't fair," he says bitterly, turning his face to the wall.

Anna doesn't believe that he's in love with Tinky Burlingham. A ten-year-old boy doesn't have feelings like that.

"I was laughing and crying at Breitenstein," he tells her. "I couldn't stop."

"You were running a temperature."

"I got the fever because of her."

She says that his feelings for Tinky are a substitute for the love he feels for Mem. She has already told him the story of Oedipus, and about how boys want to be the husbands of their own mothers.

"Why don't you have a husband?" he asks her.

"Why are you asking me that now?"

"Is it because you're the wife of your father?"

Anna is startled that this is coming from a child, but she doesn't let on, merely reminding him that they are there to talk about *him*.

Maybe Mem is right about Anna, Peter thinks; maybe she doesn't know anything about love. She's always with her father, who looks more and more bent and frail. Maybe all she cares about is taking care of him, and one day taking his place.

"Does it bother you that your father is so famous?" he says to her.

"Why should it bother me?"

"Aren't you afraid that you'll never be as great as he is?"

As usual, she doesn't answer him, telling him to focus on himself.

One day he comes into her office and throws himself down on the couch, complaining of a headache.

"Shall I take your temperature?" she asks.

"Where? Under my arm?" He feels a rush of heat between his legs and covers himself with a green blanket, complaining that she is embarrassing him.

She takes up her knitting and says, in a quiet voice, "I know that when you like someone like me or Mem, you want those feelings to come from above. But sometimes the lower part wants to join in too. This is only natural, but it can't happen yet. It will happen later, with a woman."

So he isn't a filthy pig, as the maid Thesi says; his feelings are perfectly natural. There isn't anything wrong with him; many boys have the same reactions as he does, so there is really nothing to worry about.

Their work together moves forward much more quickly now, so that Anna is very pleased with him. He makes such great strides in his analysis that she begins to talk about their work together as something in the past. But then Mem writes Hans a long letter about how she misses her son and how she wants to see more of him. Against Anna's urgent advice, Hans agrees to give Mem the use of his house in Grundlsee for half of July and all of August.

Nobody in Grundlsee has a house like theirs; everyone says that Fellerer, the architect, did a brilliant job. Hans laughs when people say that the balcony, which juts out over the lake, is in violation of the building code.

"Let them complain all they like," he says. "They'd give anything to have a balcony like mine."

It isn't as though their house is an eyesore, like the ultra-modern bungalow up on the hill, more like a barracks than a house. "A monstrosity," everyone says. No one says that about their house. Built of local pine, it faces directly onto the lake, like a ship that is about to take off. The view from any of its windows is grand, but the view from his window is the best of all. When Peter wakes up in the morning, his room is filled with liquid light, and the snow-covered mountains greet him from across the lake. In the afternoon, the reflections fly off the water and cover his walls with flashing swords.

Mem loves Grundlsee as much as he does; she cries when they first walk into the house. She picks mountain flowers and puts them in every room, throwing open all the windows to let in the mountain air. She wants to sit out on the balcony all the time, even when the sky is grey and overcast. Before breakfast, they take the canoe out onto the lake, and when they get to the middle, Peter dives off the side and swims alongside her. Rowing as quickly as she can, she laughs, saying that she'll make an Olympic swimmer of him yet. They hike all the way to the top of the Backenstein. As they rest at the foot of the mountain cross, she tells him how important it is to live the life of the body instead of living in one's head all the time.

"If you can't feel, you're lost," she says to him. Even though he notices that she's jumped from one thing to another – isn't that what Hans calls being illogical? – he doesn't point it out.

"What if you feel too much?" he asks instead.

"That means you're alive," she says to him. "Don't listen to anyone who tells you to hide your feelings away."

In the evening, she reads *The Count of Monte Cristo* to him, using different voices for each of the characters. The voice of Edmond Dantès is his favorite: light-hearted and cheerful before he has been betrayed, but deadly serious as he plots his revenge. They drink fresh milk every morning, and after their hikes they go to a little café that specializes in raspberry tarts.

Peter isn't that surprised when the visitor appears. Mem acts as though she expected it all along. It's Fellerer that Mem ran off with years ago, and Mem says that he still has feelings for her. Mem says he designed their balcony just for her, which is why it's so unfair that she's been kept away. Peter doesn't mind it when Fellerer comes around; he just wishes that he would leave after an hour or so. Mem seems more tired and lazy now; she doesn't get out of bed as early as before. They don't go out in the canoe as frequently. When he wakes up in the morning, he is often on his own.

If Hans were here they would be fishing all the time, straight off the balcony, or the canoe, or even their old sailboat, which isn't seaworthy and is really falling apart. But he can still fish with the local boys, who know exactly when the trout are biting and how to be quiet so as not to frighten them away.

What he doesn't bargain on are the visits of Karl Frank, a sleek-looking man with quick black eyes who reminds him of a shark. Mem says that Karl Frank is a communist; Peter wonders if he's ever blown anything up. He'd like to ask him what it's like to plot a revolution, but when he comes to the house, he's always in a hurry. Mem gets very excited when he's around – her voice becomes higher and sharper than usual, and she tells one story after another, like the one about the general who ran away from Russia after the Revolution and became a film extra in Hollywood.

"He ended up playing the part of a Russian general!" she laughs, waving her hands and laughing too much. Peter has already heard about the general, but Frank hasn't, so she doesn't care. Peter hates it when she gets like this. "Rumor has it that Sternberg is going to make a movie about him," she goes on. "But of course, they'll use a professional actor, and the poor man will never see a cent!"

One day, Mem tells him to play on the balcony so that she and Frank can talk over some grown-up matters inside.

"But there's nothing to play," he says to her.

"Then go get your fishing rod and catch a trout for me."

"It's the middle of the day! The fish aren't biting now."

"Try anyway," she says over her shoulder, as she and Frank go into the house.

He fills a bucket with water and gets his rod, but as soon as he hears Mem's bedroom door close, he goes into the living room and puts his ear to the floor.

"Take that off," he hears Frank say. "No, not that. Leave that on."

"Aren't you full of orders!" Mem laughs.

"Do as I say!"

Peter's foot knocks against a side table and a pewter cup crashes to the floor. He freezes, holding his breath.

"I think we have a spy," Frank remarks, after a pause. "I'm coming upstairs, and I better not find anybody there!"

Peter tiptoes out to the balcony, his heart pounding in his chest. He puts some bait on his hook and casts his line. If Frank comes out and questions him, he'll say that he was out here fishing all along. But when he realizes that Frank isn't going to come looking for him, he starts getting bored. How long are they going to stay down there? He hasn't even had his lunch. Then all at once, he feels a sharp tug on the line. Despite everything, he's gotten a bite! As he's reeling in the fish, Frank comes out onto the balcony, smoking a nasty-smelling cigarette.

"You like fishing, don't you?" he remarks, watching the fish – a good-sized trout – flop wildly on the wooden planks.

"I like fishing with my father," Peter says, unhooking the fish and throwing it into the bucket.

"I can see how your father would go in for fishing," Frank remarks. "After all, fishing is the perfect capitalist sport. But what am I thinking of? You probably don't even know what a capitalist is."

"Of course I do!" Peter bursts out. "It's a factory owner who is bad to his workers."

"That's part of it," Frank says, puffing on his cigarette.

"My father is good to his workers," Peter says. "He built them their own tennis court."

Before he can finish, Mem appears, wearing a pink satin wrapper that keeps sliding off her shoulder.

"What are you saying to my son?" she demands.

"That fishing is decadent."

"He likes it. Leave him alone."

"I still don't see why it's capitalist," Peter puts in.

"It's what we call exploiting nature," Franks says. "Ask your papa what that means."

"Don't talk to him about his father!" Mem interrupts.

"Why not?" Frank answers, with a little smile.

"What do you think?"

"Are you afraid of losing your little stipend?"

"Aren't we gallant today!"

"I don't give a damn about being gallant. I care about the truth."

In the midst of their quarreling, they go inside, and Peter hears the bedroom door slam shut. Tucking his fishing rod under his arm, he slips away, afraid that Frank will throw his rod into the lake the next time he comes out.

Later that day, he hears Thesi telling the cook that after the summer, Mem is going back to Berlin so that she can live with Frank. Thesi says Frank is seeing the actress Liesel Viertel too and that Mem had better watch out or she'll end up catching something from him. What could she catch? Some kind of flu? And what about Fellerer, who still has feelings for her? What if Mem has a baby with one of them and no longer has any time for him?

More and more friends of Mem's show up at Grundlsee, and Mem is happy to see them all again. "I have so much in common with these people," she says to him. "Artists, poets, intellectuals – this is really where I belong."

The women like to sunbathe naked, but luckily they don't use his balcony, gathering at the house of Liesel Viertel instead. They lie in the sun for hours on end, rubbing oil into each other's backs and gossiping.

During these times, he goes around with a group of local boys. The older ones find excuses to swim near the ladies' porch, and to show that he is also grown-up, he follows along, but he prays that Mem will be lying on her stomach, or that when she sees the boys approaching she'll cover herself up.

He sees less and less of Mem as the days go by – Fellerer and Frank are always popping up, and when they aren't around, all she wants to do is lie out in the sun. Peter and his friends spy on a man with a bald head and a paunch who is sitting on the beach with Margitta, a local girl who waits on tables at the Hotel Sommer. The man has a towel on his lap and he is leaning back, his face lifted toward the sun. Margitta's hand is under the towel and she is leaning forward, with her eyes half-closed, as though she's trying to remember something. Straightening up, she takes away her hand and the man adjusts his trunks. They slowly get up and walk out into the lake, until the water reaches their waists. After they leave, Peter and his friends inspect the spot, like detectives searching for evidence.

Why does Frank say that fishing is sick and corrupt? Why doesn't his mother take his part? Is it really true that Hans wants to marry Inge? When he tells his mother that Hans and Inge aren't doing *that* together, she is annoyed with him.

"I always think of you as so grown-up," she says, "but then I see that you're really just a child."

"I'm not just a child!" he says, his eyes filling with tears, so that he has to turn away.

He hears the men talking about how bad the economy is, and about how everyone is blaming the Jews. In the afternoon, the women sunbathe; in the night, there are wild parties that last until dawn. The locals spy on these goings on through binoculars, hiding in the hills or watching from canoes. "Let them look!" the women say. "And if they're handsome, let them come a little closer, so we can take a look at them!"

Should he fish or shouldn't he? Should he be like Frank, the revolutionary, or should he be like Hans? He fishes off the balcony when Frank isn't around and makes Mem promise not to say anything about it.

After Peter comes back from the vacation, he isn't himself: Anna notices the change in him right away. She says that the turbulence of Grundlsee hasn't been healthy for him, and that given the chaos of his parents' lives, he should really go to boarding school. Hans doesn't agree with this assessment at all. Like a lawyer, he lines up his arguments. He tells her that he and his son are very close. He reads out loud to him almost every night; sometimes he even shares his own writing with him. (Never mind that Peter has come to dread the moment when Hans turns to him and says, "Well, what do you think?" because of the pressure it puts on him.) The boy doesn't like hunting, but he takes him along to his hunting lodge in Klausen nonetheless, in the hopes that he will come around. (He has no idea that Peter is afraid of the gigantic stag's head that stares down at him from above the fireplace.) He points out the fact that they are starting to play little duets and that soon they'll be good enough to play a piece at one of his parties. (He doesn't notice that Peter is already better on the piano than he is on the violin, a situation that makes for a certain awkwardness.) With the help of the maid Thesi, Hans has given Peter the kind of life that his mother couldn't provide. (Peter still hopes that Mem is going to come back – even though Hans says that she won't – and that the maid will go away.) How could losing all this do Peter any good? It's out of the question. Hans won't hear of it.

And so the arrangement stays as it is. Peter continues to live with Hans, to see Anna five times a week, and to attend the Hietzing School, that little patch of ground where utopian ideals thrive and grow. On the other side of the fence, dark forces are gathering, forces that will soon uproot the enlightened consciousness that Anna and her colleagues are desperately trying to sustain.

Looking back on it all, Anna would probably have resisted the temptation to say something dramatic about the contrast between the high-minded goals of the Hietzing School and the barbarism that was taking hold beyond its gates. Narrowing her wise old eyes, she might have remarked, "Yes, it was an experiment – an experiment conducted in unstable conditions." And she would have sighed deeply.

3.

The Hietzing School

Vienna, 1927–32

PETER loved Tinky, but most people loved Mabbie, who was older than Tinky by two years. When Peter traveled to England to speak to his old schoolmates, the image of Mabbie was still fresh in their minds. Victor Rosenfeld said that Mabbie was a golden angel: "No one else compared to her." Ernstl Freud admitted that he had been in love with her, a fact that took Peter, even at 60, by surprise. Mabbie had been Victor's, while Tinky had been his – it had all been decided when they were ten years old. But how could anyone not love the "stunning Mabbie," as Ernstl called her?

Her parents were in a bitter fight over custody during her time at school, but her caretakers showered their attention on her. Anna Freud made no secret of her fondness for her, telling her how God had taken a bit of blue out of the sky to make her eyes. Peter Blos remembered sitting by Mabbie's bed with Anna, one of them on either side of her. Mabbie asked them to tell her a story, and so they took turns, while Dorothy listened from a rocking chair. "We did this to the delight of the child and to the amusement of ourselves," Blos wrote. And yet, all this time, Bob, another patient of Anna's, was lying alone and forgotten across the hall. "Mabbie was the most lovable and charming of the four children," Blos confessed, "a fact that must have made the scene even more intolerable for the boy in the next room."

Erik Erikson puts Mabbie first in a series of psychological portraits that he composed about the children of the Hietzing School. Erikson's analysis of Mabbie, whom he refers to as "the Bright-eyed One," draws on "fieldwork" done by Mabbie's mother. Two or three times a year, Dorothy entered the schoolhouse with a notebook in hand, reading out a question and asking the students to write an essay or short story in answer to it. Some of Dorothy's questions were surprisingly cruel: "What would you do if your parents were to die? How would you make your way in the world?" Others were less harsh: "If you could have anything in the world, what would you wish for?"

Many of the children stumbled over these questions, but Mabbie wasn't one of them. As Erikson tells it, Mabbie "laughs merrily when the theme is given, as if to say 'Now I'll show you!'" And then she writes:

> Once in spring, I got spring fever. All I wanted to do was to look out the school window to see whether the sky was still blue and whether the buds had already burst. I was so excited. After school I ran off and let my hair fly behind me. That was so beautifully cooling.

There is so much hunger for life in these sentences – but nothing is as simple as it seems. Erikson, an analyst in the making, interjects his analysis, tying Mabbie's desire to a history, placing her yearnings under his lens.

Erikson: "The first of the impetuously realized wishes is to let her hair fly loose." This, he notes, is significant. Mabbie has told him that she once had beautiful, long hair that her mother decided to cut. The cutting of her hair against her will has been "the focus of all resentment against her mother."

And so the little girl sits and writes, innocent of how fully she is revealing herself. In her story, she goes out without putting on her socks:

> I stormed all over the lawn and threw myself on the cool, moist grass. I rolled around and squinted into the sun and did not move for a long time, but I was baked like a pudding … Suddenly I saw a horse running as wildly as I had done. So I jumped up and over to the horse and onto his back. And it stormed away. Throughout gallop and gallop, through racing and trot, I sat on the horse, but then I fell down and stretched my arms and legs in the burning spring sun. The bees hummed and buzzed, and the red sun shone through my lids …

Erikson's analysis: the release that comes from letting down her hair accounts for the spirit of abandon that dominates the entire piece. In a later composition, Mabbie returns to the theme of hair, but now she handles it very differently:

> The story is about a family that's very well-off; they have two cars and riding horses at their disposal. They have a girl, about fourteen years old who was very vain about her long, curly hair. Then came bad luck. The father had an accident, became an invalid, was debt-ridden, drank, and ended in jail. The girl's first idea was to rush out to the edge of the city to pick many flowers and sell them. While her mother searched for work, she picked flowers, huge bunches, and tied them together with her gorgeous hair. Then she ran back, asking her way again and again, until she arrived exhausted at home. On the next day she tried unsuccessfully to sell the bouquets. Only one man came, asked for the flowers, and gave two pennies. He told her she had splendid hair and could get a whole lot of money if she sold it. She thought, "That's a good idea," and ran across the street to the hairdresser and asked him if he wanted her hair. "Oh, what lovely hair you have, but it is dirty. Let me wash it and then I'll buy it." She was given a very small sum, with which she ran to her mother, who was so happy and who found her daughter clever and kind.

Erikson: "The girl who feels that her mother has robbed her of her hair tells a story of a child who sacrifices her hair for her mother's sake." (It's significant that the little girl in the story is given such a small sum, and it's interesting that Erikson doesn't notice it, although he notices so much else.)

Erikson goes on to discuss the many possible meanings of cutting hair – as a price that has to be paid, as a punishment for unbridled narcissism, as an outward sign of the beautiful appearance covered up in real life and manifested in art, drawing connections to the Old Testament story of Absalom, King David's ungrateful son, who took fatal pride in his long hair, and to the Oedipal theory of psychoanalysis.

On the face of it, the stories that Mabbie told as a little girl were a full expression of the Mabbie that everyone knew and loved. As she grew older, a buried theme became predominant – the theme of self-sacrifice.

In Anna Freud's writings, Mabbie appears as the tearful eight year old who comes to her because her parents' marriage is falling apart. Anna thinks of her as the most successful of her child patients. She remains in analysis for the rest of her life. During her formative years, Anna becomes Mabbie's mother's closest friend, and psychoanalysis becomes her mother's religion, making it doubly hard for Mabbie to break away from it. Anna is her mother's constant companion. Confiding in her mother means confiding in Anna Freud. In an early letter to her mother, Mabbie writes: *I would like Anna Freud to read my letters but when I think of her reading them, I get shy so I thought I won't write it to you …*

At age 13, she breaks out in a complaint, using the garbled language of an American girl who is growing up in between English and German:

> Oh, it's awfully blöd (stupid) because everything has unknown reasons. I with my many troublys (troubles) and unknown reasons. Everything has an unknown reason. Oh reason after reason, everything with its reasons. It nearly makes me mad. Wide shoes have it, fears have it, things with Daddy and you have it, well … nearly everything. But hard to live with these sogennante (so-called) reasons, it is not only sometimes.

(misspellings in the original)

But despite this resistance, Mabbie becomes, according to her younger brother, a virtual "ambassador of psychoanalysis," appearing as a success story in the psychoanalytic literature. Her openness seems to work against her here; the ever-elusive Tinky, for example, manages to retain more of her privacy. (The Burlingham children come in two distinct sets – Mabbie and Bob are more exposed to the disintegration of their parents' marriage; Tinky and Mikey grow up in the shade that their older siblings provide.)

The Mabbie that Erikson conjures up is very attractive, full of joy in simply being alive. But for those who knew her as a young, and then as a middle-aged, woman, Erikson's notes point to an area of extreme vulnerability.

When he was 60 years old, Peter began writing a recollection of Mabbie, but then he broke off, saying it was impossible for him to be objective about her. She was the older sister of Tinky, his first love; she was also the heart of the school's community. She was always ready to help the younger ones, like him, a fact that he never forgot. But she wasn't merely a "goody goody" – she was creative and humorous, as is reflected by another school document that Peter managed to retrieve.

This mock-scientific treatise is entitled "Authentic Proofs of the True Kinship Between the Two Old and Honorable Families of Freud and Burlingham." In this piece, which is written in an upright, diligent, solid script that does its best to navigate around several comical drawings, Mabbie postulates the descent of the Burlinghams from an ancestral "Tiftank," who married an "infamous woman," identified as an "Indian." Invoking the "well-known theory" that the Indian descended from the lost tribes of Israel, she surmises that the Burlinghams are actually Jewish. She draws a connection between the dark, lustrous, "undegenerated" eyes of the Freuds and the eyes of the Burlinghams, which are pale to the rim, presumably as a result of the mingling of Nordic and "Indian" (read Jewish) blood. But although here the Nordic or Aryan becomes the degenerate, the Freuds don't always play the part of the Pure. Thus, according to Mabbie, the summer residences of the Freuds "sprout up like mushrooms" wherever the Burlinghams happen to be.

The intimacy of Anna and Dorothy is evenly mocked in Mabbie's descriptions of how they dress. The "revered ladies" "dress attractively" in clothes "which for all average ladies would be quite impossible." Mabbie gives herself the license to conjure up an odd and eccentric couple: "Who else could wear the caps, drawn deep down to the very eyebrows, as a charming adornment? Who else could so trippingly and gracefully move ahead in such widely drawn skirts?" And "Who else could move their feet like gazelles in such heavy and gross rubber shoes and snow boots and set them so gracefully on the ground?"

Mabbie's drawing of the "revered ladies"

Mabbie's drawing of the "revered ladies" depicts two figures in shapeless coats and baggy skirts; they are seen in profile, facing each other. The space that divides them is bridged by their hands; these little old girl ladies seem to have eyes only for each other. The essay acknowledges that the imitation of the Freud/Burlingham families goes both ways, so that the Burlinghams set their clocks by Freudian time. Apart from its rewriting of the *Rassenkunde* (racial) diatribes of the time to make a case for the oneness of Aryan and Jew, Mabbie's humorous treatment is also a witty report on the phenomenon that she has witnessed at first hand and that has transformed her life – namely, the fusion of her family with that of the Freuds.

In her last years, Mabbie fell into a deep depression, convinced that she had never lived for herself, only for others, and that she had never accomplished anything in her own right. Overcome by a sense of her worthlessness, she traveled from the United States to England, returning to her old bedroom at Maresfield Gardens and taking an overdose of sleeping pills. Although she was discovered and rushed to the hospital, it was too late and she died four days later, after great suffering.

When the news reached Peter, he was shocked. Why hadn't Anna Freud and Dorothy Burlingham seen this coming? Hadn't they both spent their entire lives honing and refining their insights into human nature? Whenever Mabbie's name came up in conversation, he shook his head, unable to connect the radiant girl he had known as a boy to what she had become.

Another person in Peter's world was Elizabeth Iona, referred to by Erikson as "the Gentle Girl." She positioned herself at the margins of the community, but in her very aloofness she created an opening in the invisible wall that surrounded the Hietzing School. Beyond that wall, hostile forces were on the rise, forces that would hit progressive Vienna like a tidal wave. Elizabeth Iona, independently of everyone, set out in search of a refuge that would be indestructible.

Although she was the same age as Mabbie, in a school that never had more than 20 children, the 2 girls never became friends. Dorothy Burlingham tried to bring them together, but her efforts failed. In a taped interview, Elizabeth speaks of Mabbie in a cool, detached way, as though Mabbie had somehow disappointed her.

One can see from their school compositions that the girls inhabited very different worlds. In Mabbie's stories, there is a conflict between strong sensuous wishes and maternal restraint. Elizabeth's writings are darker and more violent, like the following story, written when she was ten years old:

> A maiden got lost in the woods and finally, by evening, sank down, exhausted. Sadly she said, "The brook" – she had to stop to get her breath – "the brook misled me." In the middle of the night, a hissing awakened her, and not far from her, she saw two stags and a snake; the stags fought each other, and the snake steadily bit one of the stags; the maiden fled up a tree; from there, she watched the merciless battle, always thinking: "What is going to happen now?" The moon illuminated the landscape; only now she noticed that one of the stags lay sick next to the snake, who continued to bite him; the other stag kicked him; so then the maiden jumped from the tree, took the sick stag, nursed him till he was well; with his help she got home on his back, and her poor mother was happy.

Erikson's reading: the "merciless battle" played out before the maiden's eyes is a version of the sexual act. The immediacy of the question "What is going to happen now?" makes him suspect that "the Gentle Girl" directly witnessed "the primal scene" and that this early shock is registered in her composition. (Curiously, stags play the female part in Erikson's reading, subject to the male violation of the snake.) Erikson goes further: the maiden feels sorry for the sick stag that has been bitten by the snake. This pity is carried over to her "poor mother" when she finally finds her way home.

Two years later, Dorothy asks her grim question again. "What would you do if your parents died? What would you do if you found yourself alone in the world?" In the story Elizabeth writes as a 12-year-old girl, her parents are disposed of very quickly, and instead of mourning them, she mourns the loss of Yvette, a made-up friend she lives with briefly before Yvette's family moves away to India. Her only consolation for losing Yvette is her encounter with a "weeping boy" whose mother is slowly dying. At last, Elizabeth dies and goes up to heaven, where she rejoins Yvette.

Erikson's analysis: the story is motivated by Elizabeth's desire to do away with her mother in order to be with her father. Repressing this desire, she wishes both her parents away. But in the end, not even this is enough – she has to die too, rising into heaven.

In a third composition, the narrator becomes Yvette. The story is entitled "How a Girl Meekly Bore Her Mother's Death," and it describes the moonlit walk of a girl whose father has been sent to Siberia and whose mother is once again dying. In this composition, Yvette receives heavenly assurances that after death, everything will be better. She watches her mother die with a "blessed glow" on her face, after which she falls into a "deep, healthy sleep."

Erikson may have come to Vienna as a young man who was out of a job, but now it is four years later and he has mastered the Freudian idiom. He reads Elizabeth's story through an Oedipal lens, noting that this time she dispatches her father to Siberia, disposing of her mother in a way that points toward salvation and absolves her of guilt.

Erikson's "Gentle Girl" wasn't as gentle as she seemed – she was capable of being cruel to her classmates. Her twin brother Mario was an extension of her and she was fiercely protective of him. When he was threatened, she didn't stop at fending off his opponents; she could be vindictive, even sadistic.

This combination of gentleness with a harsher element surfaces again in Peter's remembrances of Elizabeth Iona. He describes her as "on the small side, with pigtails, diligent, bright, and gentle, with soft blue eyes which she retained in her later life." Like Mario, Elizabeth was methodical and disciplined, not really suited for the loose, improvised structure of the school. But she wasn't as academically gifted as her brother; she had great trouble with spelling, a source of constant frustration to her. And she wasn't always soft and mild; she prided herself on being physically tough. She could also be "devastatingly honest," according to Ernstl Freud, a characteristic that emerges when she talks about the school. In an interview with Peter, she makes it clear that the school wasn't a magical place for her. It simply marked a phase in her life, one that she didn't feel nostalgic about.

The truth is that Elizabeth and her brother were outsiders at the school. Their home life wasn't falling apart; they weren't looking to the school to provide them with a surrogate family. Their mother was clear about what she wanted from the school: she wanted her children to receive a progressive education, but she didn't want them to undergo analysis. After 12:00, when the others went off to see Anna Freud, or

August Aichorn, or Dorothy Burlingham, Elizabeth and Mario Iona walked home (their house was only 20 minutes away). And while they walked along the tree-lined streets of the Hietzing district, they chatted about the events of the day. How they must have marveled over certain things that the other students took for granted. What did they say to each other, for example, on the day that Walti Aichorn, a strapping, healthy boy, ran all over the playground yelling at the top of his lungs, "They've finally found out what's wrong with me!"

The fact that her mother didn't approve of therapy reinforced Elizabeth's skepticism. As time went on, she began to suspect that this thing called "therapy" was a kind of soul-stealing. Thinking back to her failed connection to Mabbie, she recalled:

> I had the impression that Mabbie was under analysis and there was nothing left in her, it was all taken out. It was an empty shell with which one could not have a relationship. I want to be myself, not have it all taken out. That was my impression. The Burlingham children were like empty shells.

There is a spark of resentment here, a desire to puncture the bubble of privilege that surrounded the Burlingham family. Peter lived for the evenings he spent with the Burlinghams; Elizabeth, preempting her exclusion, didn't try nearly as hard to enter that charmed circle.

If she was an outsider at the school, where exactly did Elizabeth belong? Secretly, she was building a society of her own, separate from the Burlinghams, separate from the school, even separate from her science-minded brother, who was so much better at spelling than she was. From the time she was ten years old, she was drawn to the darkness and mystery of churches. Even as a little girl, she was capable of sitting for hours in the *Stefansdom*. It wasn't the ascetic ideals of Christianity that attracted her, it was the "glittering stuff," or what she later called the "Bijouterie," a term taken from her grandfather's custom jewelry business. The candles, the carvings, the touches of gold – all of it captivated her senses.

Elizabeth's mother was the daughter of a Lutheran minister, and although she didn't pass on her belief to her children, it was still important to her. Elizabeth's father was half-Jewish, but completely secular. In her liberal family, religion was never imposed on Elizabeth – her mother believed that if she came to it, she should come to it on her own. During

Elizabeth's years at the school, religion was her secret love, giving her a ground to stand on that was completely her own.

Years later, when he came to interview her, Peter was struck by the way in which the themes of Elizabeth's early life had worked themselves out. She had married a clergyman; religion was still the great passion of her life. But what was most striking to him was the way in which she had managed to hold psychoanalysis at bay. When he asked her to comment on Erikson's analysis of her, she didn't enter into the terms of psychoanalysis at all, saying that at the time of those school compositions, she had been sexually naïve, so that she doubted that there was much sexual content in them. Her yearnings for "Yvette" simply reflected her yearning for the friends she was forced to leave behind when her family moved from Dresden to Vienna. Whatever harshness was reflected in her compositions corresponded to her toughness as the protector of Mario. Unlike Mabbie, she had held psychoanalysis at arm's length and had made religion her guiding light. In this, she was assisted by a mother who was suspicious of psychoanalysis, unlike Mabbie, whose mother embraced psychoanalysis as her family's salvation.

Struggling with dyslexia, overshadowed by her high-achieving brother, surrounded by privileged classmates who were being treated for invisible illnesses, Elizabeth Iona turned to religion. Years later, when Peter spoke with her, she told him that she had never been disappointed, a fact that was impressive to him, given his own lifelong entanglement in psychoanalysis. Her piety was a little alien to him, but her life had a logic, a coherence that somehow made perfect sense. He had been consistent too, but it had taken the form of contradiction, of doubt, of ambivalence.

There were also wilder figures in Peter's scene, wilder and more dangerous, like Sigurd Baer, the older brother of Basti, the school rascal. Both of the Baers had something subversive about them, but where Basti was admired, Sigurd was feared. Peter remembered him as a "lean and angry" bully, an "unpredictable menace to us little ones."

Sigurd and Basti didn't come from money, yet they seemed to inhabit a fairy-tale. They lived in a fantastic castle in Laxenburg, near Vienna, where their parents ran the Laxenburg-Hellerau School for Rhythmics, Dance and Gymnastics. Basti loved the castle, even though at night he was a little afraid; its catacombs, chambers, and winding halls were a source of endless fantasies. But for Sigurd, the castle was a place of loneliness and suffering. Their mother, an American woman with ambition and flair, loved both of her sons, but she didn't have much time for them, consumed by the demands of the school. Their father, a big, bearish man, was "very ordinary" according to the unsparing Elizabeth Iona. But even ordinary men can do great harm when they recognize one son and ignore the other. Basti was the golden boy who could do no wrong; Sigurd held his father's attention only when he overstepped his bounds. When Basti came home from school, a journey by streetcar, bus, and foot that took him almost two hours, he found the halls of the castle filled with the fragrance of girls, and even as a little boy, he took a keen pleasure in amusing them. For Sigurd, coming home was a bitter reminder that he was unloved, and he often took out his frustration on his younger brother, who knew to get out of his way when he flew into one of his rages.

Erikson presents Sigurd as an impulsive boy who combines shyness with belligerence. Asked to write a "free school composition," he stands "lost in dreams," "tossing his knife so hard against a wooden wall" that it sticks there. At last, he reluctantly comes inside, walking into the classroom with his head down. Erikson writes: "At his desk he grabbed the first sheet of paper and drew on it with hard strokes. Then he pushed the sheet carelessly aside. I looked at it: on it was an erect male organ, which, because of its angularity, appeared like a curious symbol of aggression, probably made unrecognizable for the dreamy boy himself."

And then Sigurd writes the following composition, which seems to go along with the gesture he has already made. Even as he writes the story, he crosses out certain words – "mother," "school," "child," "father." (The crossed-out words appear in brackets in Erikson's text.)

It is evening. Father Alfred comes home and is as nervous as he usually never is. He has two children: one girl – eighteen – who also goes to work, and another girl, four.

At six the next morning the father and the [mother] older daughter get up and go to work. The father arrives at [school] the factory fifteen minutes late and has five per cent of his salary deducted. The [child] little girl wakes up and realizes that her mother is not awakening her. So she gets up, dresses, eats a piece of bread, and goes to school. The [father] elderly man who comes every day suddenly hears someone scream in the apartment. He goes in and sees the [mother] old woman lying on the [floor] covered with blood. Now she's no longer screaming – she is dead. The father is brought home from work. An investigation ensues. It turns out that the father (who as we know arrived at the factory late) returned home again and murdered the mother. Despite his denial he was "condemned to life imprisonment."

When Sigurd is done writing, he squirms in his seat and then crosses out the whole composition, leaving one last sentence: "The only remaining relatives who the children now had left were very stingy and the children should fend for themselves."

Erikson notes that in the story, the author is missing, but then he points out that he is merely concealed, and not all that carefully: "When the boy tells us by mistake that the father went to school, he only confirms that he feels he is also the father in the story." In other words, the boy is the murderer of the mother. But murder isn't what it appears to be: it's really a depiction of (Oedipal) sexual desire.

The key to this puzzle is found in a story that Sigurd writes when he is two years younger:

I often went on little digs – and once I found a stick which appeared very weird to me. There are so many different kinds of sticks, but this one in particular struck me very much. I went to my room, looked at it more closely, and saw nothing remarkable. In the evening my wife came home. "Well, did you find something again?" she asked me. I said, "No." Once in bed she said, "How shall we live, then, if you don't find anything?" and she was in such a rage that she went to bed. While she was asleep, I sneaked around, took the stick which I had found, and beat her on the brain with it. She shook a little, and then it was over. The neighbors did notice something, though, and notified the police. The police came and asked me where my wife was. I said, "She's sleeping." But they didn't believe me, and I had to lead them to my bedroom. On the chair lay the stick. They asked me, "What's this stick?" "That's a stick which I found on one of my digs." They looked at my wife and said that she was well. They left again, I was happy. I realized that my stick had magic in it. So I had not murdered my wife after all. The two of us lived happily with our magic wand until we died.

Erikson's analysis: here the rage between man and woman turns into the magic of an act of murderous violence that is survived. Rage is the common theme, the thread that ties the two compositions together. This rage can be traced back to the boy's premature weaning from the breast, after which he began to suffer asthma attacks. This was the beginning of the pathology that set the stage for his suffering as an older boy. Providing a glimpse into the psychoanalytically informed bureaucracy of the school, Erikson remarks: "When we examine the pupil's childhood record in the school files, we find it all points to a central phase of a still earlier period, when the mouth was a pleasure-giving and pleasure-denying organ."

Erikson draws up an image of a pent-up, rageful boy that corresponds to Peter's remembrance of Sigurd as a bully. But Erikson goes on to add some softer strokes: "In truth I know hardly anyone who is more gentle and shy with little girls than he is, who, when he is in love with one, is so close to tears. This is no contradiction, since every erotic wish for possession, as we have seen, arouses in him simultaneously some stormy aggression, which finds its expression in its antithesis: shyness and tears, the expression of inner-directed torment."

Erikson's portrait of Sigurd doesn't square with the way in which Elizabeth Iona remembered him. She recalled that Sigurd was always groping the girls in gym, and that he was a nuisance to them. But despite Sigurd's transgressive behavior at the school, it became a place in which his aggression was contained, as is reflected in the drawing of an Eskimo kayak that he contributed to the Christmas journal.

D e r   K a j a k .

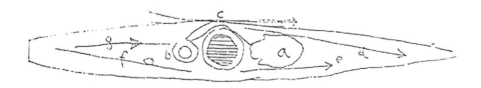

Sigurd's drawing of an Eskimo kayak

47

The male inserts himself into the female boat; the boat is perfectly fitted out with everything he needs. Sigurd uses letters to indicate where various weapons are kept – spear, knife, birding arrows, harpoon – and in his accompanying text he notes that the entire boat must be covered with skins. When the Eskimo is on board, he fastens fur jackets over the hole, so that no water can get in. "One with the boat," he can now navigate the rivers of Greenland to his heart's content; although he is alone, he is supported and sustained.

This homemade utopia broke apart when Sigurd transferred to the public Gymnasium. During this same period, his mother died at the age of 43, throwing him onto the indifference and violence of his father.

After doing badly at the Gymnasium, Sigurd joined the Austrian Military Labor Service, where he was called *Saujud* (Jewish pig) constantly. He was given this epithet purely on the basis of his looks – he didn't have a trace of Jewish blood. "He was hook-nosed and wore horn-rimmed glasses," Basti said. Even before the Nazi period, this was enough. The insults of his fellow soldiers ate away at him – when he was 22 years old, he gave up on the military and went home. And yet, with his mother gone, there was no homecoming for him. It was becoming more and more clear that he had no place in the world. After a violent fight with his father, he went up into his room, put a rifle into his mouth, and killed himself.

Erikson had isolated oral deprivation as Sigurd's problem when he was a boy; in the manner of his suicide, Sigurd bore Erikson out. The predictive power of child analysis was very much on Peter's mind when he looked up his classmates as an aging man. He wanted to know how his classmates had evolved; he wanted to discover the leitmotif that had announced itself early in their lives and that had played itself out in a series of variations that, taken together, became their destinies. He sometimes laughed at this desire in himself, as though there was something childish and naïve about imagining that one could fully understand another human being. And yet, given his upbringing in analysis, he was almost born to this search. By trying to get at the truth of his schoolmates' lives, he was testing the method that had been applied to himself. Were the interpretations, the judgments, accurate? Had the passage of time borne them out?

And so he looked his old classmates up and compared what they said about themselves as adults to what had been said about them when they were young. In some cases, this attempt failed because the classmate wasn't inclined to be forthcoming. Walter Aichorn, for example, the son of August Aichorn, an analyst who collaborated with the school, and who actually analyzed his own son, refused to be interviewed, writing a few comments that composed a record which, according to Peter, was "radically incomplete." Ighino Wimmer, the "Inaccessible Boy" of Erikson's essay, denied that he was the basis of that portrait, a disavowal that Peter didn't fully believe, but that nonetheless prevented him from sketching an adequate portrait of him.

The last of the three "sons," Bob Burlingham, was someone that Peter had kept track of over the years. He was the most dazzling of the "older ones," and he capitalized on it, flirting madly with the girls. Peter remembered him as a "model of elegance, talent, and charm." The younger boys in the school all looked up to him. It was for Bob that the school had been formed. His "delinquent behavior" (Anna Freud's words) and his habit of lying (she referred to him in her writings as "the boy who couldn't tell the truth") had first led Dorothy Burlingham to seek out Anna's help. Written after five years of therapy with Anna, Bob's school composition seemed to Erikson to be full of promise, both as a testimony to his emotional maturity and as a literary effort.

In Bob's story, an "old man" who is "over 50 years old" sits in his comfortable living room, surrounded by half-read newspapers. He is married, has children, "a fortune, a house" – but because he has been "lazy" and "lacking in willpower," he has "failed to take advantage of all the opportunities that life had to offer him."

According to his custom, he leaves his house and has his driver take him to his favorite restaurant. Here he has a coffee, and more newspapers are brought to him, which he reads through, in the name of self-improvement. The waiters make a fuss over him, knowing that he will tip them generously. But then "a young lad, poorly dressed" saunters into the restaurant. Without paying much attention to anyone, he sits down at a nearby table and puts his head in his hands. His weariness doesn't point to any weakness in him; it seems to come from physical work. The old man feels the young man's competence right away. He senses that he is the kind of person "who will go far, who will make his way everywhere." The waiters are contemptuous of the shabbily dressed young man, convinced that he won't be able to pay for his meal. The young man, oblivious to the commotion he has caused, puts his elbows on the table and "shovels his soup slowly and greedily." The old man, who is intensely focused on his every move, is disturbed by this young man, who clearly "has no manners" – the waiters look at each other as if to say "How this guy eats!" The young man gets up, pays for his meal, but leaves no tip, to the outrage of the waiters, who have no choice but to let him go. As for the young man, he seems energized by his meal. "His broad shoulders swing a bit" as he goes out. The old man eventually leaves too, but as he is driven home, a shadow keeps growing within him. He is unnerved by the decisiveness of the younger man, but he tries to hold onto his disdain for his poor manners and his shabby clothes, fretfully assuring himself that he's better off.

Erikson notes, in his analysis, that the young man represents an "ego ideal" and that the older man represents "the dangers of inner bankruptcy." In Bob's composition, these dangers are "taken in, penetrated, and finally rejected." The older man is held in contrast to the younger man, who doesn't have any part in the corrupt harmony of the well-paying patron and the waiters. In terms of Oedipal frustration, "infantile hatred is heightened, and out of it is created an exaggerated personage on whom all discontent can be projected." And yet the conflict between the old man and the young man isn't black and white; the author has achieved a level of maturity that allows him to reveal the older man's dilemma from the inside.

Erikson reads this composition as a cause for optimism, mixing praise with analysis. He sees the author as being ready to take on the challenge of his own life. The optimism that he feels regarding Bob is inseparable from his belief in the saving power of what we now refer to as "talk therapy." The style of the composition, according to Erikson, reveals a mind that has benefited from the "enlightened environment" of psychoanalysis. Rather than reducing the world to "crude dichotomies," Bob renders a complex reality in "small particular strokes."

In his comments on Erikson's analysis, Peter notes that Erikson correctly identified the conflict between "inner bankruptcy" and self-determination that was being played out in Bob's psyche, but that he underestimated its intensity. Moreover, he can't help wondering whether the "rosy picture" painted by Erikson wasn't subliminally influenced by a desire to please Dorothy Burlingham, who was, after all, his employer, and Anna Freud, who stood at the gateway of his career as an analyst. And then there was the Burlingham charm. Maybe Erikson was just as susceptible to it as everyone else.

If the Burlinghams were "handsome, gracious, ingenuous in manner," Bob Burlingham possessed all these qualities to the highest degree. He was also legendary in the school for being a risk-taker. Ernstl Freud, who considered Bob his best friend, remembered how he had scaled the walls of the wooden schoolhouse "Douglas Fairbanks style" and raced down Vienna's steep Cobenzl Hill standing on the seat of his bicycle. He delighted in all kinds of pranks, including dousing the elegant Peter Blos with bathwater. He was passionate about the cello, photography, cars, electrical trains, and internal combustion machines, and when he was enthusiastic about something, he had a way of making it his own. His spirit was magnetic and outgoing; Ernstl remembered his "open face over which would spread the most engaging smile so that one could not help taking him into one's heart."

After he had been in analysis for five years, Anna Freud found him to be "radiant and blossoming." He was cured of the lying and stealing he had exhibited before. To her mind, he had been diverted from the path of homosexuality, a "danger" that she and Dorothy had done their best to shield him from. He was also less prone to anxiety. He was at the height of this improvement when Erikson wrote about him; not only had Anna Freud's assessment of his prospects turned around, but he had affirmed the benefits of psychoanalysis.

But his life didn't continue along these tracks. His first marriage to Rigmor "Mossik" Sorensen, a Norwegian woman, broke up, leaving five children in its wake. His next marriage, to Annette Mueller, a nurse, was overshadowed by manic depression. He suffered a breakdown in 1956, from which, according to one of his daughters, he never fully recovered.

Although he blossomed in therapy when he was young, his later analyst, who reported to Anna Freud, was pessimistic about the chance of a cure. Robert's stability was extremely precarious; with constant analysis, a psychotic outbreak might be prevented. Like his sister Mabbie, he died before his time, in the house of Dorothy Burlingham and Anna Freud. The circumstances of his death are still unclear – whether he died of an overdose of sleeping pills or an asthma attack brought on by smoking and drinking remains unknown.

In trying to make sense of Bob's tragic life, Peter came back to Erikson's optimistic portrayal of him, which identified the inner decay of a failed father figure as a danger confronted and overcome.

How strange it must have been for Peter to read Erik Erikson's analysis of Bob Burlingham, the dashing brother of Tinky, his childhood sweetheart. How strange it must have been to hear him hailed, in unambiguous terms, as someone ready to take on the conflicts of life – especially in hindsight, once everything had failed. And yet it must have been even stranger to encounter himself as "the ten-year-old" member of Erikson's triad of three "Sons." Erikson didn't have all that much to say about the story Peter told, which went like this:

> Mr. Morningstar was in a very bad mood because he realized that his workers were demanding higher wages. While he was arguing with his wife, some street kids were fighting in the factory yard. They fought awhile until suddenly one of the boys picked something up and ran away. The others ran after him. After a while one could see all those boys calmly sitting and smoking on the barrels of the Morningstar petroleum and gasoline storage houses. They thought that they were all grown up and that cigarette smoke was wonderful. Suddenly one heard steps in the factory yard. The boys quickly threw their cigarettes into the gas and petroleum barrels and ran away. After several minutes there was a dreadful crash; one saw a few walls fly into the sky. Then it was over.
>
> Some people came running. "What happened??" "The Morning-star factory has exploded into the air!" "Who has done it????????" A young worker stands there swaying back and forth, and he is as white as paper. "He did it," everyone thought. Several called loudly, "He's the one who did it!!!!!!" The young worker falls to the ground. "Here's the proof that he did it!!!!" Several people go to the worker. They say softly to him, "Hey you, Fritz. I wouldn't have thought it of you. Say, did you really do it?" They looked at the face of the worker. It was still as white as chalk. The two workers went away.

The door rang at the Morningstar home. "Mr. Morningstar, there's a worker outside, and he has something dreadfully important to tell you," says the maid. "I never receive anyone during the day. Send him away!" But the worker at the door didn't go away. Mr. Morningstar got worried. But no, he thought. "My factory is safe, nothing can happen to it." Mr. Morningstar goes outside. "Get out of here," he screams at the workers. He opens the door; the worker goes out the door and throws a tenpenny piece toward Mr. Morningstar. "You should be grateful to me, Mr. Morningstar. You have less than I have. Your factory has exploded into the air." Mr. Morningstar faints. The worker runs down the stairs and laughs.

Peter was probably a little flattered by Erikson's remark that "there's little one can add to this story," even though it was a psychoanalytic rather than a literary observation. But despite this disclaimer, Erikson went on to say that the story was about an attempt, on the part of the boy, to "settle his accounts with his father," noting that he does this in three different ways: "As a boy he exploded the factory into the air with his cigarette (attribute of his already being grown up) and disappears. As a worker, he humiliates his father with the news; he proves to him that he is now superior. But as a younger worker, lying pale on the ground, he cannot free himself from an oppressive feeling of guilt."

In his writing about Erikson's assessment of his "little essay," Peter concedes that the analysis reveals "a basic character trait" of a person who "throughout his life benefited and suffered from a pervasive ambivalence" revealed in wavering between "rebellion against a father-figure and guilt-ridden submission." He feels that Erikson's remarks, brief as they were, were in keeping with Anna Freud's identification of the "central problem" of the boy as consisting of indecision "as to whether he should assume a 'masculine' or 'feminine' role." Like Bob Burlingham, Peter was seen as being vulnerable to the possibility of homosexuality, a great risk for all boys, in Anna Freud's mind, and one that her therapeutic interventions were designed to prevent. This ambivalence is again borne out in Peter's attitude toward his analysis. In the passage above, he embraces it as correctly identifying the truth of his own ambivalent nature. And yet, at the same time, he continues to question the process that he was submitted to as a child, a process that initiated him into a language and a way of seeing that he could never forget, expel, reject. He reentered this process in the middle of his life, retrieving his case history, making it into the basis of his own search, using it as a key to examining and retelling the story of his past. Maybe it was through writing that Peter finally settled his accounts, since writing afforded a way of submitting (internalizing) and rebelling (revising) at the same time.

4.

Lessons in Self-defense

Vienna, 1929–31

IN *The Ego and the Mechanisms of Defense*, Anna Freud tells the story of a ten-year-old boy who made a thrilling discovery: "During a certain phase of his analysis he developed into a brilliant football player. His skill was recognized by the big boys at his school and to his great delight they let him join their games."

But the pride that came with being accepted by the older boys soon gave way to anxiety. Her patient dreamt that he "was playing football and a big boy kicked the ball with such force that [he] had to jump over it in order not to be hit." The boy who jumped over the ball was Peter, and the big boy in his dream was Sigurd Baer. Peter had reason to be terrified of his older teammate – at school, Sigurd bullied the "little ones" and, at home, his fits of rage were so extreme that his younger brother was afraid for his life.

Anna Freud doesn't deny that the dream was a response to a real threat, but this isn't what catches her eye. It is the symbolism of this dream and of a subsequent fantasy that enables her to find what she is looking for: "The same theme reappeared soon afterward in a fantasy he had when going to sleep. He thought he saw the other boys trying to knock his feet off with a large football. It came hurtling towards him and he jerked his feet up in bed in order to save them."

For Anna, there is no longer any doubt as to the source of her patient's anxiety: "We had already found out in this little boy's analysis that the feet had a peculiar significance for him. By the roundabout way of olfactory impressions and the ideas of stiffness and lameness they had come to represent the penis."

According to her interpretation, the threat of castration was triggered by success; it was his father, not Sigurd Baer, that her patient really feared. Sigurd, as menacing as he was in real life, was merely a stand-in, a substitute.

Not long after his acceptance by the older boys, Peter stopped excelling at the game. As Anna tells it, "His skill diminished and he lost the admiration it won him at school. The meaning of this retreat was 'There's no need for you to knock my feet off, for anyhow I am no good at games now.'"

According to Anna, by withdrawing from the game, Peter unknowingly imposed a restriction on his ego. But the enthusiasm that was so sharply pulled back quickly found a way of reasserting itself: "He suddenly developed another side of his powers, namely a bent which he had always had for literature and for writing compositions of his own."

And so Anna announces the birth of her patient's true calling. She admits that he had always had a "bent for literature and for writing compositions of his own," but it was at this critical juncture that "the footballer was transformed into an author." As evidence, she cites a graph Peter drew up "to show his attitude to the various masculine professions and hobbies": "In the middle was a large thick point which stood for literature, and in a circle around it were the various sciences, while the practical callings were indicated by more remote points. In one of the top corners of the page, close to the edge, there was a tiny little point that stood for sport, which but a short time ago had occupied such a large place in his mind. The little point was meant to indicate the supreme contempt which he now felt for games." She goes on to say that although he had written from the age of seven, the "superabundance of [his] production" at this time was astonishing.

What was responsible for this dramatic shift? Anna sees it as a way of averting a threat. In her estimation, "the reactivation of his rivalry with his father was responsible for his acute anxiety that the bigger boys might revenge themselves upon him."

The story ends happily, but is it really true, or is it a fairy-tale? Did writing really represent a safe haven for Peter?

During the years of Peter's psychoanalysis, Hans was taking his doctorate in economics at the University of Vienna and learning how to run a large-scale business. But "above all, he was writing," Peter recalled, in a phrase that recaptures a child's sensitivity to the deepest frustrations and yearnings of his parents.

In his memoirs, Hans nostalgically recalls his study in Vienna:

> My entire library, consisting of over 1,000 books of literature and art history, was there. The place was decorated with modern paintings by Schiele and Kokoschka, medieval woodcuts and copper etchings by Dürer, Beham and Holbein, a portrait of Maria Theresa and other antiques, as well as my hunting trophies: chamois, buck and stag antlers and the hide of a huge brown Rumanian bear.

As opulent as it was, this study was more than a showcase for Hans, it was the theater of his ambition. Here he would write deep into the night, trying his hand at newspaper columns for the *Weltbühne*, poems, essays, novels, stories, plays. The male friends that he valued the most were those who served as mentors to him, like Alfred Polgar, a prominent culture critic, and Willy Schlamm, a well-known political journalist.

At some point, Hans must have discovered that his son had a surprisingly good ear, and he didn't hesitate to make use of it. "What do you think of this, Peter?" he would say to him, bringing him into his study and closing the door. And then he would read a passage like this, from his novel *Ein Mann Sucht Seine Heimat* (*A Man Searches for his Homeland*):

> The cable car from Grigno is the major artery of transporting ammunition and other material to the Austrian lines on the Southwestern Italian Battlefront. Since the Austrian Offensive of 1917, it runs day and night to relieve the continuously blocked mountain road, which the Italians had blasted into a vertical rock wall. It's a five-hour trek uphill for the exhausted foot soldiers: sixty-four hairpin curves, climbing two thousand feet up to the plateau of Monte Milleta. The old lumber crate makes it in ten minutes, but the transport of personnel is a hazard to life and limb and strictly forbidden. The arhythmic coughing of the motor and the smashed remnants of the broken crates reinforce the warning notice on the door of the shack. That's where the sergeant is sitting on an oil barrel, enjoying his pipe and the mild warmth of the sun on this late October day.

"Well, what do you think?" he would ask him the moment he was done. "Does it make you want to hear more?" A son knows when his father needs to be reassured. He can feel the pressure bearing down on him. Although his father might tell him to be honest and not to hold anything back, he knows better than to say exactly what he thinks.

And then there was the problem of distinguishing the father he knew from the heroes of Hans' stories and novels. Was Hans writing about himself or was he writing about someone else? Were his stories true or made up?

Some of the scenes in Hans' novels were already familiar to him; he had heard them in the form of war stories, but they had sounded different before. When Hans told these stories rather than writing them down, his voice became monotonous, quizzical, and flat, and there was a faraway look in his eyes. He tended to repeat the same phrases again and again, so that Peter knew them by heart:

In the mountains of Rovereto I listened to the screams of dying men who couldn't be rescued from the line of fire ...

When the snows melted, frozen corpses grew out of the ground, the bodies of friends, the bodies of enemies.

Listening to Hans, he saw him as a young, sorrowful man, picking his way among the dead. *Being a soldier made a man of me*, Hans said. But he wouldn't recommend being a soldier to anyone, because war was horrible and meaningless. No one was a hero if you looked behind the scenes; everybody died by accident.

The first dead man I saw was our own cook. He was hit by shrapnel while he was taking a crap. The most harmless member of our regiment in the middle of the most harmless act. That's what war is really about.

Although Peter could repeat these sentences word for word, they made him feel empty inside. It was different when he listened to Mem, especially when she was telling a story just for him. It didn't matter whether she had told him the same story before; he never got bored. There was one story he liked best of all. "Tell me the story of the falcon!" he would beg.

"Well, somewhere in Italy there was a rich young man," she would begin, turning all her attention on him, "and he fell in love with a married woman. Apart from her husband, this woman had a son who was about your age, or maybe a little younger, I'm not sure. The point is that the young man showered the lady with fancy gifts, but she acted as though he didn't exist, which is something that ladies often do, especially rich, beautiful ones. After a few years of this, all of the young man's money was gone, so he had to dress in rags. All he had left was his falcon, but his falcon was very important to him – it was so perfectly trained that it seemed as though it could read his mind. The boy knew all about the falcon, and about the amazing tricks it could do because the young man had shown it to him – they were neighbors, by the way, because at some point the young man had moved into a little hut near the lady's estate so that he could see her go by in her carriage every day. Anyway, one day the boy got very sick and his mother called in one doctor after another, but none of them could make him get well. 'What can I do to make you feel better?' his mother finally asked him, beside herself with worry. 'Bring me the falcon,' said the boy, sitting up in his bed. 'If you bring it to me, I promise I'll get well.' So she ran out and jumped onto her horse and galloped down the little side road that led to the young man's hut. When the young man saw her coming, he ran into his backyard, called down the falcon and broke its neck."

"But why did he do that?" Peter would interrupt.

"Think about it. What choice did he have? He had dreamt of this moment for years, and now she was finally coming to him, and he had nothing to offer her."

"I would never have done it!"

"Ah, that's what you think, but love makes people do very strange things. Anyway, he roasted the falcon and served it to her, and when they were finished the lady told him why she had come."

"But why didn't she tell him right away?"

"Oh, she was much too refined for that. Really refined people never come straight to the point. When she finally told him, he turned so pale that she apologized for offending him."

"And what did he say?"

"He couldn't say a word. He was much too miserable. He left the room and came back with the falcon's claws, tail, feathers and head, which he laid out on the table in front of her. Only then could he explain why he couldn't give her what she asked."

"But what about the boy?" Peter always asked, even though he knew what she was going to say.

"The little boy died, and it broke his mother's heart. But years later, after her husband died, she married the young man, and they lived happily ever after."

When Mem told that story, every detail came alive because of how she used her voice and her eyes and her hands. Peter could see the falcon circling high up into the sky and he could see the little boy sitting up in his bed and begging his mother to bring it to him.

"When Mem tells a story, no one can take their eyes off of her," Thesi said. Even though Peter resented it when Mem told her stories to just anyone who came around, he admired the way she cast a spell on them.

And yet, for all her brilliance as a storyteller, Mem floundered when she faced the empty page. She needed to have an audience; she couldn't be alone. But a writer needs to know how to be solitary, and here is where Hans had the advantage over her.

Hans wanted his writing to astonish the world, but this hadn't happened yet, and Peter secretly wondered if it ever would. But he knew better than to admit this suspicion to anyone else, except for Anna, who liked that kind of thing.

Permitting himself to trespass, he wrote stories of his own, stories in which factories were set on fire or blown up, or poems that satirized the meaninglessness of life. Maybe *he* was the one in the family who would be great – people said that he was a good storyteller, like his mother was, but unlike her, he loved to write his stories down and to speak to an audience that was always there, if he paid attention, inside his head.

But was it really all right to have the same ambition as his father did, especially if it turned out that he became more famous than him?

In the afterword to his case history, Peter adds some memories of his own to what he refers to as "The Dream of Sigurd" and Anna's treatment of it as a classic case of ego restriction:

What Anna Freud describes in the book does not coincide entirely with my memory. The game in which Sigurd throws the ball was not soccer but a kind of dodge ball (*Volkerball*) in which you have a choice either to catch the ball or to avoid being touched by it, frequently by jumping (as the ball was preferably aimed at one's feet). It hurt to catch the balls thrown by Sigurd, who was anyway the most threatening of the big boys. And yet, A.F. is right. I was afraid to play too well – especially later in the public school and in particular at soccer, to be hit in the ankles, so that I never became a good soccer player but concentrated my ambition on handball, skiing, and so on. I took up fencing after having been hit hard on the nose by my boxing instructor.

Even as he revises the story told by Anna, he acknowledges that in his life he has tended to shy away from successes that he thought would endanger him. He reflects, with unsparing honesty, that this pattern didn't always work smoothly for him as he almost always "accused himself of cowardice and failure in the field from which I withdrew."

The boy who withdrew from the fray becomes the man who has learned how to protect himself but fears that he has learned to do this all too well. And yet this very habit of second-guessing himself is a legacy of his psychoanalysis. *Every emotion can be translated into a thought.* When he was a little boy, this saying of Anna's brought him great relief. But it also taught him, for better and worse, that no emotion is simply what it is.

Thus his love for Anna wasn't really love but a transference of his feelings for his mother. His love for Tinky was a transference as well, an interpretation that shadowed their romance in the years to come, like an inescapable chaperone.

"What is that woman teaching you?" Mem exploded one day, when he told her that he was starting to see that many of his feelings weren't real. "That you shouldn't trust your heart? What a wonderful thing to tell a little boy! Are we really as complicated as they make us out to be?"

He didn't repeat this question to Anna – he was afraid that she would think it was naïve. "Psychoanalysis is hard work," he could hear her saying. "It's something that most people resist." Certainly nothing that Mem said in defense of the truth of emotion would have prevented Anna from making her case. The external threat – the adolescent bully throwing the ball at the smaller boy's feet – is doubly menacing because it stirs up an even more primal fear. The danger that comes from the outside may be very real, but the intense anxiety it stirs up reveals a hidden inner structure that can only be brought to light with the aid of psychoanalysis.

But what about the moment of reckoning that is happening *now* and that will never happen exactly the same way again? The big boys are lining up against each other in the field and Peter is taking the place that they have assigned to him. He is stocky and solid at ten years old, and he's wearing *lederhosen* and a soiled white shirt. Sigurd has the ball in his hands and he's looking straight at him. Will he catch it or dodge it? It could break his shins if it hits him full on. He hears Basti shouting to him from the sidelines, urging him on, and he sees Tinky from the corner of his eye. Sigurd hurls the ball with terrific force, aiming it directly at him. Why did he have to throw it so low? Just a little higher and it would have been his. *Tinky, watch, I'll catch the ball for you!* But at the last instant, he jumps.

Everywhere he goes, there is talk of war. If Peter listens hard enough, he can hear it all the time. His father's friends speculate about it whether he is in the room or not; Thesi and Cook talk about it in code. This constant hum that is sometimes loud and sometimes soft finds its way into his dreams. Anna Freud jots down one of these dreams while he is lying on her couch:

> There is a war. He and Basti are in Belvedere park or the Schwartenberg gardens. They wage war against the Germans. The Germans are 150 men with a bath attendant in charge as their leader. Then they run downhill. Tinky and Basti's fathers are standing there. He recites lines from a poem by Claudius: There is war, etc., I do not want to bear the guilt for its outbreak. He falls down in time with the rhythm to the last verse.

After he tells Anna this dream, other images come to him, which she comments on in her notes:

> Remembers seeing his father naked, taking a bath, quickly looked at the penis. Germany big.

> Wages war with the father about the big penis, has to check all the time whether all men have such a big one. Therefore fear of the father. Therefore going to [public] toilets, therefore incessant comparisons. Guilt, death.

Half a century later, Peter will read these notes and try to make sense of them. He will still remember the lines from Claudius because Hans and his left-wing friends were in the habit of repeating them:

It's war, alas, it's war
And I desire to bear no blame for it

He will also remember that the rivalry of Germany and Austria held particular significance for him because his mother had lovers in both countries. Would she choose Berlin over Austria in the end? Would he have to travel to a different country just to be with her?

He remembers seeing Hans naked in the bath after a session with Herr Urban, his masseur. But part of the shock of seeing his father's penis was that it was smaller than he thought it would be. He writes in his postscript to his case history: "The penis, small and short, floated upward."

Was Hans identified with "little Austria" or "big Germany"? Apparently this wasn't always clear. Was Germany superior to Austria, or was Austria superior to Germany? Another topic that the grown-ups loved to debate. Germany's theater was superior, everyone said, but Vienna had better music and better art. And so the terms of the rivalry swirled around, like murky water in a sink.

Many different threads follow from this dream of war, but Anna Freud manages to weave them into an Oedipal pattern. In psychoanalysis as she practices it, everything is eventually drawn inside, nothing remains tied to the external world. The unconscious is large enough to contain the family romance, but not the world of politics. If Austria is little and Germany is big, this is not the key to a political unconscious. The little boy is afraid that his country will be swallowed up not because of the speculations that he hears wherever he goes but because he is in the grips of an Oedipal rivalry.

Peter dreamt of war in June of 1929; on October 29 of that year, the American stock market crashed, bringing on the Great Depression. In the chaos that followed, Austria's economy collapsed, setting the stage for the country's embrace of Nazism.

In 1929, the newspapers were full of the Halsman case, which would go down in the history books as the Austrian Dreyfus affair. The story went like this: Two Lithuanian Jews, a father and his 22-year-old son, were vacationing in the Austrian Tyrol. They hiked up a steep mountain path called the *Zammerschinder* without a guide, a bad decision, as everyone said afterward. At some point, the father left the path to relieve himself while his son, Philippe, went on ahead. But when his father didn't reappear, Philippe became worried and retraced his steps. He found his father lying in a mountain stream, in a pool of water and blood. Pulling his father, who was still breathing, out of the stream, Philippe was forced to leave him by himself so that he could run down the *Zammerschinder* to get help. By the time the police came, Max Halsman was dead and Philippe was beside himself. The police found evidence of murder, but they didn't reveal this to Philippe, who believed that his father, who was prone to dizzy spells, had fallen and cracked his skull. A search team went out, but no suspects could be found. And now Philippe was in for a second shock – the police arrested him and took him off to jail.

When news of this incident came out, hatred started seeping into the Austrian press. "Dentist killed in the Tyrol!" the papers read. "Son Arrested. The Mother an Accomplice? Insurance Motive Investigated!" Even though two unsolved murders had recently happened in the Tyrol, the non-Jewish jury (Jews didn't usually settle in the remote mountain areas) found Philippe guilty of second-degree manslaughter.

Condemned to hard labor, Halsman went on a hunger strike, and his sister mounted a campaign on his behalf, organizing a rally where many famous people spoke, including Jacob Wasserman, Thomas Mann, and Sigmund Freud. After a drawn-out battle, the charges against Halsman were finally dropped, but there was no apology, let alone compensation, for the harrowing months that he had spent in jail. In fact, he was told never to set foot in Austria again, as though, despite his innocence before the law, he was still guilty of some fundamental breach of behavior.

How much of this story did the nine-year-old Peter hear? Did he know that Sigmund Freud spoke on Halsman's behalf, or that even before this, he was called to Halsman's Innsbruck trial to determine whether the defendant was suffering from an "Oedipus complex"? Freud told the court that the case against Halsman was ridiculous, and that there was no way that this young man was capable of murdering his own father.

So the Halsman case found its way into 19 Berggasse, but did it find its way into Peter's consciousness? Jews talked about it in coffee houses throughout the city, growing silent when Gentiles approached their tables. Anti-Semitism was a given for Viennese Jews, but the Halsman case threw it into sharper focus. How sturdy was the invisible wall that protected the students of the Hietzing School from the voices of hatred that were growing louder and louder all around them?

They couldn't have chosen a better day for a field trip, the teachers say. Even though it's late October, it feels like summer. The Danube is a soft, dreamy blue, uncoiling below the battlements of the Greifenstein. They've made sketches of the castle, or at least some of them have, and they've knelt in the hollow of the rock just inside the castle gate. Each of them has repeated the required oath – "As truly as I touch this stone, so do I honor the hospitality of this house" – which keeps criminals and thieves away. Looking out over the hills from the top of the yellow–grey tower, they've listened to the tale of the lord of Greifenstein, who banished his daughter to the woods for falling in love with one of his hunters.

Peter and Tinky are sitting together on a stone wall that faces the hazy river. She's wearing a navy-blue skirt, white socks, and tennis shoes, and her short bobbed hair reminds him of honey. Does Tinky believe that the castle is haunted by ghosts? They say that the mean old lord fell down the castle steps and broke his neck on the night of his daughter's wedding feast, even though he had made amends and forgiven her. The story is probably an old wives' tale, but still, you never know. What if some small part of it is true? Tinky doesn't say, one way or another. She is making a little chain out of flowers. Her hands are very clever, much cleverer than Peter's are. He tries to copy her, but his chain falls apart.

In the middle of trying to explain what socialism is to her, Peter remembers that it's never a good idea to talk to other children about "grown-up matters." But Tinky doesn't seem to mind and they get on so well that he doesn't want the day to end.

That night he has dreams that wake him up and send him running to Thesi's bed. In one of the dreams, he sees two yellow sandstone statues of David and Goliath. He becomes terribly angry at the David figure, rushes at it, and smashes it with his fist. Why is the smaller of the two statues so hateful to him? Why do his dreams have so much power over him?

Anna says that Goliath is Hans in disguise, and that the reason that he smashes the other statue is that he doesn't want to kill his father the way that David killed Goliath. The figure of David recurs in Anna's notes, becoming a symbol of Peter's fears of triumphing over Hans. Being passive is safer ... but Anna is afraid that this will lead to homosexuality, an outcome to be avoided at all costs. (Does she pass on this prejudice to Peter as well? Does he grow up believing that homosexuality is a failed development?)

The psychoanalytic reading of the dream is pure and clean, as though it has somehow escaped the messiness of the external world. David must eventually confront Goliath, according to Anna, or he will never become a mature human being. But in the larger picture – and there is no way of knowing this in advance – there will still be a huge army of Philistines at the gate. The insular, protective, utopian world of the school is a version of David too, but it is powerless to combat or even to anticipate Goliath.

While the forces are gathering, the little boy dreams, and some of his dreams are about missing trains. In one of the dreams noted down by Anna:

> He takes a train with Margot and others. She is still outside and he is terribly afraid that she will not get on in time. However she manages to hang on at the last moment.

Anna puzzles over the meaning of this dream, finding part of the answer in Peter's associations:

> On a trip to Cannes … his father and he were out to eat, while Mem and the governess were on the train. He was terribly afraid that they would leave without him, then he would have been left behind alone with his father.

And so an earlier anxiety about being abandoned by Mem and left alone with Hans plays itself out in a later dream, after that anxiety has actually been fulfilled. By the time of the second dream, trains have already become the sites of joyful reunion and anguished separation from his mother.

As he approaches puberty, train stations evolve into scenes of sexual disclosure. In the train station bathroom, he sees other men, comparing them to his father, and he is also privy to encounters between men who eventually step out of the stalls and disappear without anyone knowing what happened there. What is meant to be casual leaves its trace; what is meant to be fleeting has an afterlife. The boy lingering in the corner takes a risk, and as he grows older, this becomes part of the game.

For the moment, sexual curiosity starts to play into an original dread of departures. Thinking back to this fear as an adult, Peter writes:

Another memory comes to mind. When, as a little boy, I travelled alone to Berlin to see my mother, my father ran for a little stretch alongside the slowly moving train, which excited me terribly, as if he could end up running all the way and so come with me.

Here the journey to see his mother becomes entangled with mutually exclusive possibilities. Was Hans out to take his place on the train or did he want to come along in order to bring Mem back home to both of them?

In 1938, when Peter was fleeing Austria, the train proved to be more untrustworthy than ever, cutting him off from everything he knew even as it afforded him a means of escape.

"Is there such a thing as *Wahrträume* (dreams of prophecy)?" Peter asks Thesi one day. He already knows better than to ask Anna. Thesi, who will one day become a respected analyst in her own right, tells him, without hesitation, "No."

There are no Wahrträume. This teaching goes along with the principle that every emotion can be translated into a thought. Reason can illuminate and disentangle the maze of the past. Imagination without reason can't tell us what we will become. There are no *Wahrträume* – this is not only an assertion of rationality but an assertion of faith. And yet how fragile this inward-seeking faith will seem in just a few more years!

Peter reads Traven's *The Death Ship*, a picaresque novel about an American sailor who spends a night with a prostitute and misses his ship. Without identity papers, he becomes an unwanted alien and is kicked around from one port to another. In the midst of reading this book, he has a nightmare that he is drowning and runs screaming to Thesi's bed. Anna notes:

> He doesn't want to admit that he has screamed, says it was because of the fever. To explain his exclamation: while sick, he read the novel "The Ship of the Dead" [by B. Traven] that deals with the destiny of stateless people who have no passport and are shipped from one country to another.

At the end of this note, she sums up her thoughts: *stateless – parentless = Peter.* But why would a little boy be interested in a book about what it means to be stateless? The question is not important to Anna Freud. What is key is that he feels parentless. Immediacy borrows its intensity from what it draws up; the family romance is primary. And so Anna continues to write her notes. Meanwhile, it's 1931 and the clock is ticking.

As a 60-year-old man, trying to feel his way back into his own past with the aid of those notes, Peter will regret the fact that he was told that there was no such thing as a prophetic dream. He will wonder how he would have developed if he hadn't grown up in such a skeptical world; he will regret the fact that so little real authority was granted to the synthetic power of poetic imagination and so much emphasis was placed on analysis. He will think there was something admirable about his mother's commitment to telling stories and realizing herself as an artist, despite all the pain she caused him. And he will point out, with stubborn insistence, that not everything that Anna said was true.

When he and his cousin were fleeing Austria, for example, they had to show the books they were carrying, and his cousin happened to be carrying Traven's *The Death Ship*. The guard questioned his cousin about the book and Peter talked back – with the result that they had to clean out the train station bathrooms on their hands and knees. He never forgot this moment at the border, which could easily have cost them their lives. Perhaps his childhood dream, triggered by reading the Traven book, had contained some seeds of prophecy after all. Perhaps there really were some other ways of reading dreams and reading reality – but during his formative childhood years, those ways had been closed off to him.

5.

The Real Berlin

Berlin, 1929

WHILE Anna Freud teaches Peter that every fantasy can be translated into a rational thought, a small army of directors, producers, cameramen, set designers, script writers, and ogling assistants initiate Mem into the secrets of creating celluloid dreams. Although she's full of uncertainty, Mem has pulled up her roots and come to Berlin. Käthe Leichter's voice is always in her ears: "Go make something of yourself. If you stay in Vienna, you'll suffocate."

Berlin is a tougher city than Vienna, but she feels more awake here, more alive. The stipend from Hans is barely enough to cover her expenses, but she would rather struggle to make ends meet than end up like her mother, Jenni, who traded her acting career for a position in high society. *You underestimate Jenni*, she can hear her father saying. *Not only is she a devoted mother – she has created a brilliant salon.* But how many times has she seen her mother standing in the center of a group of distinguished men with a restlessness in her eyes? *She isn't restless, she's charming*, her father would say, *and you have inherited that charm from her.* Charm, charm. She knows she has it, and she knows how to use it too. But what is charm? Is it anything more than pent-up aggression, a game of cat and mouse?

Hans was charming when he was courting her – so charming that she didn't see what a bastard he really was. She only realized that a few days after the miscarriage, when he finally saw fit to come home from his so-called "business trip." They were sitting together in the living room, or rather, he was standing and she was lying on the couch because the doctor had told her to stay off her feet. Hans was going on and on about a "slight stomachache" and how it was probably the result of the food he had eaten on the plane. He didn't have the vaguest idea of what she had just been through, and he didn't want to know. The mere sound of his voice was unbearable to her after that.

And yet her father was "strongly opposed" to her decision to break the marriage off. He understood that she was dissatisfied with Hans, but how could she walk out on Peter, her own flesh and blood? "Don't you see?" her father had argued with her. "You're doing something you'll regret for the rest of your life."

"But many men leave their children for periods of time."

"It isn't the same for men. Women are tied to their children by a sacred bond."

"But we've made an agreement, Hans and I, that I can visit Peter whenever I like."

"That means nothing. Will you be there when Peter cries out for you in the night? Or when he falls and hurts himself? Or when he finishes some little project that he desperately wants to show to you?"

What her father refuses to understand is that she and Peter are soulmates and that whenever they come together, they share everything that is important to them. And she's convinced that one day, when Peter is more grown-up, she will be infinitely more interesting to him than a mother who has given up her deepest ambitions in exchange for bourgeois domesticity.

On the Sunday after she arrives in Berlin, she goes to the Tiergarten and sits on a bench, watching the passersby. A nicely dressed young mother is sitting across from her with her little boy, watching an old woman feed the birds. All at once, the little boy gets it into his head to throw a rock at the birds, causing them to fly up into the air. The old woman shakes her fist at him and tells the mother that she better discipline her son, and then she wanders off, muttering to herself.

"What's gotten into you?" the mother says, but the boy can barely sit still and doesn't want to listen to her. She takes him by the arm and speaks intensely to him, until he finally hands over the arsenal of stones that he's collected in his pockets. Watching the two of them, Mem notices that the mother's face looks tired and washed out, even though she can't be much older than she is. What does that woman really want from life? Does she ever stop to ask herself that question anymore or has she already given up on it?

As the mother and the boy walk away, Mem remembers how she

agonized over her decision, going back and forth in her mind. Should she try to make things work with Hans? Should she stay in Vienna so that she could see Peter every week, or would that just be confusing to him? If she stayed in Vienna, could she still pursue her career?

One morning, she ran upstairs to her mother's room and knelt by her bed. "I don't know what to do!" she said, pouring out her feelings. Her mother stroked her hair the way she did when she was a child, and listened. "There's really no question," she said at last. "You have to go to Berlin."

Mem threw her arms around her mother and cried.

Mem takes an apartment on the fifth floor of a run-down building on the Luisenplatz that has no elevator and smells of mold. There is only one window and it looks out onto a blackened air shaft, but she doesn't care. She adds a few touches to make the place feel like her own – a small Persian rug, an embroidered tablecloth, a shawl to cover the battered couch. She eats bread, apples, and cheese by candlelight, and while she's eating she scribbles down screenplay ideas. *I'm living in an absolute hovel*, she has one of her characters say, *and yet I feel more free than ever before.* She puts up pictures of her favorite stars – Conrad Veidt, Elizabeth Bergner, Pola Negri. But her favorite picture is one of her mother dressed in a white, low-cut gown, playing the part of Desdemona in *Othello*.

Before she left Vienna, she had sent a film treatment to F.W. Murnau and to her amazement he wrote back, saying that her idea was interesting and that she should come to UFA and work on scripts. Carrying that letter in her purse, she takes a series of trams and trains to the *Filmstadt* (film city) of Babelsberg, 50 miles outside Berlin. She doesn't meet Murnau on that first day: instead she is driven around by a pug-nosed boy in a black leather jacket and a black leather cap. As he drives her along Babelsberg's crowded streets, he rattles off various facts – Babelsberg covers over 80 acres of land; in addition to its two gigantic ateliers, it has a total of 22 buildings that house woodworking shops, sculpture studios, glass-working shops, costume collections, and so forth; it has its own power plant that transforms 10,000 volts of power into normal current and that delivers 15,000 amperes of light; it has underground chambers that protect against explosions caused by spontaneous combustion, etc.,

etc. As he is talking, they pass various sets: a medieval fortress, a village square, an elegant club with tennis courts, a racetrack, a train station, a riding school. He points out the greenhouse, where they raise tropical plants, and a barn-like structure where they keep whatever animals they need. (Did she hear a lion roar or is she just imagining things?) All at once, the boy jams on his brakes to let an ambulance pass.

"Is that a real ambulance?" she asks.

"It looks pretty real to me."

"Why is it here?"

"Could be for a stuntman, or for a construction worker. Who knows? People get hurt here all the time." At the next intersection, he puts his hand on her leg, but she pushes it away.

"You're no fun," he complains, making a pouting face.

"Do you think we're all sluts?"

"No, I think you're generous and kind and when you see a poor man suffering ..."

"Don't hold your breath."

"Sooner or later you'll do it," he says, with a sidelong glance at her chest.

Before she came to Berlin, she heard all about "the miracle of Babelsberg," but what she finds is a set designer screaming at a crew of scene painters; a street that has been blocked off because some quickly built structure has fallen apart; a row of cameramen on a catwalk with their legs dangling down; a janitor scrubbing a swastika off a wall. Yet she never stops feeling a thrill when she passes through the gates. When Babelsberg is taken over by the Nazi propaganda machine in 1933, she feels as though she has been cast out from a place where anything seemed possible. It will take many years before she is able to see the sheer energy of Babelsberg in the larger context of 1920s' Berlin, with its delusions of stability and its doomed dependence on steady infusions of American capital. Later, the excitement surrounding her apprentice days will seem as unreal as the façades that were continually being built and demolished in Germany's film capital.

She's brought in to work on the shooting script of *Karl and Anna* with the director Joe May. One of May's assistants, a Hungarian who smells of cheap cigars, runs through the plot for her.

"Here's the novel it's based on. It's short, you can read it in a night. For now, just listen to me." He takes a sip of something from a metal cup and wipes his mouth on his sleeve. "It's 1917. Karl and Richard, two German soldiers, have been stuck in Siberia for two years. For prisoners-of-war, their life is pretty good. All they have to do is ferry other prisoners across the river. For shelter, they have a little hut, and they supplement their rations with fish from the river. They don't see anyone else for days on end, so they've become very close."

"Are they lovers?"

"Of course not!" the assistant snorts. "We could never get away with that! They're close the way that soldiers are and they make the best of things because they don't have a choice."

"I see," Mem says, turning red. She racks her brains for something intelligent sounding to say. "What do they do to pass the time?" is all she manages to get out.

"They sit around talking about Karl's wife Anna – they've even named the stray cat that lives with them after her. Richard is obsessed with getting back to her and Karl wants to know everything about her that he can, down to the smallest detail."

"Even intimate things?"

"Very intimate, I would say."

"That's interesting," she says, "but how do we get that across without dialogue?"

"Not a problem," the assistant says, with a wave of his hand. "We just let the actors' expressions do the work."

"If only the actors could talk," Mem remarks.

"But we're not putting on a play here, are we?" the assistant says irritably. "We're shooting a film. Are you sure you want to be here and not somewhere else?"

"Oh, definitely," she stammers. "This is where I want to be."

"Then stop making useless remarks."

"Sorry," she says, wishing she could disappear.

"The point is, they talk about Anna endlessly, but it doesn't help Richard, it only makes him more obsessed. It gets so bad that one day, he can't take it anymore. He tells Karl that he has to try to escape, otherwise he'll go out of his mind."

"What does Karl say?"

"He wants to go along."

"Interesting," she says, noticing for the first time that the assistant's eyes are very red. 'Maybe he's drunk,' she thinks to herself, 'and he'll forget all the mistakes I've made.'

"The two of them start off across the Steppes," the assistant goes on, "but it turns out that Richard doesn't have as much stamina as Karl does. He falls on the ground, grabs his throat, and begs for water. Karl runs off and by a miracle he finds an underground spring. (This is going to be a great moment by the way: they've already painted some of the scenery.) Anyway, while Karl is off filling the canteens, a Russian rides in on horseback, slings Richard over his saddle, and gallops away. Karl comes back to the clearing and Richard is gone. For the first time in the film, he is completely alone. After that – well, for now all you need to know is that after a hard journey, Karl makes it to Hamburg, where Anna lives. It takes him a year."

"How will we show that?"

"They're working with a couple different ideas – maybe just an image of trudging boots that get more and more beaten up until there's practically nothing left of them."

"Hasn't that already been done?"

"Of course it's been done!" says the assistant with a shrug, staring at the behind of a girl who is passing by. "But we're going to do it better because we have a fantastic crew. And you know what? Nobody will care!"

"I'm sure you're right," she says hurriedly. What if he's completely sober and he remembers everything she's said? But if she tries to fix it, it will only get worse. Better just keep her mouth shut. But then he'll think she has nothing to say.

"Anyway, Karl looks up Richard's wife," the assistant goes on, "and the minute that he lays eyes on her, he feels as though he's known her for years. As for Anna, she's completely amazed by how much he knows about her and her place."

"She's probably frightened – but also flattered," she says tentatively.

"We'll work all that out when we're shooting the scene. The point is that the two of them end up falling in love. But just as they're about to have their first kiss, Richard walks in."

"Isn't that too much of a coincidence?" Mem asks.

"In real life, yes, but audiences love that kind of thing."

"I see," Mem says, convinced that regardless of whether he's sober or drunk, the assistant thinks she's an idiot. And maybe he's right, she suddenly thinks, flooded with self-doubt.

"When he realizes that Anna has fallen in love with Karl, Richard wants to murder him, but then he remembers how Karl saved his life in the desert, and he goes away, signing on to the next outgoing ship. Karl runs after him and tries to get him to stay, but Richard says something like, 'What use do I have for a woman who doesn't love me?' and then he adds, 'Be good to her.' Two intertitles. Two sentences. Finis."

"A fascinating plot," Mem says, leafing through the manuscript that the assistant has handed her. "But there's one thing I don't understand. We never see Karl saving Richard's life on the Steppes because he never gets to bring him the water."

"You're right," the assistant says, after a pause that seems very long. "That's an inconsistency that we'll have to iron out." He settles back into his chair and looks at her, this time a little more benevolently. "Would you like some cognac by the way?" he says at last. "I'm sure there's another cup around here."

Over the next few days, Mem works hard to perfect the shooting script, but something keeps getting in the way. One night she scribbles into her notes, "There can be no homecoming from the trauma of the war: even the new, tender love of Karl and Anna is like the play of light on the churning sea. They are only lighthearted in the first hours of knowing each other, then the weight of reality settles on them. The ghosts of the war can't be driven away." She thinks back to when Hans came back from the war, and she remembers how cold and distant he seemed. From this point on, Mem's vision of the film is clear and she's less uncertain of herself on the set.

But now the real labor begins. How to maximize the expressiveness of the actors? Gustav Frohlich, the brilliant lead of *Metropolis*, plays the part of Karl. His face seems to radiate a light, an electricity, of its own. There are points in the script where that light must turn dark, transforming itself into a maniacal fervor. The same goes for the mournful expression of Dita Parlo, who plays Anna in the film. There are moments when her eyes light up like a child's and then suddenly darken again, taking on a haunted look. And it isn't only the actors that they have to worry about: the most common object – a chair, a coat, a tablecloth – must sometimes be charged with enough electricity to transform it into a portentous sign.

"You ask me about how films are made," she writes to Peter. "It's all about the play of light and dark. Shadows are just as important, sometimes even more important, than light. That's where the real poetry lies. As for words, they hardly matter at all. I can't tell you what a relief that is to me! No matter how hard I try, I'm no good at telling stories on the page."

"I like the part about shadows," he writes back to her.

When Mem comes to UFA, the company is in the midst of an internal crisis of its own. Erich Pommer, the brilliant Jewish producer who has taken a huge gamble on expensive and ground-breaking films such as *Metropolis* and *The Cabinet of Dr. Caligari*, has been blamed for UFA's financial problems and has resigned and gone to Hollywood. One hundred directors, cinematographers, actors, and clerks have been fired in his wake, throwing UFA into even more confusion. Then, after a tough period in Hollywood, Pommer returns, bringing with him new insights and knowledge gleaned from the American scene. *Asphalt*, directed by Joe May, is one of several comeback films, and its aim is to prove that entertainment and art can be combined. Based on her previous work with May, Mem is part of the team.

Asphalt is a street film (*Strassenfilm*) par excellence – it actually begins with an image of workers laying asphalt down. With each thrust of their sinister-looking implements, another rough letter of the title appears on the screen. The wheel of a roller looms up on the screen, huge and vaguely menacing. A foreman passes in front of the workers and they collapse into a montage that opens out onto an image of the finished street.

After this introduction, the film goes on to tell the story of the seduction of a young traffic cop by a beautiful diamond thief – but the true subject of the film is Berlin. For the making of this drama, an artificial Berlin is constructed at Babelsberg. Film architect Kettelhut constructs a set that is 760 feet long and includes a street covered with real asphalt. Fake shop windows display brand-name goods. Cabs, trolleys, horse-drawn carriages and hundreds of extras are brought in. "We're not creating a fantasy world, we're trying to capture the pulse of the city," May says. "For that, we need to open with a documentary style."

And yet, as everyone knows, that style is just another façade. The point is not to reflect but to intensify reality, using any method that does the trick. Like the naïve young traffic cop, the viewer must be seduced. To this end, ten different camera locations serve as mounts for the newly invented mobile camera crane that moves in all directions to create the illusion of urban speed. Up in the artificial sky, 2000 lamps emit a quantity of light equal to what would be needed to illuminate a medium-sized city. Below this fabricated sky, Mem helps to recreate Berlin. When she walks home from her tram stop at night, she scans the streets of her neighborhood to see if there is any stray detail that might still be useful for them. She also notes what they are leaving out – the Nazi slogans splashed across walls and signs, the Brownshirts who roam the streets in violent groups, the Nazi newspapers and leaflets that are appearing everywhere, with their screaming headlines, the street fights that are multiplying between the Nazis and the Communists as they struggle to dominate Berlin.

Everyone knows that the Weimar Republic is being torn apart. Who is going to grab control? On both sides, she sees faces filled with murderous hate, and in the threats and lies that fill the air she hears a bloodlust that terrifies her. When the Republic dies, where will she go? She can't see beyond the chaos on the streets. But none of this is visible in the Berlin of *Asphalt*, a modern city wiped clean of political conflict.

With May and company, she views the montage that happens in the first part of the film – a kaleidoscopic image of streaming traffic that converges on the dutiful cop, who is standing on a tiny traffic island. They decide on a sequence in which the camera takes the viewer away from the traffic and into a crowd that has gathered in front of a shop window. Behind the glass, a pretty girl pulls a nylon stocking onto her leg. Is she a prostitute? No, she's there to sell the stockings and nothing else, and the crowd is enjoying the free show. A thief seizes this opportunity to pull a wallet out of a middle-aged woman's purse while the thief's accomplice throws her off balance by rudely bumping into her.

"Wouldn't they pass the money to a third guy?" Mem asks, as they're watching the rushes. "Somebody just told me that's how it's usually done."

"You've got to be kidding," one of the cameramen says.

"Thank God the audience won't be like you," the assistant remarks.

May tells them that they need to create a contrast between the sheltered life of the young cop and the criminal vitality of the street. The dingy but cozy apartment where the cop lives with his aging parents has to convey the purity of his heart. The details come to them one by one – a songbird in a cage, a shelf with jars of marmalade, sunshine streaming in the window, the bowls of food that the cop's mother lays out for him. And now all these details must be brought to life by the play of expressions on the parents' faces – caring, open, worried, affectionate.

Once all this has been established, they are finally ready to put the cop to the test. To make his seduction credible, the viewer must also be led astray, and here a great deal will depend on the acting skills of the alluring, slightly masculine Betty Amman. She first appears in a long, form-fitting, white sheath dress with a huge fur collar and a cloche hat. The lighting that is used on her succeeds in making her skin and her costume glow. (By the end of the day, that same light has made the entire crew's eyes burn and sting. Betty Amman collapses onto a couch and applies cold compresses the instant she gets her make-up off.)

It takes a tremendous amount of work to get the angles right when Betty Amman's character is stealing a diamond from under an old jeweler's nose.

"Is that old letch supposed to be Jewish?" Mem asks at some point.

"If you have to ask, it's not a problem," the co-director replies.

"What kind of answer is that?"

"What do you care?"

"Because I'm Jewish myself."

"Okay – he's Catholic then. Let it go."

At last May is satisfied with the scene and everyone breathes a sigh of relief. Now they're on to the arrest of the diamond thief by the cop and his bungled attempt to take her to the police station.

Mem is enlisted to help shape the seduction scene, in which Amman has to overcome Frohlich's resistance. By now, Mem has grown used to working with Frohlich, but she is even more impressed by him than she was before. In *Heimkehr* (the new title for *Karl and Anna*), his performance was exuberant and extroverted, but he plays the part of the cop with a virginal restraint. She does her best, however, not to focus too much on him, so that she can see the scene as a whole. The result: a half-crazed encounter in which Betty Amman, wearing black satin leggings trimmed with lace and a black chemise that reveals her dazzling, muscular back, jumps onto Frohlich like a tiger. (Frohlich is standing up and she has to come running at him. They do one take after another to make the jump seem to catch him off guard.) Once she has landed in his arms, Amman wraps her legs around his leather gaiters and shining boots in a way that makes it clear she is going to overcome whatever is left of his resistance. The camera lingers on the image of their intertwined legs and the police cap that has fallen on the floor.

"That's it! We've got it!" May exclaims.

"The ultimate humiliation for a German cop," the Hungarian assistant chimes in. "She desecrates his uniform!"

'Who's talking like a film critic now?' Mem thinks to herself, but she doesn't say anything.

"I can't do one more thing," Betty Amman says, collapsing into a chair. Frohlich pulls off his boots, massages his feet, and tells one of the onlookers (where do these people come from and who lets them in?) to go get him a beer.

"That's it for today!" May says. "Everybody go home and get some rest!" But Mem is too wound up to go home; instead she joins a few co-workers at a bar on the Potsdamer Platz.

"Well, how did you like it?" one of the clerks, a young Aryan type, says to her as she's waiting for her drink.

"I think it works."

"Was it sexy enough for you? I bet if you were in her place, you'd have even kinkier ideas …"

The bartender, a bald-headed man with a protruding belly and a face that makes her think of a fish, slowly revolves his bulging eyes to where she is sitting, looks her up and down, and then moves his glance away again.

"I'm tired," she says to the clerk. "If you need a woman, go sniff somewhere else." She takes her drink from the bartender and walks over to the table where Frohlich and Amman are sitting.

"The two of you were fantastic today!" she says to them.

"Yes, but I think I pulled a tendon," Betty Amman complains. "He better not ask us to do it over again!"

When Mem finally gets back to her apartment, she finds the door unlocked and sees a coat draped over the back of her chair.

"Who's here?" she calls out. She walks into the bedroom, her heart pounding in her chest. Karl Frank is lying in her bed in his underwear and calmly reading the newspaper.

"You frightened me!" she exclaims.

"You're not very clever when it comes to hiding your key."

"I didn't know who I was dealing with," she laughs, stroking his cheek.

"How professional you look!" he says, tugging at the waist of her skirt. "You make me feel quite undressed."

"Then I'll take these off ..."

"No, leave everything on."

"But I want ..."

He pulls her down and puts his hand over her mouth. "Shhhh. Don't say another word." She resists him for a moment. "I like you this way."

Afterwards, she tells him about *Asphalt*, how it's coming along, how she feels that the end of the film will be a compromise.

"The girl goes to jail for the cop in the end," she sighs. "It seems so boring and predictable."

"If you had to choose between film and sex, which would it be?" he interrupts, playing with her hair.

"I'm not sure," she says, wrapping her body around his.

"That's a bad sign," he says as he puts his arms around her. "If you're really serious about your work, it should come before everything."

"Does your politics come before everything?" she asks.

"Of course. What do you think? Especially now that I'm acting on my own."

"Have you really broken with the Communist Party?"

"With the Party, yes, but not with the Revolution. I don't trust the Party anymore."

"What does that mean practically?"

"It's a complicated business," he says, running his hand along her back. "To really answer you would take all night."

"It wouldn't take all night," she says, rolling to her side and lighting a cigarette. "Stop patronizing me."

"You're angry!"

"Why shouldn't I be? You talk to me as though I'm some silly girl."

"Look, the truth is that I'm going through a tricky time and my path isn't very clear to me. The one thing I know is that wherever I go, I see a terrible divide between ideals and realities."

"Why didn't you just say that instead of putting me off? Do you think I can't see how distorted things are? Just last week, one of the scene painters read us an article from the *Red Flag* and I still can't get it out of my head. It was about a factory worker, a young woman of about my age, who killed herself by slashing her wrists. Her husband died of pneumonia two years ago and she had fallen into debt from paying for his funeral. 'Female workers shouldn't commit suicide,' the article said. 'We should not die, Capitalism should.' There was something so awful about putting that slogan at the end. Not a single word about the loneliness or the desperation of that poor woman."

"But the message is right," Karl says quietly. "These personal tragedies are part of a general disease."

"Look, I'm not a sociologist, I'm an artist, but I'm sensitive enough to know that the mindset behind that article was inhuman."

"You see? We're not going to agree."

"What's wrong with arguing?"

"Alright, let's fight," he says, pulling her close again. But although she yields to him, she still feels upset. There's some part of himself that he's holding in reserve. She wants to ask him if he's seeing someone else, but she restrains herself. There have always been others, even in Grundlsee – some of them were even her friends – but now she has no idea of who they are.

At four o'clock in the morning, he tells her that he has somewhere to go – a political meeting that he doesn't want to talk about.

"Why should I believe you?" she says to him.

"Easy. Because I'm lying," he says, putting out his cigarette. "I'm going to see my other girlfriend. What difference does it make?"

"It makes a big difference to me."

"Maybe you should think about that," he says, sitting on the edge of the bed and pulling on a sock.

"What's that supposed to mean?"

"Do you want a husband or a lover?"

"Not a husband. I'm done with that."

"So you want a lover."

"Karl, stop playing with me!"

"I'm serious. Did I satisfy you or not? Because if I didn't, I understand why you're upset." She doesn't say anything, watching him buckle his belt.

"I don't like being lied to," she gets out at last.

"And I don't like being interrogated. I never ask you what you do when I'm not here."

Now he's fully dressed and she wants him all over again. He looks keen and alert, like a young cadet.

"Don't be angry with me," she says, putting her arms around his neck. "I'm not angry, I just want us to be clear."

After he goes, she stands by her window and stares out at the soot-blackened windows across the way. If only she could follow him down the street! Maybe she wants to own him after all.

On her way to work, she falls asleep on the train, so that when she finally gets to Babelsberg, she's only half-awake. She passes two knights standing in a doorway, smoking cigarettes; workmen setting up a façade with palm trees and a seascape painted onto it; a crowd of extras dressed in ragged clothes – are they supposed to be peasants? Convicts? She isn't sure. And the usual clusters of adventure-seekers.

She is soon in the thick of a discussion of the closing scenes, in which Betty Amman comes to the police station to prove the cop's innocence. (He has killed the crook who has been keeping her, but he did it in self-defense.) Betty Amman is accompanied by the cop's mother, who is desperate to save her son. (His father, a retired policeman, has persuaded him to turn himself in.) In the final sequence, Betty Amman is marched off to jail – the authorities have finally caught their diamond thief – and the cop goes free.

"In the seduction scene, we took some risks," Mem hears herself say, "but now we're just buying into the status quo."

"I couldn't agree with you more," May says, "but this is the ending that will sell, and we have to sell big-time, just like the Americans."

What would Karl and Käthe say? They would fight for their principles. They wouldn't back down. But working at UFA is everybody's dream and she doesn't want to risk her position by pushing too hard.

For the rest of the day, she keeps thinking about what Käthe or Karl would have done, and she finally comes to the conclusion that in the end, she isn't as principled as they are. For an artist, it's different. Any scene can be done in countless ways, and you have to remain open and flexible. But you also have to think about the final message of the film. Where do you draw the line? And then there's the question of how much power you really have, because in a collaboration there is always a boss, and that boss is almost always a man.

In a few years, she will no longer be in a position to ponder questions like this. As a free-thinking artist and a Jew – a *Saujude* (Jewish sow), as the Nazis will say – there is no place for her in the Third Reich. But it's only 1929 and there is still room for artistic soul-searching.

On opening night, she goes with everyone else to the UFA Palast am Zoo (a 1740-seat cinema adjacent to the Berlin Zoo, where all the premières are shown). As she approaches the grand Romanesque building, she sees Kettelhut's light display projected onto its outer wall, a miraculously detailed rendering of Berlin etched in light (the same image will come up with the credits when the film is shown) complete with miniature illuminated signs – LICHTSPIELE – GRAND HOTEL – VARIETÉ – and images of cars speeding by. The rectangles that indicate windows are streaming with light – as she looks up at this flashing microcosm, she feels hypnotized. She imagines seeing her name projected up there for the whole city to see, along with F.W. Murnau … Joe May … Gustav Frohlich … Betty Amman …

She is swept into the theater with the rest of the crowd, but then she parts with them, taking one of the reserved seats. And yet she is apparently still part of the same organism as they are, since their reactions go straight into her nervous system. When they murmur at the skill of the diamond thief, who picks a diamond off the floor with the adhesive tip of her umbrella, or when they gasp at the moment when the cop kills his rival in a fit of rage, she feels it physically. For the rest of the audience, watching the film is an escape, but, for her, every gesture, every shot, every camera angle, is fraught. She watches the film so intently that she gets a splitting headache. "Can you give me an aspirin?" she whispers to Albert Steinrück (the cop's father in the film), who is always handing out aspirins on the set. He gives her two, plus a slug of whiskey from his hip flask.

After the film is over, they go to the Hotel Adlon and she orders one vodka after another. In the early morning, they find themselves at the Romanisches Café, where they wait for the reviews to come out.

Tommy Ulrich, an aspiring journalist, is tagging along with them. Hypercritical and dissolute, he can't get enough of their company. "What a shame!" he says. "You had something really good there for a while. The vamp spits on the cop, with his stupid ideals. Wonderful! But then she surrenders. No! She grovels at his feet. Blind idiotic slavish obedience. Welcome back to the Middle Ages!"

"Oh, shut up Ulrich!" they tell him. "You're a pain in the ass!"

The reviews come out. They read them out loud. One says that *Asphalt* is a groundbreaking film and another says that it's a craven attempt to bring in big audiences at the expense of real art. In the end, they throw the papers down and Ulrich orders a bottle of *Schnapps*, which they pass around to stave off their hangovers.

At the same time as the première of *Asphalt*, an SA man by the name of Horst Wessel scribbles a marching song onto a napkin and sings it to his ex-prostitute girlfriend. She likes it and so he sends it on to his friend Goebbels, who publishes it in the *Angriff* [*The Attack*], his newspaper. Before long, Brownshirts are shouting out the song wherever they go, spreading it throughout Berlin. Comedians sing parodies of the song in the cabarets, but their anti-Nazi versions aren't as widely appreciated. When Horst Wessel is killed by two Communists in a domestic fight (his landlady is the widow of a Communist and two of his friends come to help her out when Wessel and his girlfriend threaten her), Goebbels calls on every Nazi in the country to dress in black and Wessel becomes a Nazi martyr. The Communists try to disrupt the funeral procession by stealing the coffin and yet another street brawl ensues. All of this is spun and twisted in the Nazi newspapers in a way that adds to the success of the Horst Wessel song: in fact, it ends up becoming the anthem of the Nazi party. But it's only 1929, and Mem has no inkling of all of this yet: for her the song is just another expression of the menace growing all around her. That menace has infiltrated the studios and workshops of UFA as well, stirring up endless speculation about what will come of Goebbels' infatuation, not only with film actresses but with Berlin's film industry.

In the lull that comes after *Asphalt* is done, Mem avoids reading the newspapers, afraid that they will only make her more depressed. She hates this time of waiting for the next project: What if they don't call on her again? She tries to work on a screenplay of her own, but she's too anxious to concentrate. She hasn't seen Karl for weeks on end – either he's spending all his nights with someone else or he's gone completely underground.

One morning, when she's walking along the street, she hears the sound of shouts and laughter and she follows it to a schoolyard where children are chasing after balls, jumping rope, standing in little circles, and talking together. She stands at the fence, watching them, until the school bell rings and they go back inside.

She walks around the building, passes through an iron gate, and finds herself in a high-ceilinged hall. "Can I help you?" says a man with a thick gray whiskers, heavy-lidded eyes, and a watch chain dangling from his vest.

"I'd like to see the Principal," she hears herself say. The man peers at her curiously, as though he's examining a specimen.

"You have an appointment?"

"Not really, but I was hoping that …"

"You probably won't have any luck, but follow me."

He takes her to a waiting area on the second floor with wooden benches running along the walls. A boy who can't be much younger than Peter is waiting there, and he's kicking his feet back and forth.

"Are you in trouble?" she says to him, after they've been sitting in silence for a moment or two.

"I don't know," he shrugs, avoiding her eyes.

"Well, good luck with your meeting, I hope the Principal is nice to you."

"It wasn't my idea!" he bursts out. "It's all Effi's fault!"

A secretary pokes her head out of the door and the boy goes into the office with his head down.

As she sits there waiting, she loses all sense of time, carried away by a rush of fantasies. Maybe she could actually bring Peter to Berlin and he could go to this school and make a new existence here. She could hire a nanny to pick him up in the afternoon and stay with him until she comes back from work. They would be together, really sharing their lives. She can picture it all so clearly in her mind!

"The Principal has gone home for lunch," the secretary says in a high nasal voice that snaps her back into the present again.

"But I was sitting here this whole time," she objects. (What happened to the boy? Did he leave by a different door?)

"You'll have to go. This office is now officially closed."

She comes by the next day, and the next day after that, trudging up the wide stone steps to the second floor and waiting on the wooden bench, where she encounters several more children who seem either worried or sullen or distracted. Finally, on Friday, the secretary ushers her into the Principal's office, introducing her by saying, "Here's the person I was telling you about."

The Principal is a heavy-set woman with a broad flushed face and a pudding-bowl haircut that makes her look like a monk.

"I'm interested in having my son attend this school," Mem begins, "and I was wondering if you have any openings."

"Where does he go to school now?" the Principal asks her, looking her up and down. (It was probably a mistake to wear a brightly patterned skirt; why didn't she think to wear her navy-blue suit? The Principal is dressed in a woolen skirt and vest, with a starched white blouse that is buttoned all the way up to her chin.)

"He's not in Berlin, he's in Vienna," Mem replies. "He's with his father."

"But you live here?" the Principal cuts her off.

"Yes, I work with UFA ..."

"So you've been living apart?"

"Only for a few months," she lies. The Principal raises her eyebrows and makes a note in her book. In the silence, Mem hears the sound of a mop flapping against the other side of the door.

"Is your son Catholic or Protestant?" the Principal asks, finally looking up.

"Neither," Mem replies.

"I see."

"I mean he's Jewish, but he hasn't been brought up to be religious."

"Ah," says the Principal, slowly laying down her pen.

"Would you like to know anything about his schooling so far?"

"If you like," the Principal shrugs, with a casualness that Mem doesn't expect.

"He's been attending a small progressive school that was started by Anna Freud. It's called the Hietzing School."

"The Hietzing School? I've never heard of it."

"It's very small, and it's been quite good for him, but I think he's ready for something more academic. You see, my son is very bright."

"Well, that may well be, but we have our own standards here. I'm sure you understand."

"Would he need to take an exam to get in?"

"Yes, but there's no need to go over all that now. Why don't you see

to getting him a visa first? There's no point in getting ahead of yourself."
After a few more remarks of a very general kind, the Principal gets up
from her chair and tells Mem that she has some urgent matters that need
attending to.

Out in the hallway, an old cleaning woman with a flowered kerchief
tied around her head comes up to Mem and whispers to her. "There's only
one Jewish girl left in this school and they're looking for an excuse to kick
her out."

"But she just told me ..."

"Only one, do you hear? A good student too. Your boy doesn't have
a chance."

Mem leaves the building as quickly as she can, but in the days that
follow, she puts the words of the cleaning woman out of her mind. The
Principal sat down with her, after all, and she told her to look into the
visa as a first step, which was perfectly reasonable advice. She hears about
a two-bedroom apartment on the floor above hers that will be vacant in
a month. What would the rent be, she wonders? Two bedrooms would
work. But she would have to make friends with someone in the building
for the nights she had to stay out late. If Peter didn't understand why
she sometimes had to go out at night, she would explain – it would be a
good example for him. But what about Karl? Karl, Karl – she never knows
when he will come! He would have to start letting her know in advance.
But the main thing is to get Hans to agree. If she can get that to happen,
she can deal with everything else.

A new film project comes up and she has to work around the clock,
so she isn't able to make any progress with the visa. She writes a long,
pleading letter to Hans, telling him that she's come to realize that as a
mother, she needs to live with her son, but she never sends it to him,
afraid of what he'll say in response. One day, when they're dismissed early
due to an accident on the set, she walks by the school again and watches
the children playing in the yard. A woman in a school uniform steps up
to the fence and tells her with distaste that if she doesn't move along, she'll
call the authorities.

6.

The Zobeltitz Plan

Vienna, 1931–32

IN 1931, when he was 11 years old, Peter started talking to Anna Freud about the Zobeltitz Plan. He wanted to write *Zobeltitz* on every public surface he could find – billboards, kiosks, pavements, store windows, construction sites. There was no limit to how far he might go: he saw himself standing on a scaffold and painting *Zobeltitz* in huge letters across a building wall. It was an idea that the practical joker Basti Baer might have been interested in, but he didn't feel like including him.

Why *Zobeltitz*? It was a ridiculous name, which was exactly what he liked about it. Hanns Zobeltitz was a bad novelist; he had written the worst kind of kitsch. Ridiculous, with an odor of trash, *Zobeltitz* was the perfect name for a movement dedicated to Nothing. Thanks to the Zobeltitz Plan, Nothing would be on display everywhere, finding its way into every neighborhood. People could commit themselves to Nothing without paying a cent; all they had to do was to write their names in his nice little composition book.

Thesi was completely fed up with him. He was running up to strangers and asking them for their signatures. "You've stopped with the public bathrooms," she said to him, "but now you're doing something just as bad. Haven't you learned anything from Anna Freud? You're sliding back into your piggish ways."

Anna was against the Zobeltitz Plan too. "If you walk up to strangers, they may try to seduce you," she said to him.

"I'd like that to happen – just once," he replied. "Then I could practice saying no to them."

As Anna saw it, the Zobeltitz Plan was nothing more than an excuse for exploring homoerotic impulses that could easily lead him astray.

In his case history, she entered the Zobeltitz Plan under the heading of "Masturbation as discharge of oedipal excitement."

But even assuming that there was an erotic agenda here, there were other elements at play. "Kitsch is dangerous," he had heard Hans and his friends say. "Just look at the damage that can be done when a failed painter turns to politics." If bad artists were trying to take over the world, he would mount his own absurd and tasteless campaign, and he would call it, rather cleverly, the Zobeltitz Plan.

In the same year that Peter came up with the Zobeltitz Plan, the *Creditanstalt* collapsed, plunging Austria even deeper into financial crisis. How could the largest bank in Austro-Hungary go down? It was owned by none other than the Rothschilds, the most powerful family in all of Europe. After Black Tuesday, not even the Rothschilds were safe, let alone lesser capitalists like his father.

The next year, Engelbert Dollfuss became chancellor of Austria, establishing an authoritarian regime and unwittingly paving the way for a Nazi takeover. Although Dolfuss banned the Austrian National Socialist Party in 1933, and tried to make sure that Mussolini would back up his efforts to keep Austria separate from Germany, the Nazi presence was felt throughout the city, with pamphlets, graffiti, posters appearing everywhere. Not only was the Zobeltitz Plan a way of writing on the sheltering wall that kept Peter from the world, it mirrored the turmoil of interwar Vienna.

When he dreamt up the Zobeltitz Plan, Vienna was a patchwork of conflicting ideologies – the brown National Socialists, the red Eastern Communists, the pink Western Socialists, the green Conservatives. Outside his school, children were being pulled into youth groups and clubs that offered them classes, outings, even vacations for free. He and his schoolmates didn't belong to any of these clubs, and they probably made fun of their badges, oaths, and uniforms. And yet there was something intriguing about the idea of a club, especially a club that broke a number of grown-up rules.

What he liked best about the Zobeltitz Plan was that it earnestly promoted the idea of Nothing. Founded on Nothing, it couldn't be crushed, for the simple reason that it was too ridiculous.

Pre-adolescent silliness? Homoerotic exploration? A desire to venture beyond the walls of the Hietzing School? Peter felt compelled to disavow the Zobeltitz Plan when he grew up, as is reflected in a curious note in the postscript to his case history. "The grotesque idea, however dimly perceived by me, was to build on Nothing to the greater glory of nothingness. For the declaration of allegiance to a mere word – akin to the alleged 'centrality of language' – is the emptiest form of nihilism."

An 11-year-old boy takes a few excited steps toward a movement that will celebrate the idea of Nothing. As a grown man, he looks back and is embarrassed by a scheme that, in any case, he was never allowed to fully act out. In the interim, the Vienna that he knew when he was young has been systematically destroyed.

"It's much easier to destroy meaning than to create it," he likes to say. And he comes down a little heavily on his boyhood scheme, at once elevating it by taking it so seriously and rejecting it as a sterile nihilistic exercise.

The December after the *Creditanstalt* collapsed, Dorothy Burlingham had a long conversation with her oldest son about how terrible times were for the poor people of Vienna. Cold, hungry, sick – how desperate they must be! They really must find a way of helping them. Wouldn't it be wonderful if they could organize a program of *Winterhilfe* – Winter Help – at the school?

As a result of their conversation, a collection was taken up and before long, the worktables were piled with second-hand clothes. Dorothy's father-in-law donated $100, Sigmund Freud donated $15, and the children themselves donated $20, thanks to a circus that they put on as a fundraiser. Forty boxes arrived from the Heller Candy factory, filled with chocolate stars, angels, etc. from the Christmas line. Shortly before Christmas, Herr Wimmer, the Burlingham chauffeur, loaded all the boxes and clothing into the family car and drove off into the night with them. None of the Burlinghams accompanied him; after all, there was a risk of disease. The mere smell of the houses was so repugnant to Herr Wimmer that when he came home, he couldn't eat his dinner.

Although classes are going on as before, everyone is talking about going away. Vicki's mother has been offered a job as the matron of a sanatorium outside Berlin and, if she takes it, Vicki will have to go along with her. When Vicki tells him that he may be moving to Germany, Peter says it sounds like a stupid idea.

"Some people have to work," Vicki says. "Not everyone owns a candy factory."

"What will your father do?" Peter asks.

"I'm pretty sure he'll stay behind."

"That part makes sense," Peter says. "My father stayed behind when my mother left to pursue her film career."

But is Vicki's mother running off to be with another man? It doesn't seem likely that Muschi, plump, clucking, and jittery, has a lover hidden away in another city. Vicki says that Muschi has been invited to run a psychoanalytic sanatorium that's the first of its kind in the entire world. To Peter, it sounds like a depressing job, especially since Vicki also says that the sanatorium is in danger of shutting down. Maybe Muschi does have someone else, Peter thinks, but no matter how hard he tries, he can't picture it in his mind. Then again, Muschi and Valti barely say a word to each other and, when they do, it's because one of them is annoyed.

Unknown to Peter, Eva Rosenfeld is in the midst of a marital crisis and everyone is waiting to see how it will turn out. A flurry of conversations is taking place, not only between Eva and Valti but also between Eva and Anna, and Anna and Dorothy, with Sigmund occasionally chiming in as Eva's analyst. Eva keeps going back and forth, torn between a passionless marriage and the promise of a real career. In one of her letters, Eva turns to Anna to tell her what to do and Anna replies:

> I really don't quite know what to say. I understand perfectly well that you can only do what you want to do from Berlin. But at the same time, I don't want you to go away. I am simply afraid to be without you, and am also afraid that you won't come back, once you are there. But you can't stay and protect me either. Besides, this isn't about me at all.

Yet, despite Anna's protests, Eva knows that if she goes away, Anna will still have Dorothy, who will never leave her side.

In the end, Eva leaves, taking Vicki along with her, and Valti remains behind.

Without Vicki to challenge him at every turn, Peter's world is reduced. As for Eva Rosenfeld's kitchen, which was once so lively and warm, it now smells of the mildewed Goethe volumes that Valti loves to collect, and

Peter hardly goes there anymore.

Next comes the news that Peter Blos is leaving too, and that Erik Erikson is planning to do the same. Without Peter Blos, there will be no one to direct the school and, without Erik, there will be no one to plan out projects and do woodcuts with them. Hans says that he understands why Peter Blos and Erik want to go, especially now that they've both been accepted into the Psychoanalytic Institute.

"They have ambitions of their own," he shrugs. "They can't just be the underlings of Freud and Burlingham."

Peter isn't sure of what an underling is, but he knows that it's bad, especially for a man. Still, he's shocked when he hears that his teachers are leaving, and he goes out of his way to get on their nerves in class.

Tinky says that her American relatives keep begging her mother to bring them all home, even though Dorothy has told them that her real home is Vienna. "They think we're crazy to be here," Tinky says. "They keep asking why we're going to a Jewish school."

But Basti isn't Jewish, he points out, and nor is Mario or Elizabeth or Ingho.

"I know that!" she says irritably. "I'm just telling you what they think."

A few days later, he asks Mabbie if they're planning to move back to the States and Mabbie looks at him with surprise. "Mutti will never leave Anna," she says, shaking her head, "and Anna will never leave Vienna, because Doctor loves it here." These words immediately calm him down, because Mabbie always tells the truth.

Bob decides to go to Antioch College in the United States, but Mabbie chooses an art school in Vienna, partly so that she can stay by her mother's side. So far, Tinky isn't going anywhere, but there's no telling what may happen in a year or two.

And so the little community starts to break apart, with the school officially closing in 1932. Peter's psychoanalysis runs parallel to all of this, stopping and starting again. He and Anna Freud had terminated his analysis in April of 1930, but, due to a period of agitation following his vacation with Mem in Grundlsee, he resumed his analysis in the fall of that year. He goes back to seeing Anna nearly every day; in the beginning of 1931, he suffers what she refers to as "The Great Relapse."

This time, there is no roller or gravel path; instead he dreams of two sleds that crash into each other and plunge down into a black abyss. He calls out for Margot, Tinky's governess, but she doesn't come. He wakes up sobbing in Thesi's arms.

Anna says that the sleds are Mem and Hans. He thinks this interpretation is absurd, and it annoys him that she's so convinced.

"... when the sleds crash together, it might mean a number of things ..." he hears her say. He watches a bug crawl across the wall, slowly heading toward the portrait of Sigmund Freud.

"You cried when Thesi woke you up because you wanted Mem to wake you up instead." *What's the use of lying on this sofa?* he thinks to himself. *It doesn't solve anything.* Mem was supposed to arrive right after Christmas, but she still hasn't shown up. Hans and Inge have gone off to Grundlsee just so that Mem can spend time with him at the house. So far, he and Thesi have been there all by themselves, even on New Year's Eve. Has Mem completely forgotten him?

A few days later, Mem finally arrives, but she isn't herself. Her face looks splotchy, her eyes are dull, and there are shadows around her mouth. She can barely focus her attention on him, and when they do talk, she snaps at him. Every morning, the maid goes in to change Mem's bed, and whenever she does, she closes the door. But one day, she leaves the door open a crack and he sees a streak of blood on the sheets.

"She's making herself sick," he hears Thesi murmur to Cook. "She really has to stop carrying on with two men."

Mem lies on the sofa in the living room and says that she's too tired to leave the house. Doesn't she at least want to go to the Belvedere Gardens with him? It's only a few steps away, and if she needs to rest, they could sit by the Sphinx. She tells him they'll go there later, but later never comes. Cook and Thesi keep whispering behind Mem's back, but as soon as he comes into the kitchen, they stop. One night he wakes up screaming. "Memka, you're a monster! Go away!" And then he's terrified that Mem has heard him, and that when he wakes up in the morning, she'll be gone.

Hans and Inge come back from Grundlsee the night before Mem

leaves, laughing and glowing from their skiing trip. Mem tries to be brilliant at dinner, but doesn't succeed, and he feels embarrassed for her.

That night, he wakes up screaming "Mem! I'm going to die this night!" This time both Mem and Thesi come to wake him up, and Mem kisses him and holds him in her arms.

The next day, Mem goes back to Berlin and everybody talks behind her back. He overhears Hans talking to Inge about Mem's breakdown, and he hears Inge say

"That poor woman is running herself to the ground."

In the kitchen, Cook and Thesi gossip endlessly. Thesi says, "I've always had a special feeling for Gretl. I wish that there was something I could do for her."

He goes up to Mem's bedroom and inspects her bed but the sheets are as white as snow. *Fellerer or Frank? Vienna or Berlin? The woman can't take it. Poor, poor thing.*

All through January, he has terrible dreams that send him running to Thesi's bed. The facts of life that Anna Freud revealed to him over a year ago are monstrously rearranged; she notes that his imaginings are "much more obscene than what he was told." Anna is convinced that he is groping for some "missing sexual scene" that he saw when he was very small. Every time they meet, she tries to help him remember it. He loses his temper over the smallest things and then feels guilty for being so nasty to Thesi and Cook.

"Why did Mem go back to Berlin?" he asks Anna one day.

"Why do *you* think she did?" Anna asks.

"She said it was because she had to pursue her career, but was it really just so she could be with Frank?"

"This is a question for your father," Anna replies.

"It's none of my business," he shrugs.

"Then why do you think you brought it up?"

"I just would be surprised if she could lie to me that much."

He doesn't feel like lying down, so he sits on the couch, drawing on bits of paper.

"What are you drawing?" Anna asks, sitting down next to him. But being near her doesn't calm him down.

"This is Frank ... and so is this," he says, tossing his scribbles onto the table.

"What about this one?"

"That's Frank too."

Frank, hater of fishing, the capitalist sport, is a genuine Stalinist revolutionary. He has many women because he is so wonderfully full of life, and Mem, his mother, is one of them.

He pokes holes in all his drawings, taking special care to poke out all of the eyes.

"Why are you ruining your work?" Anna asks.

"Because I feel like it."

At the end of the month, he dreams that he's out hunting with Hans, Thesi, and an old forester. The two men walk in front, while he and Thesi walk behind. The trees stand in rows: there are oxen and bulls, and they keep moving in and out, between the trees. *Why can't you shoot them?* he asks Thesi, tugging at her sleeve. *You can't shoot those animals*, she replies. But Hans kills a bull, slits it open, and tears out its guts, and he also pulls out a syringe that's wobbling in the ground.

"Does the forester remind you of anyone?" Anna asks. "Say whatever comes to mind."

He tells her about Grinner, a forester that Hans knows. Grinner has a habit of farting while he walks, "just like the aging Emperor Joseph," as Hans always says. And yet Grinner always warns him not to step on crackling twigs, even though he himself makes so much noise. The bulls move silently in and out of the trees just as men move in and out of women. He saw those same bloody entrails when Cook cut open a bird – was it a partridge or a cock? The wobbling syringe reminds him of the penis of a dirty old man who exposed himself to him in a public bathroom. When men go into women, they make them bleed, and that's how babies are made.

"There would be very much less in this world without love," he tells Anna, "even if children could be produced mechanically. For one thing, there wouldn't be any art."

"Would there still be technology?" she asks.

"Yes, because we would still need technology for defense." They decide that the world is made up of fighting and love: these are the two great principles. They keep trying to uncover the meaning of his dreams, like detectives tracking clues.

When he shows his writings to Anna, she still talks about them the same way that she talks about his dreams. He wishes that she would talk about the way his stories are written, because he's quite proud of them. He reads her "A Fairytale without Meanings or Morals" in which a princess beheads 100 suitors for failing to come up with the answers to three riddles. The 101st suitor is very attractive to her, so that she actually fantasizes about marrying him. But when he fails to answer the third riddle, she cuts off his head, treating him exactly the way she's treated all the rest. The only sign that she liked the 101st suitor a little more is that she keeps his head in her bedroom. But first – he really likes this part – she has it hollowed out so that she can use it as an ashtray.

Anna says that the princess is Mem in disguise. None of her suitors wins her hand; she kills off every one of them.

"Are you like one of Mem's suitors?" she asks.

"No," he says, "because I'm her son, and I'm also the author of the story. If you're the author, you don't get killed off."

Hans is always out with Inge now, and Mem is probably with Karl Frank in Berlin. He wants to live in an apartment full of children, like the Burlinghams', where no one is ever by themselves. Sometimes, when he's lying on Anna's couch, the floorboards creak over his head and he wonders what Tinky and the others are doing upstairs. At home, he kills birds with his slingshot and refuses to tidy up after himself. "Wherever you go, there's a mess," Thesi says. "I didn't think it was possible, but you're getting worse."

On the rare occasions when Hans joins him for dinner, he does everything he can to annoy him, which includes using Jewish words like *schmatte*, *schlump*, and *schlemiel*. "Stop talking like an *Ostjude*," Hans says to him. "You'll never get anywhere if you talk like that."

Anna asks him to write a little composition on "How to Become Unattractive and Disagreeable" or "How do I Revenge Myself on my

Father?" and he throws together a little list that she summarizes in her notes:

Imitate disagreeable qualities in others (for example: use Jewish jargon, be fresh, thumbs in armpits, sharp criticisms in wrong place).

His Jewish shopkeeper routine is especially irritating to Hans; it gets to him every time.

Acquire characteristics that displease Hans (disorderly, unpunctual, secretive, spying).

The spying is what Hans hates the most. He's always telling him that he listens in too much, and that he should mind his own business. But in a way, Hans' girlfriends *are* his business because he might decide to marry one of them some day.

Conceal real feelings, pretend false ones. All of this only in father's presence, otherwise nice: "What does the father want of the boy?"

Hans is always telling him to be genuine, not to be fake. So he resolves to act fake in a way that gets on Hans' nerves and then, when Hans scolds him, to pretend that he genuinely doesn't know what set him off.

Trade parents' gifts (steam engine for typewriter).

Read only trash.

This last one is a particular sticking point. "If you remain *ungebildet* – uncultured – you'll sound like a dope and people in better circles will look down on you," Hans is always saying to him. So he leaves his Karl May all over the house and takes a perverse pleasure in the red-faced sermons that this provokes.

"How far back can you remember?" Anna asks. "Do you have any memories that go back to when you were still in your crib?"

"I remember touching my cousin under her dress in the back of the car," he says to her, a subject that seems more interesting.

"We've talked about that already," Anna says, "and about how you were disappointed at finding there was nothing there." She must have written all of that down in her notes. What other grown-up would write down a thing like that?

"Today I want you to reach farther back," she goes on. But they don't make much progress, going around and around until all his thoughts have flown out of his head.

"I remember being taken through the park in a carriage that made a creaking sound," he tells her on another day. But she only wants to hear about his crib.

"Do you remember seeing anything that you weren't supposed to see?" she asks. "Something that might have frightened you?" He digs a bit of wax out of his ear and examines it, rubbing it between his fingers. "None of our experiences is ever lost," he hears her say. "If we try hard enough, we can usually bring them up."

One afternoon – it's a cold, damp day in spring, and his nose is running, so that Anna has to lend him a handkerchief – they're talking about this and that and he starts to draw a sketch of his bedroom, before they stripped the wallpaper off. He draws his crib and the old, mirrored armoire, and the little monkey that watched over him from the shelf.

"How far away was your parents' bedroom?" Anna asks.

"Right here, across this little hall."

"Could you see it from your crib?"

"Only if the closet was open and I was facing the mirror."

"And what did you see in the mirror? Can you tell me that?" An image flickers up out of the darkness like a moth; he adds a few details to his sketch.

"Tell me about these lines ... and also this face ... whatever comes to mind."

"White legs standing upside down in the air. My father looking at me over his shoulder, from the bed."

"Anything else?"

"He doesn't have his glasses on. His eyes are red. He's angry at me."

"Why is he angry?"

"I'm not supposed to be looking at him. He and Mem forgot to close their door."

Anna goes over to her desk and makes a few quick notes. The room is so quiet that he can hear the water running down the hall. He turns over the paper and makes a sketch of the Goddess Fate holding up her scissors.

At the door, Anna tells him that he has worked very hard and that she's proud of him.

When he gets downstairs, he realizes that he still has her handkerchief, but he doesn't want to go back. He stuffs it into her mail slot and runs down the street, feeling the sharp cold rain on the back of his neck.

At school they make fun of Ernstl Freud. His eyes are as droopy as a basset hound's. The fact that he misses Muschi is no excuse for acting as though he can't do anything by himself. Peter misses Vicki too, but that's life: you have to make the best of it.

Tinky tells him that her American relatives are angry at Dorothy for refusing to bring them home. They say that Austria will never hold out against Germany, and that it's irresponsible to stay there any longer.

Who *are* these relatives back in the States? He hates it when Tinky talks about them.

"Believe me, those people are rich," Hans says. "There's no telling how much money they have."

"But they don't live in a fancy place. Our house is a lot fancier than theirs."

"Dorothy Tiffany Burlingham may like to live simply here, but I bet that her family doesn't live that way in America."

Peter imagines Tinky returning to a house made entirely of stained glass, in which every window tells a story about cowboys and Indians. When it's dark, all the lamps give off rainbows of light, and there's a winding, red-carpeted flight of stairs that leads up to a velvet-hung turret, which is where Tinky goes to read her books. If she does have to go back, he'll find a way to follow her. He won't just let her disappear. To get to America, he'll have to stow away in a ship, because Hans has no interest whatsoever in going there.

"The Americans are crude and primitive," Hans always says. "They put business before everything."

"But don't you want to see the Wild West? You could go hunting there."

"I'd rather go hunting in Africa."

The idea of being a stowaway frightens him, but he thinks about it all the time. One day, Tinky talks about how she loves going to her grandfather's house – she calls him "Bompa" – and he explodes.

"Go back then, why don't you," he blurts out.

"Maybe I will. And never come back."

For the next few days, he's angry at her, but when Dorothy invites him to spend a few nights with them, he's beside himself with excitement. Thesi packs his bag and warns him not to lose anything, but he doesn't pay any attention to her. He's a little lost when he first gets there; he's never lived in a household that's run like this. The children do whatever they like and, as a result, you can never predict what's going to happen next. One day, they listen to the latest hits from America on Bob's gramophone; another day, Bob unveils his plans for a vast electric railway. He and Tinky play duets on the piano, and then Bob gives a concert on his cello. He reads one of his latest stories out loud to them, and everyone, including Bob, is terribly impressed. But for some reason, Peter constantly loses things – his clothing, his *Winnetou*, his leather wallet. At night, he has trouble falling asleep, and he misses Mem more desperately than ever.

And then the time is over, and Herr Wimmer drives him home, and he's standing on his own doorstep again. He may have a more elegant address than the Burlinghams but there's still a smell of stale soup in the corridor. That smell has been there for as long as he can recall and, on the day of his return, it seems more inescapable than ever. He presses the button for the elevator but then decides that he doesn't want to wait, going up the stairs to the mezzanine two steps at a time. The wrought-iron cage of the elevator stupidly rises after him, jerking to a halt when it reaches his floor. Only Thesi is there when he walks in. Hans has already had his lunch, taken his nap, and gone back to work, and as usual he'll be out for the evening.

He makes a map of his apartment for Anna, marking the places that have always frightened him. The back hallway that leads from his room along the outer wall of the library to the vestibule is where the ghost-child lives. The front door of the apartment is where a burglar might slip in, in search of money, paintings, silverware. The servants' bathroom is another frightening place: dark and narrow, things could happen there that he shouldn't see, and yet the keyhole is at a perfect level for him.

"Can you draw a picture of your anxiety too?" Anna asks him. He draws a picture of a being that looks like a cross between a man and a squashed-up bug. His mandible-arms are waving angrily in the air and his gigantic black eyes are bulging with rage.

"Why do you think your parents leave you all alone?" Anna says. "Do you think that it's because you did something wrong?"

He shrugs.

"Maybe it seems as though they're punishing you," she goes on, "because long ago you saw something you weren't meant to see. Do you think that's possible?"

"I don't know," he says to her. Her questions are boring to him.

Mem comes to visit in the fall. She's feeling much better than before, and she promises to come more often from now on. "You're growing up so quickly," she says to him. "Are all boys in such a hurry as you?"

Instead of going to the Belvedere, they take a tram to Schoenbrunn so that they can visit Mem's beloved Palmenhaus. (When Hans and Peter move to the Gloriettagasse, Schoenbrunn will be very near, but Mem will be even farther away.) As they walk among the exotic plants, he feels proud to be seen with her.

"Aren't the orchids wonderful?" she says to him.

"I like the cacti better this time."

"How can you say that? They all look like they're coated with dust. Look at these colors! Don't you love this speckled one?"

"The colors are fine, but I don't like their shape. They look like puffed-up purses and sacks."

And so they argue back and forth, deliberating over every plant. Her thick black hair is pulled back from her face; she's wearing a string of seed pearls around her neck.

Afterwards they stroll through the park and she tells him the story of Xantippe, Socrates' wife. "Poor Xantippe. She led a terrible life! Always washing and cleaning up after Socrates and his crew. And what did she get for it in the end? Her husband's 'noble' suicide!"

She's been working on a play about Xantippe and the next time she comes, she's going to show it to him. When he tells her that he's been writing poems, she asks him to recite something to her, so he recites a piece called "The Regicide," all about a young man who murders an aging king and feels horrified afterwards.

When he walks into Anna's office the day after Mem leaves, she looks drab and mousy to him.

People like her don't really have a life of their own, he hears Mem saying. I don't have any respect for them. They live off of everyone else's misery and spin cold, dead theories in their heads. The arrogance of it – as though passion can be explained away!

"You're like a nun," he says to Anna.

"Oh? Maybe you can tell me why."

"Nuns don't have men," he says, his face growing hot.

"Maybe it would be good if Mem were more like a nun," she says, after a pause. "Then she wouldn't be going off to Berlin all the time."

"I never said that!" he shouts, jumping to his feet. "Why do you always twist everything around?"

He paces up and down and flails his arms exactly the way that Hans does when he flies into a rage. Wolfi watches him with his head to the side and makes a curious, questioning sound.

"I want to stop coming here," he says in the end.

"Alright," she agrees. "Let's try it for a week."

When they meet again, he tells her that he wants to come back, but only if they continue under different terms. "I'm not a little boy anymore," he tells her angrily. "I want our conversations to be more grown-up."

He refuses to lie on the couch, pacing up and down. He tells her that these last few days have been very productive for him. He's drafted plans for a full-length novel about a crazy man who goes to prostitutes all the time.

"Why prostitutes?"

"Because the only way that he can get love is if he pays for it."

"Is that how *you* feel about coming here?" she asks.

"You're twisting things around again!" he shouts. "You never listen to what I say!"

In the middle of his tirade, she sits down across from him and he becomes acutely conscious of her soft white hands, resting quietly in her lap. An ache shoots into his hands and spreads through his entire body, so that he has to turn his back to her. At the end of the session, he tears off a piece of paper and writes: *Decency alone forbids me saying it: it seems to me: that I love you.*

Thesi is furious with him because he's made a pigsty of his room. "I just tidied up here this morning!" she complains. "Here, the least you can do is straighten out your bed."

He smoothes out his featherbed and then he dives under it, watching her from inside his warm, dark cave. She takes off her sweater with her back to him, accidentally pulling up her blouse.

"What's that bluish lump in the middle of your back?" he calls out from under the covers. "Is that the injury you're always talking about?"

She tugs down her blouse and spins around. "What are you doing under there? Spying on me?"

"What was that thing? It looked like a bruise."

Her face is turning very red. She refuses to say another word, throwing herself into putting his clothes away.

This is the first time he's actually seen her injury, but he's heard her talk about it to Cook. She thinks it makes her unattractive to men, which seems ridiculous to him. Her back is a little rounded, it's true, but it's not as though it makes her look like an old woman or a witch. The real reason why she doesn't have a boyfriend is because she dresses like a governess, with stiff white blouses, silly little scarves, and sensible shoes.

"Mind your own business," she tells him when he brings all this up. She's really quite wrong not to listen to him.

Anna has problems in this area too. Why does she wear necklaces made of clunky mountain stones and sweaters that don't have any shape? Thesi is adorable, with her snub nose and her plump, red cheeks, but Anna is actually beautiful, even though she dresses like someone's grandmother.

"Do you have any silk blouses?" he says to her.

"What kind of silk blouses?"

"The kind that are shiny and smooth."

"Does your mother wear silk blouses like that?"

"All the time."

"Do you want me to have boyfriends like your mother?" she asks, after a pause.

"If you dressed better, I bet you could." He tries to imagine her in high heels and a low-cut dress, on the arm of a mustached young man.

"And if I had a boyfriend, do you think I'd stop seeing you?"

"Maybe," he shrugs.

"Do you want that?"

"No."

"And yet you're curious to see what would happen."

"I don't want to talk about this anymore."

It's close to Christmas. Mem is coming! If only the *Christkindlmarkt* by the *Stefansdom* hadn't shut down. He and Mem used to go there and pick up all sorts of things – angels made of ironed straw, silver bells that jingled in his pockets. "Times are hard," Thesi says.

"I still wish it was open."

"Of all people, you shouldn't complain."

Will Mem be disappointed if they have *Glühwein* and *Lebkuchen* at home? He gets it into his head that they should have a Christmas tree, and for once Thesi is on his side.

If only he didn't have to wait! The waiting really is very hard. He can barely cross a room without thinking of Mem, and his eyes are constantly filling with tears. *Boys shouldn't feel this way about their mothers*, he thinks. He tries his best to hide his feelings, especially from Hans. He has tantrums over ridiculous things, taking refuge in acting like a baby.

The day before Christmas, there's a knock at the door and Mem is standing there. She's wearing a red cape bordered with blue-black fur and a pair of tasseled boots. She's just arrived from Berlin, but she isn't tired. There's a sparkle, no, a glitter, in her eye. She comes in for a moment to say hello and then she whisks him away to the Hotel Sacher, where she orders two slices of cake, ends up giving him most of hers, and allows him to dip sugar cubes into her cognac until flames are burning in his cheeks.

As they're walking along the Opernring, men turn to look at her, and he feels proud to be walking at her side.

"I can only stay for two days this time," she says to him, slipping her arm into his.

"But I thought you said …"

"Things have turned out differently."

"Just two days?"

She agrees that the time is much too short but she'll be here for his Christmas performance and she'll come back as soon as she can.

She has a long chat with Thesi in the kitchen, and he overhears everything.

"Well, at least you've narrowed it down to Fellerer," Thesi says.

"He's much better for me," Mem sighs.

"Has he told you his intentions?" He listens with all his might, flattening himself against the wall of the passageway.

"My stubborn Thesi! You refuse to believe that I have no interest at all in marrying."

"Why wouldn't you?" he hears Cook ask.

"As soon as you marry, the fights begin and romance goes out the window."

So Fellerer is in and Frank is out, but Mem doesn't want to marry him. Maybe, just maybe, there's still a chance that Hans and Mem will get back together again. Fellerer lives in Vienna; Frank lives in Berlin. Maybe Peter will see Mem more often from now on. But then again, maybe Mem didn't come to Vienna to see him at all; maybe she really came to see Fellerer, which is why her visit is ending so soon.

He wanders into the dining room, takes a fork out of the drawer, and stabs a series of holes into the tablecloth. Nothing that Mem tells him is true. Everything is a pack of lies. And it's not just Mem, it's everyone, especially the grown-ups, who fill him with disgust. Anna pretends to be committed to helping him, but she wouldn't be committed if Hans didn't pay her to listen to him. Hans lies to him about what he does at night, saying that he's going to the theater when he's really going to Inge's apartment in the Jacquingasse. Inge pretends that she likes him oh so much when she's really only interested in Hans, or maybe in Hans' money – Hans worries about this himself. Thesi is the only reliable adult, but she's only reliable because she's an employee of Hans, just like Cook or Tilly, their chambermaid.

There's no one I can trust, he thinks. *There isn't a single grown-up who tells the truth.* He starts mocking and challenging everyone. At first, Hans is amused by his wit, and then he complains that he's turning into a know-it-all.

At the Christmas performance, Peter appears onstage, his entire body covered in a parchment scroll. Anna, Sigmund, Dorothy, Peter, Erik, everyone is there, and also all of the parents, including Hans and Mem. In his hand, he's carrying a little speech, but he doesn't need it, he knows it all by heart. He has dashed it off in one sitting, and he delivers it in a ridiculous voice, after making an exaggerated bow to the audience:

Honored Ticket-holders, and Patrons! It gives me an immensely, unspeakably great pleasure to have the privilege of presenting this circus which matches the prominent undertakings, to so venerable a public. No crass greed for money warms my heart at the thought of full wallets! No! The pure passion for art burns within me. This purest of fires consumes itself within itself, if it is not permitted to present itself most humbly to a high and mighty and all-judging audience. Believe me when I tell you this! Believe – that I have this ardent fire, read it in my heart, see it shine in my eyes.

Oh blissful day, for my wishes are fulfilled. Blessed is the circus director with his jingling purse, commanding all; and the poor but creative artist who is rewarded in cash. Blessed are they indeed.

After the circus, Mem comes up to him and tells him that she's very, very proud of him, and that she didn't realize that he was such a talented actor. He bows and repeats the speech's closing lines: "The eternally servile artist salutes you."

The chauffeur comes into the schoolyard instead of waiting outside and tells him that he won't be seeing Anna today. He should pack his things up quickly, they don't have a minute to spare – Herr Heller wants him at the factory at 2:00 sharp. But one end of the Davidgasse is blocked by a stalled delivery van, so they have to go around the other way. There isn't any time to stop in the display room on the way in, much to the disappointment of the girl behind the desk, who usually gives special treats to him. Instead, he's ushered into a windowless room, where he is greeted by Herr Kohldorfer, a thin man with a pockmarked face and a habit of wagging his head from side to side.

"Your father will be here shortly," Herr Kohldorfer says. His breath smells like the *Schnapps* they put inside the chocolates. "Let's see now, how old are you? Let me guess ..."

"I'm 11."

"Just like my Georg! Fancy that. What do you like to do for fun?"

"I like to read."

"You're a clever one, I can see that. So is my Georg, especially when it comes to math."

Peter's relieved when Hans comes through the door and breaks this conversation off. Hans wants to teach him something about how the business works; he asks Herr Kohldorfer for the ledgers for "1926" and "1932," laying them out on the desk and opening them to matching pages.

"The whole history of this business is stored in this room," Hans says, with a sweep of his hand. "You just have to learn how to interpret the information in these books. If you compare this column to this one, for example, you will see how sales have dropped over the last five years." The numbers seem to be hovering above the page, like a swarm of insects about to attack. "It's not because the quality has gone down," Hans goes on, "it's because of this lousy economy."

Herr Kohldorfer has retreated to a little desk in the corner. Is he laughing to himself, or is he sucking his teeth? *That boy wasn't listening*, Peter imagines him saying to his co-workers afterwards. *He isn't cut out to run this factory. Now my Georg could do a fantastic job. But of course, he won't get a chance. No, no, that's only for the boss's son, whether he's cut out for it or not.*

Not a single window, no real books, only ledgers as gray and dense as stone. "Let Georg run the factory!" he wants to cry out. But his fear of Hans' fury holds him back.

After his visit to the factory, he tells Anna a favorite daydream of his.

He's sitting outside her office, in the hall, and Sigmund Freud happens to pass by. Freud asks him about the book he's holding in his hands and he shows him the cover: *Das Kapital*. Impressive reading for a boy, Freud remarks. Tell me, what do you think of it? Without hesitating for a moment, he replies, I think that Karl Marx is a far greater man than you.

"Is that your opinion in real life?" Anna asks.
"Definitely."
"Why is that?"
"Because Freud never explains the things that happen in the outside world. He only talks about what happens inside."
Although she says this is an interesting point, she brings the conversation back to Frank, saying that he might seem superior to Hans

because he succeeded in taking Mem away. Could Frank = Marx and Hans = Freud?

He should never have told her his fantasy.

Hans is much more than a businessman; he's a sophisticated man of the world. Hans has a library of over 1000 books and he's read bits and pieces of many of them. One day, Hans' library will belong to him, but he can't wait until then – he needs a library of his own. He starts buying books from the stalls along the street, arranging them alphabetically on a shelf in his room. But one day, Hans finds Schnitzler's short stories there and he takes the book away, saying that these tales of over-heated love are inappropriate for him. This seems incredibly unjust. He hates being treated like a little boy!

The next day, he storms into Anna's office with a list of questions designed to evaluate juvenile books. "Are they didactic or anxiety provoking?" he says, in a high-pitched voice. "Are they fairy-tales? Technological? Realistic? Scandalous? Do they teach the children anything about the intricacies of love or is this a topic to avoid, since it only makes children 'feel their smallness,' something that they are always being made to feel?"

He feels like a lawyer who is appealing the case of a person who has been wrongly accused. Each question is an arrow that he is shooting into the heart of the massive hypocrisy of the grown-up world.

He has the dream of two directions, in which he envisions a vaulting horse that can be "mounted" from both sides. In her notes, Anna records the following interpretation:

> The two directions [German *Richtungen* = directions, movements, tendencies] which he has to bring together are Hans and Menga [Mem], analysis and politics (Marx and Freud.) One says: children may read everything, the other: that is not suitable for you. His sexuality is the reason Menga [Mem] left, the parents can come together again if he gives up his claims *on both, castrates himself.*

When he holds to Marx, he is holding to Mem and her world, and, when he holds to Freud, he is holding to the milieu of Hans. When he longs for a synthesis of Marx and Freud, it's the reunion of Hans and Mem that he is really looking for.

And so he and Anna continue their conversation in the sealed-off room of 19 Berggasse. Outside, beggars are filling up the streets. At the university, Jewish students are being beaten up, so they have to slip into their classes through back doors. In Berlin, Jewish books, including works by Sigmund Freud, are being thrown onto blazing bonfires. But in Anna's office, the family romance reigns supreme, and the dream of achieving full humanhood remains intact.

7.

Sex and Politics

Berlin, Italy, Vienna, 1933–37

MEM writes to Hans that she's been down in the dumps and that she needs to have more contact with her son. It's springtime and Easter vacation is coming. Isn't Peter old enough to take the train to Berlin?

After some back and forth, Hans agrees to the plan, but Mem must promise to be on the platform when the train comes in. Thesi is certain that Mem will be on time. She won't keep Peter waiting; she only does that with her men.

"On the train, you'll be completely on your own," Hans says, looking him up and down as though he is sizing him up.

"Just stay in your compartment," Thesi tells him as she sews a button onto one of his shirts. "Don't get too friendly with anyone."

He is nervous and excited about the trip. He loses his temper over the smallest things. One sharp word from Hans is enough to make him stamp off to his room and Thesi's nagging reminders are unbearably irritating to him.

In her most quivery voice, Inge sings "*Hänschen Klein*," about a little boy who sets off into the big world on his own. Although her way of singing usually seems sappy to him, the image of Hänschen with his walking stick and cap brings tears to his eyes.

Anna asks him whether he thinks he'll be able to be himself when he's staying with Mem in Berlin.

"Who else would I be?"

"Someone who constantly tries to please others."

"I don't know what you mean."

"You've been so natural lately. I would hate to see ..."

"What if Mem doesn't like me that way?"

"What about *you*? Don't *you* like being yourself?"

But he and Mem have a way of being that no one else understands. They aren't interested in what's plain and ordinary, not in others, not in themselves.

When he finds out that Hans has gotten him a ticket for the night train and that he's going to be travelling first-class, he begs Hans to trade in the ticket for a cheaper one. Why doesn't anyone understand that he wants to go to Berlin as an adventurer, not as a pampered little boy?

He can barely wait for his vacations to begin. Although he is usually very disorganized, he packs his suitcase three days in advance. In her notes, Anna writes that his agitation is due to some negative feelings about the trip that he's trying to overcome.

Finally the day arrives, and the chauffeur drives him and Hans through the streets of Vienna. In the midst of his excitement, he feels a stab of sadness, and then he tells himself that he'll soon be back again. How official the old train station suddenly seems! He usually comes here to meet trains, not to board them himself. Hans settles him into his compartment but doesn't say goodbye. Instead he hangs around on the platform endlessly, giving him bits of advice through the window.

Will Hans lose his temper if he asks him to go away? He doesn't want to take the risk. The whistle pierces the air and the train begins to move. To his horror, Hans starts running alongside the train, looking up at him with a grin on his face. As the train picks up speed, Hans starts running with all his might. His vest bursts open; he's panting from the strain of keeping up. *Go away Papa!* he wants to shout. At last, the train reaches top speed and Hans is no longer there.

When the conductor comes to take his ticket, he calls him *young sir* and Peter forgets his disappointment about travelling first class. This cabin belongs completely to him; he tries out the bed and finds it very comfortable. He wants to stay awake for the entire night so that he doesn't miss a moment of the trip, but his little bed is warm and snug and the rocking of the train puts him to sleep.

When the train pulls into the Berlin station, Mem is there. How mysterious she looks! Like a female spy. She is wearing a brown velvet hat set at a slant, so that it casts a shadow over one side of her face. He shouts, "Here I am! Here I am!" She runs up to his compartment and taps the glass with her gloved hand.

"We have the whole week together!" she says in the cab. "I hope you won't feel too bored without your friends."

"I have no friends, not any real ones," he lies. "I only want to be with you." But the truth is that if Basti had been with him on the train, they would have had a hilarious time.

One night, she takes him to the Scala, a glittering hall with a gigantic stage, where the *Würstchen* are exceptionally good. She lets him have as much of her beer as he likes, until his eyes become moist and his face feels hot. The master of ceremonies is dressed in silver and black, and his voice is a cross between a scream and a whine. He introduces the Maharajah, an old man in a loincloth with a long grey beard who stretches out on a bed of nails and doesn't bleed, and a clown by the name of Doloro, who seems to be crying underneath his painted smile. After Doloro comes an army of high-heeled women, wearing sequined bathing suits and flame-colored plumes on their heads and behinds. They kick up their legs, do splits, and twirl around, all in perfect unison.

"What do you think of the Tiller Girls?" Mem asks him afterwards at a café.

"They're like those trained horses, the ones in the Spanish Riding School, only not as horsey."

Mem laughs. "Did you find them attractive?"

"They weren't bad."

"Aren't you the little man of the world!"

She takes him everywhere – his favorite is the zoo – urging him to jot down his impressions of Berlin. "This city won't be the same the next time you visit me," she says to him. "Already they're suffocating us."

Towards the end of his vacation, she takes him to an alley that is completely hidden away, leading him down a half-flight of steps. Passing through a dank cellar, they go through a second door and suddenly they find themselves in a room packed with people who are dancing wildly in a cavernous space. On a makeshift wooden platform, a band is playing jazz, and all of the musicians are black. A woman with bright red hair and a monocle comes up to them. She's wearing a tuxedo, but with sheer stockings instead of pants.

"Where have you been hiding?" she yells, giving Mem a giant hug. "Don't tell me – this is the son you were telling me about. Your mother is a wonderful woman, do you know that? We need more of her kind here in Berlin. All the free spirits are flying away!"

She finds them a table and then hurries away, saying she has to make sure that her performers are ready to go onstage. Before she leaves, she says to Mem, "He's adorable. Keep an eye on him!"

A man steps out from behind a curtain and cracks a whip. Two girls crawl out onto the stage. To Peter's amazement, they're not wearing any costumes at all, except for garters, fishnet stockings, pumps, and a kind of tassel or fringe that dangles between their legs. They go around on all fours for a little while, which causes several people to cheer, and then they finally get onto their feet. They begin to sing a silly song about "hair up here and hair down there," but by this time, no one pays much attention to them. Their singing is way off-key, but their skin is as white as ivory. One of them is plump, with big breasts, and the other one is tall and slim, with the narrowest waist he's ever seen.

They climb off the stage and come right up to their table, and now he doesn't know where to rest his eyes. Mem hands the plump one a little money, and they move away, roughing up his hair and winking over their shoulders at him.

"That was really too much," Mem apologizes when they get home. "I was hoping for political cabaret."

"I'm glad we went," he interrupts.

"It wasn't too awkward?"

"Not at all."

She pours a bottle of milk into a pan, puts it on the stove, and mixes it with honey. "Do you have a girlfriend?" she asks, with her back to him.

"Not really."

"No? That surprises me. Are you sure you don't have a sweetheart tucked away?"

"If I did, I'd tell you," he replies, even though it isn't true.

"I bet you're still crazy about the Burlingham girl, " she remarks, as she sets the honey milk down in front of him.

"She's alright," he says, turning red.

"You know, I'm a little jealous of her."

"Why should you be jealous?" he asks, stirring his milk with a spoon.

"Why? Because she's your first love!"

"I don't want to talk about Tinky."

"That's not very nice."

"But there's nothing to talk about."

"I thought we made a pact, you and I. Don't you remember? We wrote it in that little notebook that you used to keep by your bed. We said that no matter what happened, we'd always be honest with each other."

"But I *am* being honest," he lies. "Besides, you've kept things back from me."

"Like what things?" she asks in surprise.

"All kinds of things."

"That really isn't true."

"Yes it is!"

"You're just trying…"

"Stop it Mem!"

"What am I doing?"

"You're twisting everything around!" He shoves the table away as hard as he can, spilling her wine and his milk all over the floor.

"Now look what you've done!"

"It's your fault! I told you to stop."

When he gets home, Hans wants to hear all about his adventures in Berlin. Peter describes Mem's tiny apartment, and the places she took him to, and the show they saw together at the Scala. "The Tiller Girls. Quite fun. Harmless stuff."

He doesn't mention the cabaret, but a week or two later, it slips out. "She took you where?" Hans shouts. "She must be out of her mind! What can she have been thinking of!" Anna is in agreement with Hans, and even Thesi, who is usually Mem's ally, shakes her head.

He feels guilty about betraying Mem, but he doesn't say anything in her defense. Although he really didn't mind going to the cabaret, it begins to seem shameful to him. How degraded those girls really were, with their tassels and their ridiculous song. Apart from taking him to a sleazy bar, Mem spent hours telling him about her various men, going into details that he didn't want to know. Her "honesty" about Tinky was the worst of all – why should she be jealous of her? Mothers weren't supposed to have feelings like that. Why did she always make life so complicated?

The trip works its way into his dreams, turning into a riddle that he tells to Anna and is then required to solve.

He is standing in front of the Scala. SHAKESPEARE is emblazoned on the marquee. Passing into a waiting room, he is admitted to see a prostitute. She shows herself to him; he shows himself to her.

Downstairs, Mem is waiting for him. He knows that she doesn't approve.

Nothing in a dream is arbitrary. Anna Freud records his associations in her notes:

> Both are Mem, prostitute and mother. She makes a grown-up of him, entices him, but she doesn't give him anything. The prostitute is Macbeth (?), a biblical figure, the sacred devil, the 'men let down their pants with her.'

In his dream, he is waiting. Waiting for what? That's easy – waiting to live. But somehow Mem is in the way. Mem is his temptress-guardian, watching over him on the one hand, seducing him on the other. The prostitute is "the sacred she-devil." There is no way of resisting her power. Men compromise their dignity – "let down their pants" – for her. If they give her money, she gives herself in return. But Mem doesn't give anything to him, and yet she wants to keep him all for herself. Out of loyalty to her, he shirks his responsibilities, proving that he can't be successful or move forward without her – that he needs her, no matter how bad everyone else says she is.

"The stupid thing about it all is that I'm waiting," he writes in his diary. He recognizes that waiting is a big mistake. Why do grown-ups praise patience so much? In a poem that he shows to Anna, waiting swallows up his entire life.

> Hours, long hours, must I wait
> Days, long days must I wait.
> Years, long years must I wait.
> And I am still not a youth, not a man.
>
> And again the waiting years
> And at last I'm a youth, a man.
> A boy with a slanted beret, and a girl,
> a girl, that is happiness.
>
> A day has passed, and I am an old man;
> And may not wear a slanted beret:
> Again with no girl,

And the yearning again in my heart.

Meanwhile, the school is closing: one by one, teachers and students leave, and finally the wooden building shuts its doors. The Rosenfeld garden is just a garden again; there are no children laughing and shouting in the back. Only Valti remains, lost in his Goethe library, which keeps on growing while everything else withers away.

If he wants to take his *Matura* in six years, Peter must go to the Realgymnasium, but Hans doesn't think that he'll pass the entry exams. The Hietzing School has been wonderful in many ways, but his year-long study of the Eskimos hasn't prepared him for public school. Why didn't Erikson and Blos think about this? They've thrown him to the wolves. But then Hans hires Bernard Taglicht, a Hebrew teacher from the *Schwarzwaldschule* (Schwarzwald School), and everything turns around.

"Intelligence isn't enough," Herr Taglicht says, stroking his beard. "Success depends on hard work." When Peter complains, Herr Taglicht says to him, "When your grandfather makes a decision, do you question him? Accept what's in front of you. God has a plan." Herr Taglicht quizzes him relentlessly, marching through physics, Latin, history. "Learning by doing" means nothing to Herr Taglicht: the only thing that matters is drill, drill, drill.

At last, the day of his exam arrives, and Peter walks into the huge lecture hall of the Realgymnasium defiantly, throwing himself into his chair. The test is even harder than he thought it would be, and it takes all of his concentration to finish.

"I passed!" he tells Thesi when the results finally come.

"You just squeaked by. Don't give yourself airs!"

"Why are you scolding me now?"

"Because I worry about you. Who's going to get after you to study once I'm gone?" (Thesi is leaving to teach at the Montessori School; it's high time for her to make something of herself.)

The Realgymnasium isn't anything like the Hietzing School. No one cares about "developing into a whole person" there. As Peter notes in an essay entitled "We Must Study," "Everything is taught in an astonishingly dull manner: in History we have dates, in Latin little verse, in Physics rules, in Religion faith is required, and in Physical Exercise a military drill." In the halls, the students push and shove while the monitors scream hysterical warnings at them. The physics teacher makes fun of them when they get an answer wrong, and the history teacher is a pompous bore who twirls the waxed ends of his moustache as he struts up and down the aisle.

Peter is constantly picked on for being a rich Jew's son. *"Zuckerl Heller!* When are you going to bring us some candy?"

Everyone wants to be like everyone else. No one knows how to think for themselves. To survive, you have to belong to one of two groups – the Social Democrats or the Christian Socials. But he doesn't belong to any group, and so he's nothing but a Jew. If he succeeds, he's a pampered Jewish boy, who doesn't know his head from his ass; if he fails, he's a pathetic Jew, unfit for anything.

On the playground, he gets into a fight with a boy wearing the white knee-socks of the Nazi Party (swastikas have recently been banned at school) who says that his father stinks of fish. Peter gives the boy a bloody nose and, to his surprise, the boy, whose name is Andreas, is friendly to him after that.

"Look out for Herr Achsel," Andreas warns him one day.

"I don't have him for gym."

"Look out for him anyway – he likes nice Jewish boys like you."

Peter keeps his eye on Herr Achsel after that, noticing that he often appears in the gym when the boys are changing their clothes and that he has a girlish way of smoothing back his hair. But Herr Achsel never makes an overture to him or to anyone else as far as he can tell, so that he wonders whether Andreas has made the whole thing up.

He's lost touch with Tinky – she's visiting her family in America. Although she's told him that she'll be coming back, he doesn't know whether to believe it or not. Even if she does come back, she'll be attending a different Gymnasium, so he won't even be able to see her every day. There's no question that Tinky is his great love, but sometimes the feelings that he has for her seem to dissolve into a vague, shimmering mist. In the meantime, he has to solve the riddle of who to be, which is more pressing than anything else. He can sometimes hear Anna Freud's voice telling him "Just be yourself," but that only works in her quiet room, with Wolfi snoring on his rug, not in the crowded hallways of his school, or on the playground, where he has to fight.

He doesn't get picked up from school anymore. No one at the Gymnasium has a driver and car. He already gets enough grief for being rich and, besides, he prefers coming home under his own steam. One afternoon, when he's halfway home, he sees a band of boys running down the street. They stop in a doorway and huddle together, with one of them standing guard. Andreas is among them: Peter recognizes his high, excited laugh. Two of the other boys – there are seven – are from his school as well. What are they doing? Pissing against the door? A man appears in a window and they run away.

Peter inspects the wall where they've just stopped and sees that it's covered with swastikas. The wooden door says "Jews get out!" written in drippy black paint. He looks up at the window, but the man has disappeared.

"Should I report them?" he asks Cook when he gets home.

"The best thing is to mind your own business," she replies, looking at him with an expression in her eyes that he has never seen before.

In a story about his youth, Peter describes standing on the threshold of a party and waiting to be let in. As he waits, he adopts a casual pose – one hand in his pocket, one leg thrust forward, a dreamy look on his face – but no one answers his knock. Without changing his pose, he counts to 30, then knocks again, despite the fact that he already wants to go away. This time the door opens for him. He takes a deep breath and plunges into the crowd.

Bare arms brush against him as he heads for the punch in a room that reeks of perfume and sweat. A few glasses later, he finds himself in the bathroom with Felix, his pimple-faced, gangly friend, who perches on the edge of the tub and talks dance strategy with him. Felix says Peter should dance with Sylvia, even though Sylvia is going with Robert. Felix is convinced that his prospects are very good and argues his point so excitedly that he slips into the tub. For his own part, Felix wants to dance with Lilly, but he's afraid that Peter will move in on him. "The girlfriend of my friend is sacred and taboo," Peter says to him, quoting a line that he's heard in a film.

Out on the dance floor, Sylvia dances with Bob, Felix dances with Lilly, and Peter is alone. He flings himself into a chair and drinks yet another glass of raspberry punch. How can you "act naturally" when everyone's eyes are on you, waiting to see whether you are making a fool of yourself? But maybe he doesn't give a damn, maybe he's wrapped up in his own important thoughts. Unsure of what to do with himself, he studies the reflections of the dancers in the opalescent glass. And then the flat-chested Lilly comes up to him and tells him that she wants to talk to him alone. They stand together on the balcony for a moment or two and then he kisses her with a rage that is possible "only in perfect indifference."

When they go back into the room, they find Felix staring gloomily off into space and Bob still dancing with Sylvia, whose head is resting on his shoulder. After the party is over, Peter wraps himself into his coat, puts up his collar, and strides out into the rain. If it were up to him, he would walk all night, but the chauffeur is waiting for him on the corner.

The traditional fabric of Viennese life is stamped with a pattern of *Gemütlichkeit*, that is, cordiality, comfort, cheerfulness. How pleasant it is to spend the afternoon in one's favorite café! What interesting conversations one can have at a *Stammtisch* of artists or economists or journalists, not to mention writers, teachers, psychologists. But thread by thread, the fabric is being pulled apart and reworked into an ugly pattern. Nazi posters and pamphlets are appearing everywhere and violent incidents are happening every day, overturning decades of predictability.

In the afternoon, the regulars start coming to the café, and the waiters rush to bring each one his favorite paper. Suddenly someone runs into the room and throws a package onto the ground. That was no mailman! Get out of the way! But the explosion happens too fast. The marble sideboard is suddenly vertical, pastries are splattered all across the floor, the mirrors are covered with coffee and whipped cream. Several customers have been thrown onto their backs, and one of them can't get up. Within moments, everyone else is gone, running out onto the streets. Only a few terrified waiters remain, scrambling to clean up the mess. What about that man slumped in the corner? A trembling waiter calls an ambulance.

Within a few days, the customers return, except for some of the Jewish ones, who stay away, even though they have been coming here for years. Scenes like this repeat themselves every week, altering the cellular structure of the organism that is still known as "Vienna."

If one party fails, there is always another. And, with a little luck, that party can be held at one's own house, when the grown-ups are away. Peter writes about such a party in detail, down to the wine donated by Inge. "For your orgy," she says, pointing to a case. She and Hans leave for the evening, dressed for the opera. Peter stands by the piano in his "inspired artist pose" but no one appears. Should he play the piano thunderously, barely looking up as his guests come in? But he doesn't feel like playing Beethoven to an empty room. He gazes at his reflection in the mirror instead, wishing that the pomade had worked better on his frizzy black hair.

"You look lovely," he hears a male voice say. He twirls around and finds Robert and Sylvia standing in the door. So, there will be guests after all – Felix and Lilly also appear – but will there be conversation? No one seems to have a damn thing to say. What's wrong with the four of them tonight? They're acting as though they've never met. He had the sequence of events all planned out – first, there would be conversation, then dancing, then couples pairing off, but he doesn't know how to make it all happen. He's about to take action when Robert pours everyone a glass of wine and turns out the lights. Now it's too dark to see each other, or to dance, or to do anything except sit together on the couch in a squirming pile. How badly this is turning out. He doesn't have the luxury of leaving in disgust because this joke of a party is happening in his house.

He steps out onto the terrace and tears at the purple wisteria that hangs down the walls in clustering vines. Something brushes against his shoulder and he turns his head. To his astonishment, Sylvia is standing there, smiling at him.

"From a slight touch comes a kiss," he recounts. "… he feels her tongue and teeth and is afraid of her wildness with which he doesn't know how to deal." Is he kissing her because he loves her or so that he can boast about it afterwards? After all, this is only his ninth or tenth kiss.

At recess, the boys stand in a circle, rubbing their arms. Even though it's February, they can't be bothered with their coats. Matthias Greiner comes out of the building still chewing his bread. He's wearing a red woolen jacket, scarf, and gloves.

"Look at you!" Helmut Pechel shouts. "Are you sure you're dressed warmly enough?" This remark goes over well with the girls, who giggle and whisper among themselves.

"He's even shorter than the chancellor!" Otto Weisskirch yells out. (Dollfuss is only 4' 11").

"Dollfuss is a loser!" Pechel remarks. "He lives in a cruddy house and eats vegetable soup for lunch."

"Why are all dictators vegetarians?" Willi Edelstein puts in. "The world would be a better place if Hitler and Dollfuss tried some meat."

"Don't talk about Hitler and Dollfuss in the same breath!" Pechel says. "One is a leader and the other is a wimp."

"You're just pissed because he's outlawed your party," Edelstein laughs, "and now you can't wear your uniform to school."

"Oh yeah? Well he doesn't like Social Democrats either. He's about to tear your militia apart."

The insults keep flying back and forth until Pechel pushes Edelstein in the chest. "Get your hands off me!" Edelstein shouts. Within seconds, they're rolling on the cement. A tight circle forms around the boys. The girls' attention is completely engaged.

"Go Pechel!"

"Get him, Edelstein!" Peter shouts. He's always liked Edelstein, with his long pale face and his skeptical eyes.

Pechel is crouching over Edelstein, trying to pin down his arms, but Edelstein keeps twisting away. The bell rings, the monitors come out of the doors like birds out of cuckoo clocks, and the boys and girls fall into line. But they barely have time to get into the classroom and pull their notebooks out of their desks before the lights start flickering on and off. When the lights go off for good, the teacher goes out into the hall and the room breaks into pandemonium. "It's the electrical workers. They're striking," Edelstein cries. Everyone rushes to the windows but all they can see are unlit buildings and a few people standing out on the streets. "Don't be so happy!" Pechel says. "If you're right, you can bet that they'll pay for it."

School closes early so that everyone can find their way home despite the fact that the streetcars are no longer running. Peter's favorite bookstore is open, but the bank is closed. Many shopkeepers are standing in their doorways or out on the street.

When he finally gets home, he finds Hans and a group of friends sitting in the living room and smoking cigars.

"I was worried about you," Cook says, taking off his coat. "This is no time to be wandering the streets." She sits him down in the kitchen and gives him a piece of honey-cake. Suddenly, he wishes that Thesi was still here, even though she left them months ago. As he sits eating, he hears the grown-ups talking excitedly. He tries to make out what they're saying, but only bits and pieces come across to him.

"... the government forces are sure to win ..."

"... the Social Democrats are fighting out of Karl-Marx-Hof, in the 19th District ..."

"... and the people who live there?"

"... caught in the crossfire."

"Dollfuss is a bloody dictator."

His eyelids are heavy; he can't stay awake. He hears Pechel laughing as he falls asleep.

For the next couple of days, he gets to stay home from school, and he's perfectly content to practice piano and read his books. On the third morning, he gets up before everyone else, throws a breakfast roll into his satchel, and sneaks out. He walks for what seems like a long time, but he doesn't feel in the least bit tired. As he approaches the *Wien Landesgerecht* (Vienna Court), he hears the roaring of a crowd, and then an ambulance pulls up ahead of him and comes to a screeching stop. A stretcher is lifted out of the back; on it lies a man with bloody bandages around his chest and waist. Two men in uniform pull the man onto his feet, but he can barely stand up, so they put their shoulders under his arms and drag him into the building.

"Hang him!" he hears someone cry.

"He looks like a corpse!" someone else exclaims.

The crowd now forms a solid wall, and Peter's trapped inside of it, unable to see beyond the people directly in front of him. A panic seizes him and he twists around, pushing his way back to the street and running away as fast as he can. The next day he reads in the newspapers that seven workers were hanged the day before, including a worker who had been badly wounded by the government forces. *It serves him right!* he hears the people roar. *He betrayed his country. Why shouldn't he get what he deserves?*

When Peter turns 16, Hans sends him on another trip, but this time it isn't to see his mother. Accompanied by two students paid by Hans, he goes by train to Italy, and in Italy he is taken to a brothel. There he is "initiated into the mechanics of sexual intercourse" as he puts it later. Once again, his sexual development is managed from above, in the name of arriving at a healthy outcome.

Smuggled into the brothel with a borrowed passport, he's thrilled at passing as an adult. But now he finds himself in a world of violet curtains and yellow light, where everything smells of talcum powder and mildewed plush. A black-haired woman stands before him in a barren room; he puts his hand on her shoulder but she pushes it away, as though she is brushing away a fly. She strips off her stockings in a brisk, efficient way that makes him understand that nothing, or very little, is expected of him. This nameless woman, with her pointed belly, small breasts, and hairy thighs, is utterly alien to him, even though her flesh is touching his. "Sucking, licking," she throws herself on him like "a small naked animal." The light is an unblinking yellow eye that watches them indifferently. The ending is as abrupt as the start; he barely remembers leaving the room.

The two students lead him down a narrow street overlooked by a huge poster of Mussolini. In a nearby restaurant, they buy him many rounds of drinks, until he laughs and jokes just as loudly as they do. And now he carries his new knowledge inside of him, without knowing what to do with it.

Sylvia's parents have a villa on the Wörthersee and he has been invited to stay with them on his way back from Italy. They assume that his *Bildungsreise* (educational journey) was all about seeing art, and they ply him with questions about what he saw in Florence. "Aren't the reds of Titian fabulous?" "What did you think of Raphael? We always come away thinking he's a bit too sweet." In the nighttime, he and Sylvia sit out on the dock and throw stones into the moonlit water, trying to touch the outermost circles with their bare feet. Sylvia talks about Fred, Mary's boyfriend, who seems to have a giant crush on her.

"Is there anyone here who isn't in love with you?" he asks, letting his hand brush against her knee.

"You're mean!" she says. That word is exciting to him. She presses herself against him and he puts his arm around her. With an abruptness that he doesn't like, she takes him by the hand and leads him towards the house.

In the living room, she sinks down onto a shaggy rug, smiling up at him and hugging her knees. She's wearing a short linen skirt and a linen jacket with a blue anchor on the lapel; sitting down on the floor across from her, he sees that she's still wearing her bathing suit underneath. She asks him to play the piano for her, but he can't take his eyes off the hollow behind her knee, which she is stroking with her fingertips. He leans forward and awkwardly gives her a kiss, knocking his knees against hers.

"Not here," she whispers. She runs across the moonlit floor, waving to him to follow her in a gesture that seems too rough. In her room, she throws off her jacket, pulls down her suit and lies back on her bed, offering herself to him. But he remembers the yellow light that watched him so pitilessly.

"I can't," he stammers.

She turns her head. "Don't you like me?"

"Of course I do."

"This is torture," she says, pulling the sheet over her breasts.

The next night, there is dancing by the lake and everyone goes – Sylvia, Mary, Sylvia's girlfriend, as well as Fred, Mary's beau, the one who has a crush on Sylvia. The jazz leader has a crush on Sylvia too – his greasy black hair is parted in the middle, and he conducts the band languidly, with his lips curled back in a fixed, lazy smile that grows longer whenever he looks Sylvia's way. Sylvia dances with Fred and then she disappears. Has she gone to the other pavilion, the one that everyone keeps talking about? Neither Mary nor Fred seems to know. He tosses the pin that he was going to give Sylvia into the lake. What's the point of being here?

Later that night, when everyone else has gone to bed, except for Sylvia, who is still out somewhere, he walks up the moonlit stairs and remembers the fluttering child that he used to see when he was a little boy, holding its thin white arms out to him. He isn't afraid of it anymore, but he still sees it; he sees it now. And then he hears the front door open and Sylvia appears below, humming softly to herself as she slips off her shawl. She's holding her dance shoes in her hand, and now she's raising her arms above her head, making a pirouette in the center of the living room.

"Sylvia, it's me!" he calls down.

"Why aren't you in bed?" she whispers, looking up. Like a faerie, she floats up the stairs, brushing past him as she heads for her room. She slips through the door and is about to close it again, but he puts his foot on the threshold and steps inside. Without kissing her, he unbuttons her blouse, admiring how alert and responsive she is. He searches for a detail that will impress him as obscene, "in order not to be overwhelmed by the storm of desire." Without any effort, he pulls her down onto the bed. How unresisting she is, like a body without weight. She embraces him, and for an instant he's prey to doubt – what is this feeling? Is it lust or pain? And then "a black gate stands in the midst of a white flashing sea and the network of reflections vanishes." He sees her head on the pillow and marvels over her pale forehead with the shadows at the temples, as though death is shining through her sun-bronzed skin. Afterwards, he lies back on the pillows and puts his arm across his eyes, trying to hold back the tears that are stinging his eyes. All at once he begins sobbing so uncontrollably that he leaves the bed and hides himself in the closet, without even noticing that Sylvia has begun to cry too. In his literary version of this moment, he describes the "jubilant sobbing" that comes over him. But in a still later version, he reflects on his terror, at that moment, of growing up.

He is slowly making progress in the task of overcoming the fear that makes him want to pull away. He can't talk about this fear to anyone, especially not to Sylvia. A real man has to be sure of himself.

He must be careful not to overwhelm her when they're together, not to think only of himself, which happens so easily. When they're talking afterwards, he must remember to listen to her, to draw her out, and not to talk only of his own ambition to be great. Otherwise she will soon get tired of him. When she gives him a bowl of berries in the woods, he must eat exactly half and give the rest to her. And he mustn't devour his half all at once; first she should take some, and then he should, and so on, no matter how long it takes, until all the berries are gone.

Sylvia's father is set on taking them to the *Strandcafe*, where the view of the lake is fabulous. But when they get there, the place is packed, so they can't get a table by the window. "These damn Germans!" Sylvia's father complains. "It's all because Hitler got rid of the travel tax."

"We've never had trouble finding a seat," Sylvia's mother says.

"At least it isn't dead, like last year," Sylvia remarks.

The view across from them is blocked by a table of Aryan types who keep shouting to the waitress to bring them more beer. "Too many toasts to the Führer!" Sylvia's father remarks. "Just ignore them," Sylvia's mother says.

At a table in the corner, a Jewish family sits. As far as he can tell, no one is serving them. The mother keeps pouring the children glasses of water, and the father watches the waiters hurry back and forth with a blank expression on his face.

The waiters come to their table with platters of food – trout, potatoes, peas and carrots, cucumber salad. The lunch is really very good, but he feels as though the children in the corner are watching his every bite. The youngest child is whining now, and the mother is unable to silence him. Suddenly the father jumps to his feet, addressing himself to the entire room. "This is preposterous!" he bellows, causing everyone to turn their heads. "We've been coming to this restaurant for years." But the waiters continue to hurry back and forth, without looking at him. A few moments later, the entire family files out, and the Germans across from them cheer and clap their hands.

"I've never seen anything like this," Sylvia's mother says in a lowered voice.

"This is just awful!" Sylvia bursts out.

"Why don't the two of you go explore the lake," Sylvia's father says, handing Sylvia some money. "We'll meet up with you on the promenade in an hour and a half."

They walk to the lake and rent a canoe, rowing it far out into the water and letting it drift. "I'm glad we got out of there," he says.

"I hate that place," Sylvia agrees. "I'm never going back again."

They lie side by side in the bottom of the boat, staring up at the cloudless sky.

"I'm part Jewish. Did you know that?" Sylvia says.

"You? Jewish?"

"Just a quarter, on my father's side."

"So you're not really Jewish."

"But if we had children, what would they be?"

"They'd be nothing. It has to go through the mother."

"What if I converted?"

"Why would you want to do that?"

"Because the way it is now, I don't know what I am."

"You're a *Mischling*! Completely impure. Let's be impure together," and he gives her a kiss.

"But let's say I converted, and we had children, Then our children would be …"

"I would never do that."

"Never have children?"

"Never tell them what to believe."

"Why not?"

He closes his eyes against the sun. "Because I don't know what I believe myself."

She props herself up on her elbow and gazes at him thoughtfully. "Sometimes I think that belief is something that just happens to you."

"What do you mean just happens?"

"That it doesn't come from the head …"

 Where else would it come from?"

"From the heart."

"You could use that argument to justify anything."

"But it's not an argument …"

"Neither is this." He pulls her down and kisses her on the lips.

"You never listen to me!" she complains.

"That's not true."

"You don't take me seriously."

Before he can answer, he hears a splash. "Damn it!" he cries. "That was one of the oars!"

"How did that happen?"

"I think I knocked it with my foot."

"Now what will we do?"

"I'll use the oar and you use your hands."

"Stop telling me what to do!"

"Sylvia, we don't have time for this. Just do what I say!"

They finally make it to the pier, where Sylvia's parents are waiting for them. Sylvia is silent and withdrawn, and doesn't so much as glance at him.

"Sylvia, what's the matter?" her mother says.

"The intensity of youth," her father chimes in. "All we can do is envy them."

Mem is in the process of moving back to Paris, but she'd be delighted to join them on the Wörthersee when she's settled in.

"I wish *I* lived in Paris," Sylvia says. "I can't wait to meet your mother. Her life sounds so marvelous!"

On the day of Mem's arrival, he and Sylvia have a fight because he doesn't want her to come to the train station with him. "I don't understand you," she complains.

"She wouldn't like it."

"Don't you want her to meet me?"

"Of course I do."

"I'm not so sure."

But he refuses to give in to her, setting out for the train station alone. An hour later, he is sitting in a dusty little square, flipping through his copy of *Thus Spoke Zarathustra*. He leafs through the introduction by Stefan Zweig, coming to a passage that he has never noticed before, a passage that describes Nietzsche having his dinner in a boarding house. Nietzsche's stomach is so sensitive that he has to consider the menu with great care – the smallest error of judgment will make him suffer for days. The tea has to be weak; the food can't be spiced; he doesn't allow himself to drink or smoke. Nietzsche hardly speaks to anyone and, when he does, he speaks softly, about trivial things. When dinner is over, he goes cautiously up a narrow flight of stairs – he is extremely near-sighted and unsure of his steps – to his writing table, piled high with books, papers and proofs. His room is poorly heated and completely bare, except for bottles of medicine for migraines, vomiting, stomach cramps, and vials containing the heavy sedatives that he depends on for sleep. Peter can almost see him, wrapped in a shabby overcoat, his double glasses touching the page.

To think that Nietzsche, with his bad stomach and his weak eyes, was the creator of the *Uebermensch*, of Superman! The people around him barely noticed him, but he was one of the greatest thinkers in all history. Hans says that Nietzsche is tainted now that the Nazis have embraced his ideas, but, in his opinion, this doesn't make him any less heroic and brave. This shy, tortured man, bent over his desk, knew beyond a shadow of a doubt that his ideas would change the world. Will *he* ever attain this certainty, or will he be ambivalent for the rest of his life? Anna Freud has traced his ambivalence to its source, but consciousness is only half the battle. Nietzsche says that great men transcend themselves.

Peter closes the book, his head aching from all these thoughts. There's a kiosk over there, where you can buy sandwiches and cigarettes. He's spent all the money that Hans gave him for the trip, but maybe Mem will buy him something when she comes in. In the meantime, he can look at this picture of a brunette, who is very sexy even though she has the face of a horse. He'd like to do it with someone vulgar like that. They could do it in an alleyway, standing up.

Why can't I come with you? he hears Sylvia saying, and he feels a little guilty, toward her, but the brunette is still grinning up at him ...

The whistle shrieks and he can see the train heading for the station, its black sides gleaming in the sun. *A young man threw himself on the tracks. His mother was beside herself...* But that isn't his story, it belongs to someone else, like so many stories that drift through his mind. The train pulls into the station and the passengers get off, moving quickly, as though they're in a hurry. An old crone wrapped in dusty black lace totters toward him with a faint smile on her face. That's not Mem – she's as bony as a skeleton and she's smiling at that elderly gentleman standing behind him. Where is Mem? Did she miss the train? Did she decide at the last minute not to come? But then he sees a neat little figure in a round straw hat with broad shoulders and narrow hips, standing perfectly still as the others rush past. She is, after all, a real human being, quite separate from the image that he has formed in his mind. And because she's real, he has to get used to her all over again, which is strange, considering that she's his mother.

"How long are you staying?" he asks, as he takes her bags.

"I'm not sure yet," she says, hooking her arm through his. If she actually likes it here and decides to stay for several weeks instead of a few days, what will he do about Sylvia?

The hotel is modest but satisfactory, with a pleasant view of the lake. After she changes her clothes and washes her face, Mem immediately wants to take a walk.

It must have rained while they were in her room because the air is cooler now and misty sunbeams have formed on the path. Here and there they stop to look at furry islands of moss growing over massive roots that remind them of sleeping animals.

He asks her to tell him about her life in Paris , but she has nothing to report. "You're at that age where everything is new," she remarks. "At my age, it isn't like that anymore." She stops for a moment and looks at him thoughtfully. "You seem different to me. Are you seeing someone?"

He admits to having a girlfriend and everything comes out.

"Is it the daughter?" He nods. "So that's why the parents invited me. Well, I better make a good impression."

"It's nothing as serious as that."

"Do you like her?"

"Sometimes."

"Why not always?"

"I don't know. She says that she's in love with me, but she really doesn't know me."

"Whose fault is that?"

"Sometimes she sees that I have moments of despising her."

"And why *do* you despise her, as you call it? Such fancy words."

He thinks for a moment. "Because she runs after me."

"You men are all the same!" Mem exclaims, shaking her head. "I hope that you're taking precautions at least."

Mem performs brilliantly at the dinner table, teasing Sylvia's father about the doctrine of sexual *laissez faire* that he flirtatiously expounds. Even as she flatters his masculinity, she conveys her sympathy to his wife, who has obviously put up with her husband's indiscretions for years. Mem's performance captivates everyone, but why is she working so hard to charm people who are so clearly inferior to her? If he knew that she was simply doing it for him, he could forgive her. But performing like this is a compulsion of hers, and he feels that it cheapens her to always give in to it.

As for Sylvia, she does everything she can to ingratiate herself to Mem in a way that makes him feel embarrassed for her. After dinner, they all go out to see a film, and he feels awkward sitting between the two of them. On the way home, the grown-ups walk in front and he and Sylvia fall behind. Sylvia makes a point of kissing him, whispering in his ear about "getting away with it" and "not letting Papa see." He tries to have an intelligent conversation with her about the film, complaining that the ending was weak. "But I like happy endings," she says, a statement that seems utterly idiotic to him.

The next morning, he visits Mem at her hotel so that they can have a serious talk. Speaking of Sylvia, Mem says she's surprised that such a pretty girl with such long, fine thighs would be intimidated by a middle-aged woman like herself. As for Sylvia's parents, she is amused by the fact that when they were walking home from the film, they warned her not to turn around, so as to allow the two young ones to enjoy a kiss. "A good situation for a young man who is taking his first steps in love," she remarks. "But maybe they make it too easy for you here."

She has received a telegram from her Parisian lover, asking her to come back and marry him. "He's too young for me," Mem says. "I'm going to turn him down." They talk about how her affairs have distracted her from her work. She has yet to make a decisive success.

"You could be a great screenwriter if you wanted to be," he says. "No one can tell stories like you."

"But I'm a woman. You forget. I may have a masculine intellect, but I don't have a masculine will."

"If you don't care about success, why don't you marry?" he says, frustrated with her. "I don't understand."

"Because then I would lose my monthly payments from your father, and that's what my lover and I have been living on. He's self-reliant, but if he became financially responsible for me, he would have material worries that he doesn't have right now."

"You still get money from Hans?" he asks in surprise.

"And why shouldn't I?" she says defiantly. "I didn't come into my marriage as a beggar, you know. I brought him a big dowry, and if I still had it, I'd be an independent woman."

She seems more and more bitter when she talks about men. Her anger makes him all the more determined not to be a disappointment to her. Yet there is also the problem of Sylvia, who is starting to feel neglected by him.

He takes Mem to the post office so she can send a telegram to her lover, and then to the hairdresser, so that she can get ready for him. While he's waiting, he dashes back home to where Sylvia is playing the piano, just so he can spend a few moments with her. How attractive she looks in her silky white dress with the three little buttons on the collar that hide the adorable nape of her neck! He'd like to open those buttons one by one. Why does he constantly have to take Mem around?

He accompanies Mem to the station and sees her to her train, and this time Sylvia doesn't even ask whether she can come along. White smoke and black pistons, the screeching of the brakes. He stands on the platform and watches her disappear. What is this pain that twists around in him like a knife? Anna would say the pain arises from the guilt that he feels for wanting Mem to disappear.

He imagines himself standing at a lectern with a manuscript in his hand and reading a sentence about the "feeling of irrevocable farewell" that comes over a young man as he watches his beloved go away. There is silence, and then the audience breaks into applause. Laying the manuscript down, he humbly bows his head.

Hans is never satisfied with him, hammering him with warnings and advice. "You won't pass the *Matura* if you don't work." "No one will hold your hand, the way they did at the Hietzing School."

There are parties at their house every week, with Inge flirting with the men and Hans directing the conversation. When the talk turns to Germany, Inge retreats, saying it's all too depressing to her. Whenever he can, Peter listens in, without any sense that what he is hearing will soon change his life.

How can we sit here like this, looking on while they strip everything away from the Jews who live just three hours away?

I hear that the Nazis stand outside the Jewish stores, frightening the customers away, and that if a German wants to have his coat tailored by a Jew, he ends up with his head bashed in.

What about what's happening here? There was another bombing in Innsbruck the other day.

They say the tourists left in droves. And who will the shopkeepers blame it on? The Jews!

The discussion turns into a catalog of Nazi-engineered events – bombings and beatings and book burnings. And then they talk about the friends who are trying to get out, with some of them considering places that seem foreign and strange, like Shanghai and America.

Peter is starting to wonder whether he has anything in common with Hans. All he ever talks about is salvaging the business and protecting his money. The only time Peter actually likes being with him is when they're in Grundlsee. They catch massive salmon in a crystal-clear lake above the tree line, at the foot of the Dead Mountains, and bring them back to the village to be smoked. They fly-cast for trout in the river known as the Traun, roasting them over little fires and eating off sharpened sticks. Many times, they are out all day, coming home at five or six o'clock. But before long, they feel the itch again, so they get into the peeling canoe moored at the little dock and fish on their own Grundlsee until the sun goes down.

8.

Graduation

Vienna, 1938

FAILING the *Matura* is social death – at least that's what their parents and teachers want them to think. As an act of defiance, Peter and his classmates start putting together a *Matura Festschrift* that will expose all the absurdity of the *Matura* year. Rebellion or sophomoric humor? There isn't any difference in their minds. But among all the examples of inside jokes, there is one drawing that stands out from the rest: the massive bulk of Herr Rydel, the school's principal, is seen from the back as he reads from a book to eight skinny students in prison clothes.

The beleaguered students walk together in single file, without seeing the parting of ways that lies directly ahead. Looking at this image, we can hear the laughter of teenage boys, a mix of Aryans and Jews, who know and don't know how thin their reality is. Haven't they heard rumors about the German prison camps? Haven't some of them even visited them in their sleep? Yes, but those are rumors, after all and, even if they're true, that's not the point. The point is that Herr Rydel is no better than a prison guard, and studying for the exams feels like a form of punishment.

Andreas has grown heavier this past year and his voice is scratchy and thick. He likes to brag about how the Party is going to save Austria, even though his "arguments" are laughably weak. "The Jews are parasites on our people," Andreas says.

"I see you've been studying your pamphlets," Peter observes. "Define parasite for me."

"They feed off our people. They suck them dry ..."

"And yet some of the greatest Austrians have been Jews."

"Mozart wasn't Jewish!" Andreas blurts out. His close-cropped hair seems to be standing on end. In fact, he looks like an angry porcupine.

"But Freud is a Jew, and so is ..."

"Sigmund Freud is full of shit."

"Alright, since you argue so eloquently, what about Wagner? They say that he had Jewish blood ..."

And so they go back and forth, until they get tired of words and wrestle each other to the ground. But one day after school, Andreas changes the game and comes after Peter with two of his Nazi friends. "We could destroy you if we wanted to," Andreas says, "but we're going to go easy on you today." One boy pins back Peter's arms and the other one punches him in the stomach with a fist that operates like a machine. At a signal from Andreas, the two boys back away, leaving Peter doubled over by the fence. "Poor little rich boy," Andreas laughs. "From now on you better watch your mouth."

The trip home takes forever that day. When he finally gets back, he finds Hans waiting for him. "Look what came in the mail," Hans says, waving an envelope in his face.

"What is it."

"A letter from your school."

"My report card," he says, sinking down onto the couch with a groan that Hans misinterprets.

"You're failing in two of your subjects! Why haven't you mentioned this to me? Do you even know what they are?"

"Physics and trigonometry," he manages to get out, pressing his hand to his stomach.

"What's become of your ambition?" Hans shouts. "Your mind was so active when you were a little boy. All you care about now is skiing and fencing and dancing with the girls. If you go on like this, you won't amount to anything."

The middle of his body feels as though someone has trampled on it, but he's too fed up with everything to talk about what happened with Hans. In the bathroom, he looks at himself in the mirror, but all he can see is a purple bruise on his left side. When he comes back out, Hans is talking to someone on the telephone – something about the plebiscite that's happening on Sunday and how there still may be a chance for Austria.

"I'm going to the café," Hans says, after the call is done. "I want to see you studying when I get back."

Peter sits in the kitchen while Cook prepares his dinner, comforted by the sight of her sloping shoulders and broad back. "Go on, read your book," she says to him. "Don't just sit here, staring off into space." He opens his book dutifully, but the letters look like tiny ants dragging crumbs of light across the page.

At last, Cook fills his plate with strawberry omelets, his favorite, and sets a glass of milk in front of him. She turns up the radio and through the crackling he can just make out the sentimental strains of the *Blue Danube*. "I'm so hungry all of a sudden," he says to her. "Can I have seconds when I'm done?" Before she can answer, the music stops and a man's voice shouts, "The Chancellor!" After a pause, they hear another voice, but this one is subdued and trembling.

Austrian men and women! This day has brought us face to face with a serious and decisive situation. It is my task to inform the Austrian people about the events of this day. The Government of the German Reich presented a time-limited ultimatum to the Federal President demanding that he appoint a candidate chosen by the Reich Government to the office of Chancellor and also follow its suggestions when selecting the ministers to serve in that cabinet. Should the Federal President not accept this ultimatum then German troops would begin to cross our frontiers this very hour.

I wish to place on record before the world that the reports disseminated in Austria that the workers have revolted and that streams of blood have been shed, that the Government is incapable of mastering the situation and cannot ensure law and order, are fabrications from A to Z.

The Federal President has instructed me to inform the nation that we are giving way to brute force. Because we refuse to shed blood even in this tragic hour, we have ordered our armed forces, should an invasion take place, to withdraw without serious resistance, and to await the decisions of the coming hours. The Federal President has asked the army's Inspector-General, General of Infantry Schilhawski, to assume command over all troops. All further orders for the armed forces will be issued by him.

So, in this hour, I bid farewell to the people of Austria with a German word and a wish from the bottom of my heart: God save Austria!"

As Peter listens, tears come to his eyes, not only because of the Chancellor's words but also because of the note of defeat in his voice. He looks up at Cook, whose mouth has fallen open, and slowly pushes his plate away. "I'm done," he says, but she doesn't respond, sinking into a chair.

He goes out to the living room, but no one is there, so he retreats to his room and lies on his bed. When he hears the front door open, he quickly jumps up, but Hans bursts into his room before he has a chance to dash back to the kitchen and retrieve his book. Hans places his hands on his shoulders and looks into his eyes, standing so close that he can smell the liquor on his breath. "What will happen now?" Hans says, shaking his head. "We have to stick together, no matter what." He doesn't understand what Hans is talking about. All he knows is that Hans no longer cares whether he's studying or not.

An hour or two later, they hear trucks rolling down the streets and men screaming "Heil Hitler" and "Jews get out!"

"You're not to leave this house under any circumstance," Hans says to him. "God only knows what they're up to out there."

Hans starts to build a fire in the living room, ordering the butler to bring in more wood. When the fire is blazing, Hans goes into his study, emerging with an armful of books that he proceeds to toss into the flames.

"What are you doing?" Peter exclaims.

"It's bad enough that I'm a Jew, but if they decide I'm a Communist, that will be even worse."

Peter picks up a book that has fallen to the floor, an encyclopedia of economic terms that has mystified him ever since he was a little boy. "Why would they care about a book like this?" he asks, leafing through pages filled with graphs and diagrams. "Because it contains the truth, that's why," Hans says, taking the encyclopedia from him and opening it. Peter can tell that Hans doesn't want to part with it by the way that he's holding it in his hands. "But nothing we touch is innocent anymore," Hans suddenly says angrily, hurling the heavy book into the fire.

"You better stop!" the housekeeper says, shaking her finger at him. "When they see all that smoke, they'll know exactly what you're up to."

The next day, German bombers fly over the city, releasing a blizzard of propaganda. "Hitler has arrived in Linz," the radio screams. "He has entered into his hometown … the people are ecstatic!"

The weekend drags on. Still no going outside. Cook goes out for bread and milk and comes back with a list of all the shop windows that have been smashed. As for the outdoor market, it isn't the same. "Half the vendors are missing," she complains.

"All the Jews are hiding," Hans remarks. "I want every door and window of this house to be locked at all times."

That night Peter dreams that Andreas has found his way into their sitting room, and that he's ripping down their curtains and kicking over their chairs. He stands in the corner, watching him, hoping that he won't notice he's wearing Hans' dressing gown.

On Monday, they wake up to the clanging of bells and the rumbling of heavy vehicles. According to the radio, thousands of people are pouring toward the city center and the German *Wehrmacht* is rolling in. "The most powerful military machine in the world," Hans remarks, "all for our tiny Austria. And who's standing up for us? All our so-called friends are backing off. In the absence of protectors, Vienna is opening her legs to receive her highest-paying customer."

Hans' phrases seem phony to Peter. Why does everything have to be addressed to an audience that isn't even here? He wonders where Mem is and whether she has any idea of what's going on. Maybe she's sent them a telegram and they just haven't picked it up. Or maybe she's forgotten them, taken up with her latest lover.

By Wednesday, he's back in school, but he never makes it to his desk. Instead he's told to report to the assembly room that has been designated for Jewish boys, which means any boy with a drop of Jewish blood. Here Principal Rydel informs them that they will no longer be attending this Gymnasium; they'll be attending the Gymnasium in the old Jewish quarter of Leopoldstadt instead. "You'll still be preparing for the *Matura*," he says to them. "Are we supposed to be happy about that?" Edelstein whispers in Peter's ear.

They're let out of school early that day, but the non-Jewish students remain. On his way home, Peter sees an old man kneeling on the ground with a tiny brush in his hand and two SA boys leaning against a wall. The old man is wearing a long, mud-splattered black coat; his wispy grey beard is speckled with dirt. "Is your beard getting in your way?" one of the boys laughs. "Here, let me help you with that." He takes a knife out of his pocket and with one broad sweep of his arm, he hacks off the old man's beard, knocking his skullcap off. After this operation, the old man bends even closer to the ground, brushing the pavement frantically.

Peter freezes, afraid that the boys will turn on him, but they're completely focused on the old man.

"Come on Israel," the second boy shouts, kicking the old man in the small of his back with his heavy boot. "You missed this part! Start all over again!"

"Eh, eh, eh," the old man moans, swaying back and forth over the sidewalk, his head almost touching the ground. Peter turns the corner and then breaks into a run, unable to get the sound out of his mind.

The Gymnasium on the Kleine Sperlgasse in Leopoldstadt is out of control, with students pouring in from every district of Vienna. In the absence of desks, students sit on the floor or stand in the back, and the teachers have to shout to make themselves heard.

Peter looks for Sylvia among the faces in the hall, but he doesn't see her anywhere. Maybe as a *Mischling*, she can stay where she is, in which case there's little chance that he'll see her again. On his way to the bathroom, he sees a tall, slender girl bending over the water fountain, and he starts making his way over to her. But no, that one has a coarser face, and her calves and ankles are much too thick.

When he gets home, he finds Hans pacing back and forth in the living room, while Inge watches him from the couch. "They were Hungarians," Hans is saying in an excited voice. "There were five of them, and they waved their pistols at us."

"How much money did they grab?" Inge says.

"Not very much. We've never kept that much at the plant."

Inge looks up at the ceiling and shakes her head. "That isn't the end of it. They'll be back again."

"You think I'm an idiot?" Hans snaps.

"I was just saying …"

"Believe me, I'm not going to sit around and wait."

"What are you going to do?"

"I'm going to meet with my upper-level workers."

"What's the good of that?"

"They've always been very loyal to me. We'll work out a plan."

A few days later, Hans is dragged off by the SA and interrogated in their office. His cousin and partner shows up in the middle of his "interview," appearing in his First World War regalia and wearing a medal awarded to him by Mussolini. But his decorations don't produce the desired effect – the SA men still force them to clean out their toilets. After being held for a few hours, they are finally released, thanks to the efforts of a pharmacist who has done business with the family for years and who has connections in the Nazi Party.

Over the next few days, the factory is Aryanized, filling up with men in uniforms who don't know the first thing about candy manufacturing. Hans is retained because his top workers make the case that he's indispensable to the running of the plant, and that he's also key to foreign sales, which constitute a large portion of the factory's earnings.

And so in the morning, Peter goes to the school in Leopoldstadt and Hans reports to a Nazi-run factory. Peter carries his books under his arm – he's too old for a satchel now – and Hans goes to the office with a packet of cyanide pills sewn into the lining of his jacket. Hans' Nazi bosses refer to him as "Israel," a name that has been stamped onto the documents of all Jewish men. At home, Hans loses his temper over the smallest things and Peter does his best to steer clear of him. Inge finds it more and more difficult to be around Hans, withdrawing into an alcoholic haze.

One night, Thesi comes to visit them and tells them she's no longer satisfied with teaching at the Montessori School.

"If you have a good job, hold on to it," Hans says, "especially now, when everyone is scrambling."

"I want to be a child analyst," she says, her cheeks turning red. "Anna thinks I have an aptitude."

"You see?" Peter teases her. "All your troubles with me have finally paid off!"

"Will Anna train you?" Hans asks doubtfully.

"Yes," Thesi says, "she's promised me, but it's going to mean leaving Vienna."

"But I thought that Sigmund ..."

"Don't mention this to anyone, but the Professor has finally agreed to go to England."

She tells them how the Gestapo came to 19 Berggasse, demanding that Sigmund Freud come with them for questioning, and how Anna stepped in and asked to go in his place, saying that her father was too frail to make it down the stairs.

"How brave that one is!" Cook remarks.

"So what happened?" Hans wants to know.

"They actually agreed to it."

"She was taken away by the Gestapo?" Peter repeats in alarm.

"Where did they take her?" Cook puts in.

"I have no idea," Thesi says. "All I know is that they took her away, and that it was hours later before she finally came back."

"Was she alright?" Peter asks.

"She was perfectly fine, but the Professor was beside himself. No one in the house, including his own wife, had ever seen him that upset before."

"That poor man!" Cook exclaims. "At his age, to have to go through something like that."

"They say that when Anna finally walked through the door, the Professor broke down in tears."

"Sigmund Freud cried?" Peter says in astonishment, unable to imagine it.

"He cried on Anna's shoulder," Thesi tells him, "and said that they all had to leave as soon as possible."

"Soon no one will be left," Hans remarks, puffing on his cigar. "It's really quite astonishing."

The city is suddenly full of traps. You have to be on the lookout wherever you go. A classmate of Peter's was forced to clean out a barracks the other day; another spent an entire afternoon scrubbing *Schnussig* propaganda off a bathroom wall. So far, Peter hasn't been pulled off the street, despite his curly black hair and his Jewish nose. And yet he certainly hasn't been obeying all the rules, sitting on park benches at the Belvedere and flirting with Aryan girls when no one is watching him.

Hans is spending more of his evenings at home, sitting in his study behind closed doors. "If something happens to me, the business will fall into your hands," he says to Peter one night. "I don't want to be a businessman," Peter replies. "What will you do for money? Don't be an idiot!" Before Peter can answer, Hans flies into a rage, going on and on about how out of touch with reality Peter is.

A few days later, Hans walks into Peter's room and sits on his bed, telling him that there's something they need to talk about. "I think we can save the factory," he says in a lowered voice. "I've been talking to Victor Opalski. Do you remember him?"

"Victor Opalski," Peter says. "Isn't he Inge's brother-in-law?"

"That's right. He calls himself an Aryan, but if you ask me, he looks more like a Slavic Jew. An intelligent man, up on all the latest things. He's actually helped me to modernize the factory. Anyway, Opalski has an uncle by the name of Vogt, and this uncle is not only a real Aryan but he's actually done business with Goering. Now, if I sell the business to Opalski and Vogt with the understanding that I'll buy it back one day, I could maybe get a contract with a special clause granting me permission to emigrate."

"Can you really do that?" Peter asks.

"With the Goering connection, anything's possible."

For the next few days, Hans is in an exalted mood, and he and Inge don't have a single fight. But then one evening, Opalski comes to the house to have a meeting with him and the mood in the house is strained again. "What a coward!" Hans storms after Opalski is gone. "If he didn't want to stick his neck out for me, as he says, why did the bastard lead me on?"

A few days later, Peter comes home from school to find Inge lying on the couch with a bottle of *Schnapps* tucked under her arm. "I haven't gotten to anything," she sighs. "I better get up before your father comes home."

"He's been awful these last days," Peter says to her, noticing a bruise on her arm.

"It's because of Opalski," she sighs. "I knew it wouldn't work out, but he wouldn't listen to me."

"What will we do now?"

"Oh, he has a million schemes."

"But he can't seem to settle on anything ..."

"He'll get out of here one way or another, and so will we. If his visa isn't accepted, he says he'll ski over the Swiss Alps."

"Are you joking?"

"He's already asked Albin Schraml, his old skiing pal, to purchase all kinds of equipment for him. He'll get out of here – there's no question of that – and both of us will end up following him. But what our lives will be like afterwards, I can't say. There's a very good chance that we'll be perfectly miserable."

"Don't talk like that, " he says to her, irritated by her maudlin mood.

"But really, what kind of life will we have, cut off from all of our friends and from everything we know?"

"You could always leave him," he wants to say. "You're not Jewish. You could just stay behind." But he's afraid that Hans would fall apart if he didn't have Inge to criticize.

Every few days, another piece of art goes missing from their house. The Dürer etchings are the first to disappear, then the Holbein etchings, then the portrait of Maria Theresa, and eventually the "degenerate" Schiele and Kokoschka. It isn't the Nazis who are stripping their walls – with the help of the housekeeper, who is growing more and more cantankerous every day, Hans is carefully hiding his collection in the cellar. With the artwork gone, the apartment seems cold, and it seems even colder without the Persian rugs and the hunting trophies and the famous bearskin from Romania.

"What's the point of all this?" the housekeeper complains. "We don't even know where to send the boxes to." The next day she announces that she has found another post, so the already overworked Cook has to take her place, adding packing and cleaning to her long list of duties.

To everyone's surprise, Opalski suddenly comes forward, offering to store their things until Hans has established a new address. But how does Opalski even know that Hans has hidden all the art? Ever since Opalski let him down, Hans has been holding him at arm's length. "I don't trust that man," Inge says. But once again, Hans doesn't listen to her, saying that Opalski may not be so bad after all. And so a van pulls up to the house in the middle of the night and three men in work clothes appear, going about their business with great speed and energy. Within an hour, all the carefully wrapped packages are gone and Hans is paying the men in cash.

"It's like giving it away," Inge says to Peter, as they watch the van rumble down the deserted street.

At his new school, Peter's insulted constantly, both by his fellow students, who taunt him for being rich, and by his teachers, who call him "*Saujud*" when he gets something wrong. And yet, even as his teachers tell him how worthless he is, they still put him through the hoops of preparing for the *Matura* exam, drilling him relentlessly. When he passes the *Matura*, Hans is greatly relieved. "Perhaps you're not as undisciplined as you seem." "It's all completely meaningless," Peter shrugs, but he's really very proud of himself.

Back at his old school, the *Matura Festschrift* finally appears, with a much smaller cast of characters. Some of Peter's contributions have been used, but his name has been erased, along with the names of all his Jewish classmates.

If passing the *Matura* is such an accomplishment, it's strange that he has to flee his country as his reward. No party, because there isn't any time. No present, because money is suddenly tight. They find out that he has passed at the end of May and now all anyone cares about is getting him out of Austria. All that effort. What was it really for? As of June, he'll be on his way to Paris, along with Tommi, his younger cousin.

Whatever he takes has to fit into two suitcases that are light enough for him to carry on his own. How do you pack up your entire life? The best solution is not to try. He throws his clothes, including his winter coat, into the suitcases, without bothering to fold anything. (For the rest of his life, he will pack in this hurried way, and he'll pride himself on taking as little with him as possible.)

He's never lived anywhere but Vienna before, and yet he thinks of himself as a citizen of the world. He's traveled to Berlin and Paris after all, and he's fluent in English and French, with a little Italian thrown in, not to mention all the books he's read. After he lands in Paris, he'll make his way to London, where he'll be met by Jack Jones, of Rowntree Associates, Hans' new business partner. The Burlinghams are in England, together with the Freuds. Maybe he'll find a way to see Tinky again. And Mem may be in Paris for all he knows, plus he has the contacts that Hans has written down for him.

The day of his departure finally comes. Hans can't stop flooding him with warnings and advice. "If guards talk to you, for God's sake, don't talk back. Just do as they say and don't be arrogant."

Inge embraces him at the door, running her fingers through his hair. "I'll see you in England," she says shakily. "Who knows? Maybe it will be better than we think."

He takes one more glance at the apartment as he stands at the door. Where is the little girl, with her fluttering white sleeves? He has an eerie sense that at this moment, she's watching him, and that if he lingers any longer, she won't let him go.

The driver is waiting at the curb. Hans sits in the front, tense and still. As they drive away, Peter looks over his shoulder and sees a pool of golden light shimmering on his balcony.

Tommi is waiting for them at the station, sitting on his suitcases with his head in his hands. "You're early, which is good," Hans says to them. "Get on board. Use those steps over there …"

Although parts of the train are packed, he and Tommi manage to find seats across from each other. A young Frenchman wearing too much cologne is sitting next to Tommi. Whenever their eyes meet, the Frenchman looks away. He seems determined not to take notice of either of them.

"Your father is right there," Tommi says. Sure enough, there is Hans, standing on the platform and peering up at the windows of the train. Peter suddenly realizes with a pang of guilt that he hasn't really said goodbye to him. He doesn't know when he'll see him next. Should he open his window? The train is starting to move … Before he's made up his mind, Hans throws down his cigar and walks away.

As the train leaves the station, Peter's stomach turns and he has a sudden feeling of vertigo. A moment later, the feeling has passed and he looks across at Tommi, who is staring intently out the window. *Watch out for your cousin*, he hears Hans saying to him. *You're older, so you have to*

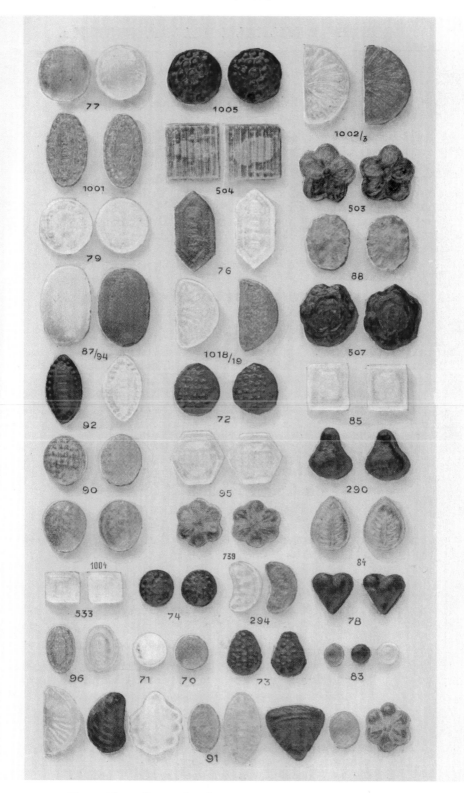

Plate 1 The Heller candy selection. Private collection. *See page 4*

Plate 2 Margaret Steiner, standing 2nd from left,
and Hans Heller, standing 2nd from right, 1924.
Courtesy of Peter O'Connor

Plate 3 Peter Heller
as a boy.
Peter Heller Album,
Courtesy of the
Sigmund Freud
Museum, Vienna

Plate 4 Photograph of the Burlingham children and Anna Freud with Wolf,
c. 1930. © Freud Museum London. *See page 18*

Plate 5 Hietzing School Children's Party. Peter Heller Album, Courtesy of Freud Museum, Vienna

Plate 6 Hietzing Faculty Portrait with Erik Erikson, seated far left and Peter Blos, seated 3rd from left. Peter Heller Album, Courtesy of Freud Museum, Vienna

Plate 7 Children of the Burlingham-Rosenfeld (Hietzing) School at play in front of the schoolhouse. Peter Heller Album, Courtesy of the Sigmund Freud Museum, Vienna

Plate 8 Children of the Burlingham-Rosenfeld (Hietzing) School in front of the schoolhouse, May 1929. Peter Heller Album, Courtesy of the Sigmund Freud Museum, Vienna

Plate 9 Prisoner of War Camp
Camp N, Sherbrooke, Canada.
Library and Archives Canada PA 114463

Plate 10 Peter Heller as a young man.
Private collection

be the responsible one. He's more sophisticated than Tommi, there's no question of that. He was the first one to tell him about prostitution and venereal disease, but, even though that was a couple of years ago, Tommi is still quite naïve.

When the train stops in Salzburg, the Frenchman quickly leaves the compartment, leaving the two of them alone. "Come on," Peter says to Tommi, standing up. "Let's look around."

"My parents told me not to get off until we get across the border," Tommi blurts out, looking at him anxiously.

"But we're on our own now. No one is watching us."

"What if something bad happens?"

"What could happen?"

"I don't know ..."

"Don't be such a coward. You're not a kid anymore. I dare you to get off the train with me!"

Tommi leaves the train reluctantly, falling in behind Peter. The platform is crowded with people, most of them loaded down with suitcases.

"I'm starving," Peter exclaims. "Let's go over there ..." They choose a table set apart from the rest, stretching out their legs and feasting on cheese sandwiches.

"What do you want to do when we get to Paris?" Peter asks, taking a sip of his wine and seltzer.

"I don't know ... climb the Eiffel Tower?"

"That seems boring to me. I'd rather sit at a café in Montparnasse with a beautiful girl, or visit the Père Lachaise Cemetery, where Chopin is buried." As they're talking, the train begins pulling out and they look at each other in horror. A second later, they're running with all their might, shouting "Wait for us! Wait for us!" A train attendant stretches out his hand and pulls them up an instant before the train accelerates.

"What did I tell you?" Tommi says, when they've collapsed into their seats. The Frenchman looks at the two of them quizzically. "We made it," says Peter with a shrug. "That's all that counts." But secretly he feels ashamed. *What's wrong with you?* he can hear Hans saying to him. *You have no sense of reality.*

Before long, the train arrives at the border of France, where two SS men order them off the train and start pulling their luggage apart. The shorter of the two looks familiar to Peter, but he can't figure out where he's seen him before.

"What's this?" the taller one says to Tommi, lifting up a worn paperback with a painting of a black ship on the cover.

"*The Death Ship*, by Traven," Tommi replies.

"Don't you think I can read?" the officer demands. Tommi laughs nervously.

"Stop laughing, or you'll regret it!" the officer shouts.

"It's a novel I'm reading. I've just begun …"

"Are you aware that it's on the censored list?"

"I didn't have any idea. A teacher at my school recommended it to me."

"Is that so?" the officer says sarcastically. "What was the name of this teacher? I'd like to write it down." Peter breaks into a loud cough and Tommi looks at him uncertainly.

"I can't remember," he falters. "It was last year …"

"Strange that you can't remember your teacher's name."

"Keep your mouth shut," Peter murmurs to Tommi.

"What was that?" the officer says angrily.

"I was just telling my cousin here not to waste your time."

"Oh no you weren't, you arrogant prick. Do you want us to send you both to the concentration camp?"

"This is all a misunderstanding," Peter says.

"Scum of the earth," the officer snorts, kicking Peter's suitcase so hard that his clothes spill all over the ground. Peter gets on his knees, trying to stuff the clothes back into the suitcase, but he can't manage to get them all in again. "It's good to see you on your knees," the officer laughs. Peter thinks of the old Jew he saw kneeling on the street, in his long black coat, covered with dust. Is he linked to him after all?

"While you're at it, you can clean out the stationhouse," the other officer says. They march them into the station and hand them rags, dustpans, and brooms. Peter takes hold of one of the brooms and looks at it helplessly.

"What's the matter?" the taller officer shouts. "Aren't we in the mood for cleaning today?"

"It's just that I don't know how …"

"Don't worry, we'll teach you, you pampered brat. You sweep like this and use the shovel so. That's it. Filthy Jewish pig!"

As they're cleaning, Peter suddenly realizes that the shorter of the two officers was a grade below him at his old Gymnasium. How far away the

Gymnasium suddenly seems. And yet he just passed his *Matura* exam a couple of weeks ago. "Didn't I know you at my old school?" he says to him. "Keep your mouth shut and do your job."

But before the job is half done, this same officer comes over to them and tells them that they can go. Did he put a word in for them after all? "Pick up your suitcases," the older officer shouts at them. "Take the rest in your arms. You can leave by foot, just as you came, carrying your bundles of rags. Jew peddlars! No one wants you here. Don't ever come back here again if you know what's good for you."

And so they walk across the border into France, following the track until the stationhouse is no longer in sight. At a fork in the track, they come upon a train that is bound for Paris, but that has stopped for a layover. To their amazement, they're able to board this train, repack their luggage, and actually find seats.

Once they are settled and the train has pulled away, leaving the station far behind, Peter takes out his notebook and pencil and tries to write, but his hand starts shaking uncontrollably. He looks across at Tommi, who is staring at his hand. "I can't believe …" Peter begins, but he can't finish his sentence. The words simply won't come. He slumps back into his seat and closes his eyes, waiting for the shaking to stop.

Does he remember reading *The Death Ship* when he was a little boy, and the fever dream that he had afterwards? In that dream, he almost drowned, but Thesi came and woke him up. Was that dream a prophecy of this day? Are dreams prophetic after all? The only thing he knows for sure is that he and Tommi almost failed to make it across the border.

PART 2

9.

Experiments in Living

England, 1938–40

O VER the next two years, Peter lived in a series of rented rooms,
moving from London to Liverpool to Cambridge. His notes on these
times are fragmentary, as though he didn't have time to sit down and
write.

His stay in France was brief, no more than two weeks at the most. It
was summer in Paris, and he was 18 years old. Did he throw himself into
the life on the streets, or did he hold back? Despite his advice to Tommi,
he probably felt overwhelmed; he didn't know Paris, he only knew Vienna.

He describes meeting up with Alfred Polgar, Hans' literary friend,
and his wife Elise, who seemed pathetic to him. He remembers how Elise
complained about not being able to find a restaurant that was friendly to
Jews, and how he found this ridiculous. What did it matter whether the
waiters were nice to her, as long as she was served?

At this point, Mem still had a Parisian address, so he must have tried
to look her up. But if he succeeded in finding her, there is no record of
their meeting.

Paris was a disappointment to him. Was this really the great city of
the Enlightenment? The people he met there seemed guarded and afraid,
completely taken up with settling their own affairs.

In July, he and Tommi finally arrived in London, where they were
greeted by Jack Jones, Hans' new business partner. Jones put them to
work in his candy factory, giving Peter his first taste of menial labor.
"From gray dawn to evening," Peter writes in his diary, he and Tommi
work in "the soot-covered industrial quarter" of London. Officially, they
aren't really there; the law doesn't allow for them to be employed. Yet, it
isn't all bad to be a ghost – most of their co-workers are lower-class girls

who greatly enjoy flirting with them. They receive their first lessons in Cockney English from them, delivered in a never-ending stream of dirty jokes.

One day in August, Peter is told to draw up a report on how chocolates are made, so he walks around the floor in his long white apron, chatting with the girls and jotting down some of their phrases on a little pad. All at once, he hears an ironic laugh coming from the other end of the room. Hans is standing in the doorway with Jack; the two of them are watching him.

"Well, are you learning something?" Hans remarks. "Something about making candy, that is?"

"What are you doing here?" Peter says, turning red and shoving the pad into his pocket.

"I finally got out," Hans replies.

"And not a moment too soon," Jack puts in.

"You don't look bad," Hans says to him. "I see that Jack here has taken good care of you."

Although Hans is wearing a good suit, it looks as though he's slept in it, and he hasn't shaven for a day or two. For the first time in his life, Peter sees his father as a foreigner, as someone who is at a disadvantage.

After they've left the factory, Peter tells Hans that he's sick of working in the factory and that he doesn't want to sleep on Jack's couch anymore. Inge and Hans have just moved into a little flat; within the next few days, Peter moves in with them. The flat is dreary: Inge can't get herself to unpack, and dirty dishes are piled up in the sink. One day she puts up some pink curtains with a pattern of small white flowers that she has brought with her from Vienna and goes on and on about how they cheer her up. She adds a few more touches after that, but then she sinks into inertia again.

Peter eats a little better, although Hans always complains about how badly Inge cooks. The flat is really very small; Peter doesn't have a room of his own. When Hans and Inge are fighting in their bedroom, he hears every word. When they aren't fighting, it's even worse – the walls of their bedroom are very thin, and from where he sleeps, he can hear everything.

At last, Hans agrees to let him live on his own and Peter moves into a boarding house. The building adjoins a train station, and there is a constant drone of human voices, not to mention the screeching and rumbling of the trains. But there's also a piano in the dilapidated sitting room, and he's free to use it whenever he likes. What does he care about how shabby the place is? The louder the trains are, the louder he plays.

He dreams of becoming a world-class pianist; he practices for six or seven hours every day. Hans finds him an instructor, Frau Hilda Pollak-Stern, formerly a conservatory piano teacher in Vienna, now a house-cleaner. "Life is treacherous," she says to him. "Don't listen to all the promises people make to you. It's not enough to work hard at what you love. You can work as hard as you like and they can still take it away from you."

Unlike Frau Stern, he can't get a permit to work – his papers say that he's been admitted into England as a Refugee from Nazi Oppression under the condition that he doesn't seek employment – and he has no desire to work off the books for Jack Jones again.

"You can be a pianist and a scholar," Hans keeps saying to him, "but you have to earn money. You can't live on air!"

"How can I earn money when I'm not allowed to work?" Peter argues with him. "What if I get caught?" Secretly, he's grateful for the laws that are buying him time. No matter how hard Hans pushes, he always has this way out, although everything could change overnight.

He practices more and more feverishly, and when he doesn't practice, he roams the streets, sometimes ducking into the cinema, sometimes chatting with girls in pubs, in parks, on street corners. When he practices well, his life seems to have a shape, but when he can't, everything falls apart.

"The Burlinghams have a place in Hampstead," Hans tells him one day, giving him the address.

"Is Tinky here too?"

"From what I understand."

"But why? She can't have finished college."

"How should I know?" Hans says impatiently. "Go there and find out."

He wants badly to see Tinky again, but he's also afraid. What is she doing here in England? Does she have a boyfriend here? Will she want to see him? Always this damned ambivalence. Seeing Tinky will probably mean seeing all of them: Dorothy and Anna and the entire clan. He can't imagine any of them here. Will they be glad to see him or not?

He doesn't do anything for a day or two, practicing harder than ever and telling himself that he really doesn't have time for anything else. But one day, no longer thinking, he goes out, making his way to Maresfield

Gardens. "They're in Number 2," he remembers Hans telling him. "Anna and Sigmund are in Number 20, a few doors down."

When he arrives at Maresfield Gardens, he is somehow reassured by the thick-walled, ivy-covered houses and by the wild roses that are growing everywhere. He had forgotten about the magic that surrounds the Burlinghams; he feels it again as soon as he enters their neighborhood. A door opens and Tinky is standing there! All of the children are there, and they keep telling him how glad they are to see him. But Dorothy seems strained and brittle, and soon retires to her room.

As they are having their coffee, he finds out that Dorothy's ex-husband Robert has recently committed suicide, and that the family is struggling to absorb the shock. If he had known, he wouldn't have come unannounced, but, if his presence is an intrusion, no one lets on.

In the late afternoon, Anna stops by to bring Dorothy a book, and she does a double take when she sees him in the living room, with his elbow on the mantlepiece. She looks him up and down, and then she says, with a knowing smile, "So tell me, are you still losing things?"

"I'm getting better."

"I wonder why?"

"Not having any possessions has done wonders for me."

Anna Freud laughs, and for an instant she seems open and warm, but then her face seems to harden again. She looks older and sterner than he remembers her, as though her youth has suddenly disappeared.

He doesn't write about his first meeting with Tinky; he doesn't say anything about how it felt. He doesn't record the first words they said to each other when they were finally alone, or whether, in those first moments, they said anything at all. He doesn't say anything about how it was that they first got together, even though it must have marked a turning point for him. Instead he fictionalizes their relationship in a novel that he starts to work on around this time and that he never manages to finish.

In the novel, a young man plays piano for a young woman, interspersing his playing with a speech about the meaning of the fugue. He shows her how, in the fugue, two voices come together and break apart, but never completely, always remaining intertwined. The girl listens, sitting on his bed, with her arms wrapped around her legs. The pianist captivates her, but as the story unfolds, it becomes more and more clear that he neglects her in some fundamental way, failing to listen to her, to fully take her into account. The girl yields to him, but holds part of herself back, so that the pianist is never certain of her. He's determined to secure her love, and he can't rest until he possesses her completely, body and soul. The girl's mother does everything she can to break up the relationship, even threatening to kill herself. In the end, the mother prevails, taking her daughter away with her to Australia.

The girl in the story shares many traits with Tinky, down to her migraines and her weariness, but most of all her detachment, which he desperately wants to overcome. The pianist, who floods his beloved with music and words, is guilty of being too insistent, too demonstrative. Tinky's charm and attractiveness are still there, but there is also a restraint, a refusal, that throws him back on himself. If he can't take away her suffering, he wants to come closer to it. He wants to rescue her from her isolation.

In real life, as in his novel, this doesn't come to pass. After their time together, Tinky goes to Norway on a Christmas holiday. While she is away, Dorothy allows him to sleep in Tinky's room, since his own place is so wretchedly cold. 'Has she accepted me into the family?' Peter wonders. Dorothy is so fiercely close to her children that it seems improbable, and yet she is allowing him to sleep in her daughter's bed.

When Tinky comes back, she confesses that she's fallen in love with a Norwegian man who is very gentle and kind. She's never felt this way about anyone before; she's discovered the real meaning of intimacy, and although she feels guilty for hurting him, she has to be true to herself.

As shocked as he is, there's a part of him that isn't surprised. After all, he's grown up with this combination of care and abandonment. To him, it feels like an old, threadbare coat, never warm enough, yet impossible to throw out.

After going through the motions of trying to win her back, he gathers up his things and returns to his cold room by the train station.

Outwardly his life hasn't changed, but inwardly he is lost. In the midst of practicing piano, he rises up from his bench, spending hours wandering the street, or in the cinema, where he watches the same movies over and over again: *Pandemonium, The Spy in Black, Shadow of Death*. When Hans invites him to move out of London to his new place in Hoylake, Peter accepts, frightened by how adrift he feels.

The house at Hoylake is an English cottage, complete with a thatched straw roof. Hans's new business venture is starting to turn a profit, but Inge is still unhappy. When they're alone, Inge tells Peter that she's miserable, making sure that he has a good view of her legs. Hans is frustrated by Peter's refusal to think about money; Peter feels that Hans doesn't think about anything else.

Hans has managed to salvage a few belongings from Vienna – one or two paintings, some drawings, a few cherished books. But one day, someone – is it Inge, or one of her drinking buddies? – leaves a cigarette burning in an ashtray or forgets to turn off the stove. The dry old beams of the cottage burst into flame and the fire licks at the straw roof. By the time the fire truck comes, all that's left of the roof is a few clumps of blackened twigs, and Hans' possessions are gone. After the fire, the fighting becomes unbearable. Peter takes a room in Liverpool.

His new landlord is almost completely blind and he spends most of his time inside the house. Tall and heavy, he rarely gets out of his chair, leaving all of the household duties to his wife. Every afternoon, he comes into the parlor to play British marching tunes for anyone who happens to be having tea. He offers to give Peter piano lessons, but Peter turns him down, to the disappointment of the landlady, who is always after her husband to get up and do something.

The writing table in Peter's shabby room is coated with a film of brownish dust. Outside his window, brown smoke curls out of the chimney stacks, slowly uncoiling in the air until it dissolves into a yellow haze.

A boxer lives in the basement and works out there; when he runs up the steps, the entire house seems to shake. Peter often thinks of the boxer when he practices, using him as a source of inspiration.

Spira, his present piano teacher, takes great pleasure in cutting him down. "You're not concert material!" Spira exclaims. "Your interpretation is completely unartistic."

"What can I do to improve?"

"I keep saying the same thing – do your finger exercises."

"But those are completely boring to me." And so it goes, on and on. No matter what he does, Spira is never satisfied.

Should he enlist as a soldier? He's never been confronted with a question as momentous as this; he barely knows how to tackle it. He makes a list of the pros and cons, scribbling them onto a beer coaster that he later copies into his diary.

On the one hand, enlisting would mean interrupting his artistic ambitions and opening himself up to the possibility of losing his life. On the other hand, it would be a tremendous experience, and he would be fighting for a cause that is undeniably just. But would he have the courage if it came down to it? Or would he suddenly become frightened and run away? Is he really capable of killing another human being? He won't know until he puts himself to the test. Maybe if he enlists, he will finally overcome his narcissism, his dependence on others, his exaggerated sense of himself. All of these questions swirl around in his mind until he can barely think of anything else.

At last, he applies to the Royal Air Force – the RAF – because it's too terrifying to contemplate fighting on the ground. He waits for a reply, but the answer never comes. So that's how it is. A refugee is no better than a ghost.

Uncertain of his playing, disappointed in love, estranged from Hans, who is fed up with him, he drifts through Liverpool, spending hours in the cinema and following women down the streets. He writes in his diary that he has sunken into "bestial dullness," but that it's still better than living "at home." "Here I am free, and misuse my freedom; am alone; make myself lonely," he writes. But at least he's living in a world that he is creating for himself.

Spira loses his temper with his playing, telling him that he might as well give up. After the lesson, he trudges through the gray, foggy night, passing his hand along the spikes of a cast-iron fence with tears streaming down his face.

He complains about Spira's "discouragement pedagogy" in his diary; he rallies, even begins to rebel. "The more that Spira convinces me that I'm unmusical, the greater my hopes of learning to write." He remembers that when he was six, he wanted to be a poet, and that his determination to become a pianist began only when he was 16 years old. He starts turning toward a friend of his father's, a tall, dignified man with bright blue eyes and a cherubic face who is just now emerging as a highly distinguished man of letters. He is teaching at Cambridge, but his background is Czech – he left Czechoslovakia in 1935. Although they share the same last name, they aren't related by blood. His name is Erich Heller, and he has taken a great liking to Peter, engaging him in long, passionate debates about literature, music, religion, philosophy. "Music is narrow," Peter writes in his diary, "compared to the comprehensiveness of the descriptive arts (poetry, prose, theater, criticism, psychology, philosophy)."

Erich believes that Peter should move to Cambridge, where he can be part of an intellectual world that has been quite accepting of Jewish refugees, and he promises to write Hans a letter on Peter's behalf. Hans will have to be persuaded, of course, because, while Erich can make the arrangements for Peter, he can't provide the funds. The letter is sent and now there is nothing to do but wait. Now more than ever before, Peter's fate seems to be hanging in the balance. As a refugee, he is here at the pleasure of the government; he still isn't allowed to work, and his status could be revoked at any time. But all of this seems much less real than the question of whether Hans will agree to Erich's proposal or become furious that Peter has enlisted Erich to conspire with his impracticality.

One morning the landlady knocks at the door and announces that she and her husband want him out. Her husband is standing behind her, fixing him with his milky blue eyes. "We want you to leave!" the landlady says. "But what have I done?" he asks, quickly throwing on his dressing gown.

She shakes a magazine in the air and points to a board in the floor, which is sticking up suspiciously. "We know what you've been up to!" she says disgustedly. "This is a decent house!" her husband chimes in. "I've never seen such filthy stuff," the landlady says. "We're giving you a week to get out."

They're lying, he thinks to himself after they're gone. *They want to get rid of me because I'm a Jew.*

Toward the end of the week, a letter finally comes from Hans. He's read Erich's letter and, after giving it some thought, he's agreed to underwrite Peter's studies in Cambridge.

Living in Cambridge is like living in a different world. At first, it doesn't seem real to him. The robed dons, the perfectly tended lawns, the Gothic buildings, all make him feel as though he's in church. But this ethereal impression quickly fades away, leaving a community of fiercely competitive young men in its place. *Who are you? What are you doing here?* Even if these questions are veiled in British gentility, he knows that he will be scorned if he fails to answer them.

He works with an organist from King's College, practicing with more focus than ever before. After one of these sessions, he writes in his diary: "Overwound: exhausted and excited at the same time. And yet, after all, a burning life, after months of dreaminess and lack of responsibility. How comfortable and pleasant it is to bask in the illusion of some capability, without testing it to the limits of its possibilities. This is completely different from winning ground inch by inch."

In the evening, he walks to Erich's house and has discussions with him that go deep into the night. Afterwards, he walks back to his rooms, passing behind the Gothic buildings that crouch on the carefully tended grounds. Eventually he comes to a grand tree-lined avenue, with fields and meadows on either side. Cattle and oxen are grazing there; he feels them watching him as he passes by. Sometimes he's convinced that he is being followed by a Nazi spy and he hurries forward with a pounding heart. Is this just a game he is playing with himself? He can barely tell fantasy and reality apart.

He is reading, reading, all the time – Nietzsche, Marx, Thomas Mann – and he's also writing a new novel about a young man who is struggling to break free from his parents. But at the same time, he's terribly worried about Mem. Why hasn't he heard from her in such a long time? What if someone has come and taken her away? He's also afraid that Hans and Inge will come upon a letter that he wrote when he was in a rage and that he was almost stupid enough to send. If they find that letter, which was all about their pathetic marriage and their pathetic way of life, he's convinced they'll take Cambridge away from him.

He is constantly pushing himself; he wants to confront – and overcome – his own "natural" limits. One night, he stands by his mantelpiece, staring into the fire. He takes a sheath of paper – a failed manuscript – and tosses it near the flames. He doesn't take his eyes off the paper, waiting for it to burn – but there seems to be a draft and the flames don't touch the surface. He keeps staring into the fire, trying not to blink. He tells himself that if he witnesses the instant at which the pages ignite, that means that he'll be a genius, but if he misses that instant, he'll be nothing. He stands there for so long that he grows light-headed, as though he's had too much to drink. At last, he falls down, hitting his head against a bucket. At that same moment, the pages burst into flame. Did he win the wager, or did he fail?

He goes to the cinema – he's avoided it for several weeks – and as he's leaving, he sees a girl dressed in a dirndl crossing the street. Their glances meet. He follows her. To his surprise, she turns around and asks if he'd like to stop for a drink. She isn't dressed in a dirndl, after all, but in a barmaid's costume, with puffed white sleeves. After they have a drink, they go back into the cinema and she kisses him with a desperate abandon that he didn't expect. They leave the cinema and go into an alleyway, where they finish what they've begun. Her neck is dirty and she reeks of cigarettes. "Not again," he writes later in his diary.

He is so affected by Erich that he sometimes wants to be free of him; he feels that his influence is too strong. And yet, whenever Erich leaves town, he feels lost and distraught.

On the morning of May 12, he gets up late and practices piano, unhappy with his playing of a Brahms Sonata. He's scheduled to perform at a tea party in Grantchester that afternoon; he wonders if his performance will be brilliant or mediocre. Vicki visits and takes his tensions away, teasing him relentlessly. He remembers his conversation with Erich of the night before and how he had said to Erich, "We may not see each other for a long time," as a back-handed way of hinting that Erich might be getting fed up with him. After Vicki leaves, there is a knock on the door, but he doesn't pay any attention to it. To his surprise, the landlady calls him down. The man in the parlor is apparently a detective, and he asks Peter to accompany him, apologizing for the inconvenience and saying it will only be for a short time. Did the girl in the alleyway report him to the police for taking advantage of her? That would be ridiculously unfair. Wild thoughts go racing through his mind, but outwardly he remains calm, so as to make it clear that on every count he's innocent.

10.

Kindly Come Along with Me

England, 1940

SO this is what it feels like to be under arrest, he thinks to himself, as he trots along at the detective's side. And yet he hasn't done anything wrong, at least nothing that could be considered criminal. People turn to stare at him on the street, or maybe he just imagines this. None of what's happening seems real to him; it's all very strange, as though he's moving in a dream.

When they finally arrive at City Hall, a thin-lipped man with sharp cheekbones and a raspy voice asks him to hand over his papers and be quick about it. Now he knows why they've come after him: he must have forgotten to show up for his last Alien Registration appointment. "Is there a fine for missing an appointment?" he asks. "My funds are a little low right now, but I can arrange for my father to wire you the money."

The clerk doesn't answer him, poring over his papers and checking something off in a ledger. As he stands in front of the table, he becomes aware of a murmur of voices coming from across the hall. A door swings open and the murmur turns into a roar. There is a huge crowd of people in the neighboring room. "What's happening in there?" he asks the clerk. "Is someone giving a speech?" "I expect you'll find out," the clerk remarks. Peter's heart begins fluttering in his chest.

A moment later, he is led into a smoke-filled room that is packed with men, some of them talking, others shouting, still others sitting in a slump. A white-haired gentleman comes hurrying up to him: it's Herr Hausig, an acquaintance of his.

"We're all going to be interned for the duration of the war!" Herr Hausig exclaims, clutching hold of Peter's arm, so that he instinctively pulls away.

"I don't understand …"

They're rounding us up!" Herr Hausig is usually very composed; Peter's never seen him this agitated before.

"But the English are friendly to us."

"Look around you! Do you see anything but Jews?"

It's true that there are many Jewish faces in the crowd, and that everyone in the room seems to be speaking German. "It's alright for you young people," Hausig goes on. "But I have thrombosis in this leg, and on top of that I have a heart condition."

Three men are talking heatedly on a bench – Peter turns away from Herr Hausig, trying to hear what they're saying.

"They'll release us after a few weeks," one man says.

"Don't believe it," another replies.

"The war is heating up," a third man says with a shrug. "In times of war, you intern enemy aliens."

"But we're not enemy aliens, we're refugees!"

"They don't know that. For all they know, we're spies."

After hours of waiting, a short, red-faced official pushes his way into the middle of the room and clambers up onto a bench. He tells them they're going to be held up for a few more days and that if they like, they can go home and pick up a few personal items: toothbrushes, clothes, that sort of thing.

A heavy-set man with a meaty face takes Peter all the way back to his house. Once again, he finds himself hurrying along the street, but this time his escort is more formidable and he's certain that everyone is staring at them. He's afraid that his landlady will make a scene about his unpaid rent and that this will make his situation worse. But she doesn't breathe a word about the money he owes, saying only that she's saved his lunch, which is waiting for him up in his room.

The detective accepts the landlady's offer of tea, allowing him to pack his suitcase in peace and quiet and to gobble down the bread, cheese, and pickled onions that the landlady has put on his desk. Shouldn't the detective be keeping an eye on him? Maybe he's already sized him up as someone who won't try to escape.

Instead of packing lightly, Peter takes as much as he can, on the theory that Hausig and the others are right. Volumes of Nietzsche; sheet music – why not? Beethoven, Brahms, Chopin; a notebook that he has just bought; Pascal, Goethe, Thomas Mann; a heavy sweater, socks, underwear, one pair of pajamas, his coat. At last he picks up his suitcase to go downstairs and right away the handle breaks. If only his father hadn't become so cheap! He's complained about this flimsy, papier-mâché suitcase countless times, but Hans has refused to take the hint.

He goes downstairs, hugging his suitcase to his chest, his coat dragging along the floor. The landlady tells him that she and the detective have been having a "lovely chat." Although it crosses his mind that perhaps she is trying to smooth his way, it seems more likely to him that she and the detective have been having a little flirt, which would explain why the detective has been so lax.

On the street he catches sight of Magda, a Czech girl he's gone out with a few times. "Farewell!" he cries out to her jauntily, tucking his suitcase under his arm so that he can wave to her. She turns her head away from him, and only then does he notice that she's walking with another man. He has no right to feel jealous: after all, he hasn't exactly been faithful to her. What moved him to wave at her in such an idiotic way? She and her new boyfriend are probably laughing at him.

The detective allows him to buy cigarettes on the way back to City Hall, and he also carries his coat for him. He asks him a couple of questions about Magda, but Peter isn't sure whether he's doing a bit of investigating or whether he's interested in her.

They walk up the steps of City Hall a second time, pushing open the heavy doors. The room is even more crowded now, so that Peter can barely turn around. He is shaking when he first comes in, and for some reason his eyes are moist with tears. But as the time drags on, all of this subsides, giving way to hunger, boredom, and a need to urinate.

A Cambridge contingent has formed in one corner of the room. There is another contingent of religious Jews who seem to be praying constantly. And there is Professor Simmel, a brilliant philologist he once met at Erich's house, a shy, scholarly man who chooses his words carefully. Simmel is worried about his pregnant wife and how she will manage without him for the next few days. She comes from a good family and has never worked a day in her life. How will she be able to support herself, especially given her condition? Peter talks to this Simmel at length, focusing all his energy on him. "Leave it to you to start making contacts as they're dragging you off to camp," he hears Hans commenting. "What good will it do you now?" But Peter likes Simmel very much; like many of the Jews who make up the Cambridge crowd, he is impeccably

British in his manner, but without being stuffy or pretentious.

At last, they are herded into buses – by this time, the sun is going down. On the running board of the bus is a soldier with a bayonet, in case anyone gets the idea of trying to jump off. He stares at the soldier for the longest time, unable to take his eyes off him. The guard looks like a bronze statue that's been welded to the side of the bus; when he stamps his foot in a salute, the whole bus shakes. How official he makes this madness seem!

They are taken to Bury St. Edmunds, a small, sleepy town about an hour outside Cambridge. When they get out of the bus, they are met by more soldiers with bayonets. "Are we really this dangerous?" he hears one man remark to another. "Someone seems to think so," the other replies.

Their new holding place is an enormous barn, with skylights cut into its 30-foot-high roof. But the skylights are plastered with blackout paint, so that the interior is grey and dim. The floors of the building are made of stone and the windows are broken, letting in mosquitoes and flies. Everything is covered with a film of grimy dust, and in the course of a few hours, his face is coated with this dust as well.

That night, they sleep on the stone floor, which is not only hard but cold. Peter spreads out his winter coat, glad that he thought of bringing it, and starts putting on his pajamas. "Very nice! Are those silk?" his neighbors joke. "Look at that! There's even a monogram!" After a few minutes of this, he takes his pajamas off and sleeps in a shirt and heavy sweater instead.

No one is allowed to go to the bathroom by themselves; they must be escorted by a soldier with a bayonet. "What do you think of this dump?" he hears a familiar voice remark as he's waiting on line. It's Vicki! He's come here on a different bus. "I hope you're able to do your business," he goes on. "Under these circumstances, it's hard to press with all your heart!"

It's a great relief to see Vicki's satirical face, which looks paler and more pointed, but otherwise unchanged. "Just think of all this as a new experience," Vicki says. "Material for that brilliant novel you're about to write." When Peter takes out his journal and jots down a few notes, Vicki teases him mercilessly. "Can't you ever experience anything directly?" he says to him. "Nothing is real to you unless you can scribble it down."

He takes note of all the different ways in which people react to the uprooting of their lives. Some grow angry and threaten to rebel; others speculate fearfully about where they will be taken after this; others, like himself, find the situation fantastically unreal, watching over the scene as though it's a play or an experiment. One man sketches his fellow prisoners endlessly; another starts setting up committees and groups as though their survival depends on it. Yet another finds a tiny hole in the surface of the blackout paint that enables him to capture a projection of the sun on a piece of blank white paper. The image on his piece of paper is so sharp and clear that he can even make out sunspots, which he shows to his fellow scientists.

Almost immediately, classes are set up, an initiative spearheaded by the Cambridgers. Peter records his schedule in his diary, glad to have a bit of order in his life: 8:45 Roll call. 11:00 French class. 2:30 Meeting of Camp Committee. 5:30 Lecture. 7:15 English class. And so he finds himself in yet another school, this time improvised by a group of disenfranchised scholars.

"I suppose you're happy now," Vicki remarks. "After all, your status has changed for the better. At Cambridge, you were just a hanger-on. Now you actually stand a chance of being part of the inner circle."

The truth is that he admires the Cambridgers, not only for their intelligence but also for their nonchalance. Nothing seems to take them by surprise; they make it seem inelegant to complain.

Like everyone else in this barn, he is lost and displaced, but he never feels lonely or bored. There are interesting people to talk to wherever he turns; in fact, he's locked into a conversation that begins the second he opens his eyes and goes on until he falls asleep. "I have the childish feeling of being at a party," he writes in his diary, "where I feel compelled to talk to everyone I meet. I'm building up to the moment at which I'll say, 'Thanks for the enchanting weekend! I wish I could stay for a bit longer, but I simply have to get home.'"

Some of the internees are much younger than him; the youngest looking of all is a 16-year-old stable boy, pale and freckled, with a shock of red hair. For most of the day, he lies in a corner and reads detective novels, wrapped in two thick woolen blankets. Everyone likes him, including the officers, who chat with him about horses and give him chocolate and cigarettes. He ends up working in the officers' kitchen and sometimes manages to bring back scraps. But his fellow inmates want more than this from him. Was the radio on in the kitchen? What did the officers talk about? The boy never has much to report to them, but they question him constantly, since he's their only point of contact with the outside world.

And then one day he comes back with the news that Brussels has fallen, delivering this with a look of satisfaction on his face.

"What exactly did you hear?"

"Just that – nothing more."

"Come on, you must have heard more than that." And they scold him for not getting more details.

The fall of Brussels depresses everyone, releasing a flood of gloomy predictions. The stable boy withdraws into his corner, burying himself in his detective novels.

Between hunger and classes and more hunger and endless debate, there are moments of reprieve. When it isn't raining, they are taken out to a field that lies between their barracks and the street. Although the field is overgrown with nettles and weeds, there are patches of soft grass here and there. While the guards look on in their stiff uniforms, the internees unbutton their shirts and bathe in the sun.

One afternoon, he and Vicki wrestle in the field, exactly as they did when they were boys. Afterwards they lie on their backs and stare up at the racing clouds.

"Do you ever think of Vienna?" Peter asks, rolling onto his stomach and picking apart a dandelion.

"I try my best not to," Vicki replies.

"But it's our city."

"Not anymore."

Peter turns his head and gazes at the street, littered with bits of paper and orange peel. Children are playing on another street; he can hear their shouts off in the distance. Three girls pass by, giggling at the sight of so many young men, and they are immediately greeted by a flurry of whistles and calls. For once, the guards don't intervene, looking on impassively.

Discussions are their main way of passing the time, but many of their discussions explode into fights. A short Polish Jew, very thin, with a pockmarked face, loves to argue with a fanatical, bitterly humorous Jew, who holds that rational thought is valuable not because it's right but because it's a means of prevailing over circumstance. They play out this same battle over and over again, never growing tired of it.

A rabbi says to a socialist, "One day the Messiah will come, and everyone will stand up in their graves."

"How can anyone in their right mind still believe something like that?" the socialist replies, shaking his head.

So many problems are taken up! Peter goes around the hall with his journal in his hand, jotting down the various topics that are being discussed: anti-Semitism, freedom of will, rights of inheritance, sin $2 - \cos 2y$. But the question that haunts all of them, even in their sleep, is the question of what will happen to them if Germany succeeds in conquering England.

He is hungry, very hungry, for most of the day, and comforts himself by thinking of *Indianerkrapfen* (Viennese sponge cake topped with chocolate and filled with whipped cream), *Sachertorte*, lobsters with mayonnaise. The food here is very bad: stingy portions of bread; watery, unsweetened tea; a bit of canned fish or boiled cabbage here and there. Writing allows him to forget his hunger for a little while, but he never forgets that he is surrounded by barbed wire.

"How wonderful it would be to walk freely through the streets," he writes, if there were no Hitler, and if it weren't for these horrible machines that I used to dream of when I was a little boy. Yes, the machine is coming up behind us, and if we walk along the manicured paths of the park and whistle carelessly to ourselves, it is suddenly upon us, snatching us up and pressing us up against its metal bars until there is nothing left of us."

And yet some are optimistic, like Simmel, who says that all the B Category refugees (aliens about whose loyalty the tribunals were not absolutely certain and who for one reason or another should be kept under a form of supervision) have been locked up so that the C Category refugees (all those about whom the tribunals were satisfied) can be released. Peter continues to like Simmel, who is now teaching a course in philology and helping his students throughout the day. He can't stand to be around the mindless optimists with their idiotic assurances that everything will turn out for the best, but Simmel, who looks more strained by the day, as his wife's due date draws near, is a person he trusts.

The word goes out that they are going to be transferred to another camp, which makes him feel uneasy and excited. He washes with a bucket of water, organizes his things, and makes sure that his journal is safely packed away. At last they are loaded onto the bus, where he has a fight with Vicki, who calls him hysterical and undisciplined. It's true that his nerves are completely on edge, but he's sick and tired of Vicki's constant criticizing.

Turning away from Vicki, he talks to a very young and brilliant German philosophy professor by the name of Hans Werner Kohn, taking a liking to him right away. His pale green eyes dominate his narrow, sun-tanned face, and there are grey strands running through his stringy black hair. He has elaborate opinions on everything, from Kant to Thomas Mann. They talk and talk about everything under the sun while the bus lurches forward on the badly paved road.

For some reason that no one bothers to explain, the bus doesn't deliver them directly to the camp. Instead, they are made to walk through the slums of Liverpool, dragging their suitcases along with them. People stand in doorways and stare at them: proletarian women, prostitutes, dirty children. One woman says, in a disappointed voice, "These are no Germans – these are only Jews!" Others are convinced that they are the enemy, spitting at them and even hurling a few bricks.

A little lieutenant, who has been their friend, is disgusted by the treatment they receive, saying afterwards, "*You* were the spectators, not they!" But the memory of walking through Liverpool with his suitcase in his arms and the riff-raff shouting insults at him never completely fades away. He can't shrug it off, like the Cambridgers; in fact, as he writes in his diary, in this particular instance, their dismissiveness seems dishonest to him.

Their destination turns out to be an unventilated hall lit by harsh, electric light. Along the sides of the hall is a series of even more airless rooms that become known as the *Unterseeboot* (submarine). It's true that they have beds here: wooden frames with straw mattresses – but the air is stifling. Still, it feels better to be sequestered than to be on display now that whatever remained of their status has been taken away from them.

They have no idea how long they will be stuck in this place, or where they will be taken after this. Those who have been cut off from their families are especially irritable; the older internees are constantly wheezing and coughing, and a number of them get sick. Fights erupt here constantly, but there is one fight in particular that captures everyone's attention.

Federbusch, broad-chested, with short, muscular legs, long arms and a slightly stooped back, is responsible for doling out the rations, a job that earns him nothing but complaints. One day, he gets upset over the fact that there are six men rather than seven at one of his 40 or so tables. Goldmann, one of the Cambridgers, remarks, "My good man, why are you making such a fuss? Just dole out the rations for seven, as usual, and if the missing man shows up, he'll be given his portion."

"And what if he doesn't?" Federbusch demands, his face growing red.

"In that case, the others can divvy it up."

"And then everyone else will feel cheated," Federbusch storms, "and they'll say it's my fault."

"Come now, Federbusch," Goldmann laughs. "Are we really as bad as that?"

"Don't you dare laugh at me, or you'll be sorry!" Federbusch shouts, clenching his fists.

Lindau, another Cambridger, who has been listening to all this with a gleeful smile, says to Federbusch that he has to apologize to Goldmann immediately. Federbusch glares at Lindau and says in a furious voice, "Go to hell! I have nothing to apologize for."

Later that evening, Lindau goes looking for his friend Weitz in the *Unterseeboot* and crosses paths with Federbusch, who thinks that he is hunting him down. Confronted with Lindau, Federbusch bares his chest and roars, "I am Federbusch!" and falls on the terrified little man. By the time the two are separated, Lindau's face is covered with blood and Federbusch is completely unscathed. A former Viennese doctor is called in to inspect Lindau's wounds. Glancing over at Federbusch, who is panting like a wild animal, he remarks drily, "That man should be interned."

The encounter between Lindau and Federbusch is analyzed endlessly. The bad air is to blame, some people say – it's poisoning them, making them crazy. Goldmann started everything with his arrogance, others say; Federbusch is sick to death of being criticized. The man who struck Lindau wasn't Federbusch, still others say, it was his more nervous and neurotic brother. Lindau's version is that Federbusch was just waiting to take him down, and that in the dark passageway of the *Unterseeboot*, he found his perfect excuse. Peter's conclusion: Lindau, sadistic provoker of rage, took pleasure in torturing Federbusch, an uneducated, emotional man, and that he drew Federbusch's rage upon himself.

Meanwhile the news comes that the Germans have reached Abbeville, and that they are throwing hand bombs into every third house. The news about Abbeville leaves everyone with a feeling of helplessness: it's easier to argue heatedly about the fight between Lindau and Federbusch, which is, after all, the first outbreak of violence among the 300 men, than it is to face the possibility of Germany's conquest of France.

Shiny new buildings! Private rooms! Hot and cold water! Movies every night! If even a fraction of what they're told is true, life will be better at Huyton, their next stop.

Buses drop them at a housing estate enclosed in a double fence of eight-foot-high barbed wire. The houses are only partly built, there are piles of rubble everywhere, and the unpaved roads between the houses are troughs of mud. "Get into line to be counted," an officer yells. They do as he says, already depressed. Three new busloads of prisoners arrive when the counting is almost done. Just to be safe, they start all over again. "I never knew so many Jews were Nazis," an adjutant says to a commandant. This remark becomes a standing joke.

After the counting comes the usual medical examination: stripping down, bending over, pretending to be somewhere else. Because there are so many of them – 1600 by this last count – the healthy are assigned to tents so that the unhealthy can sleep indoors. "At least in the Liverpool hole we had a roof over our heads," an internee complains.

When the medical examinations are finally done, their Camp Father, an Austrian professor, who constantly dabs at his nose with a wrinkled handkerchief, delivers a speech in an effort to boost their morale. "This camp isn't what we expected," he says to them, "but we must do our best to put up with it. The last thing we want is to be subject to force. That would be more demoralizing than anything. "

"The way they're treating us is a scandal!" an old man shouts. "How long do we have to put up with this?"

"Be patient, my friends," the Camp Father says. "Remember, things could be much worse."

Just as he's beginning to get used to sleeping in the tent, Peter's moved into an unfurnished room along with ten other men. The room is unpainted, with a dusty parquet floor, and the amenities are minimal, consisting of a two-ounce bar of soap that is issued once a week and a small amount of toilet paper stamped with the words "Government Property."

He can't read or write in his new room, so he spends most of his time walking around the grounds. One day, when he is jotting down a conversation that he has just overheard, he walks straight into his cousin Tommi, whom he hasn't seen since they were both living in London. "Permit me to invite you to my house," Tommi jokes. A few minutes later, they are sitting on a pile of blankets in a tiny room, eating oranges and smoking cigarettes.

"Where did you get all of this?" Peter asks.

"Let's just say I have some connections in the camp."

The two of them sit together for a long time, sinking into memories of the past. "Do you remember that *Dobos Torten* that we ate at our grandfather's?" Tommi asks.

"Of course I remember," Peter says. How clearly he can see that lavish cake, with its many layers of frosting and marmalade, and the stately house in the silent street, and their grandfather, with his perfectly curled beard, so proud of the riches he had accumulated in his life. He even remembers the look on the old man's face when he came down the stairs after his nap and saw that the two boys had finished off the cake without leaving a crumb for him. (Was it their fault that his old servant had offered it to them without telling them how many slices they could have?) As they lie back on the blankets, more images come floating up: the pavilion in Klausen; the narrow, stone-filled stream where they caught the trout with their bare hands, or with little hooks that they stuck into worms that they found in the dirt; the narrow path that led into the ancient woods; the raspberries they collected from branches studded with thorns. But then they hear heavy footsteps coming down the hall, and they sit up with a start. "Report immediately for a luggage search!" an officer shouts. "Only show them the stuff you don't care about," Tommi warns. "Put your valuables in a hiding place."

Peter runs back to his room as fast as he can, hides his Nietzsche and his journal in a crack in the wall, stuffs his other books into his suitcase along with his dirty clothes, and rushes downstairs to the inspection tent – only to find the search is already over.

Hunger puts everyone in a foul mood. The cook, whose name is Joseph, is desperate. An excitable man with greasy hair, Joseph appears in the dining hall every other day, delivering a speech that is always the same, so that everyone knows it by heart: "*Meine Herren*, I don't want to intrude on your meal. I know that I can't satisfy your hunger with words. All of us here – yes, all – I am, after all, one of you – we are all hungry, and always being hungry is hard. But tomorrow, things will be better than today. Tomorrow we've all been promised an extra ration of pea soup ..." (His promises are almost always met with boos.) "*Meine Herren*," he goes on, stretching out his hands, "I beg you to give the kitchen three more days. We are exerting ourselves mightily, *meine Herren*. If it still doesn't work, I'll go back to the authorities." (More cries rise up from the dining hall, and now he begins to react.) "Among us sufferers there are many complainers and know-it-alls," he says. "And if the complainers still aren't satisfied with me, then it will be a pleasure, yes, a pleasure, *meine Herren*, to say, *You are free to take my place! You can fight with the Quartermaster! You can worry over whether there is enough cutlery for 3000 people! You can organize a kitchen that has too little coal to heat the oven! In short, it would be a pleasure to say to the complainers MAKE YOUR CRAP FOR YOURSELVES!*"

These speeches, delivered in a hysterical voice, only make them more conscious of the inadequacy of their meals. Peter jots down exactly what they're given to eat, noting that it's barely enough to keep them going:

8:30: Breakfast: 2 slices of bread, margarine, "golden syrup" (little), tea.

1:00 3 small pieces of rubbery meat; ½ potato; beans.

5:00 2 slices of bread, margarine, cheese, marmalade, tea.

Sometimes a spoonful of rice with a stewed plum thrown in.

Nothing from 5:30 pm to 8:30 am.

From the officers' quarters, plates of food come back with scraps of Yorkshire pudding or mashed potatoes or meat. He volunteers for dishwasher duty so he can eat off of these plates, indifferent to whether the food has been touched or not.

A newspaper is smuggled into the camp by an officer who is sympathetic to them. Belgium has fallen! King Leopold has surrendered what remains of his army.

The war is lost, everyone says. The older inmates are especially hard hit. Even the pessimists are silenced by this news, as though reality has outdone them.

A boy in a black rubber coat appears in the camp. He wears a gas mask that makes him look invulnerable. When he takes off the mask, this illusion disappears, revealing a pale, twitching face and feverish eyes. The stories that he tells about himself don't make any sense: he says that he wears the gas mask because he has no ointment for his face, and that he is always at the Army's service, ready to clean out the enemy with his dustpan and broom. He repeats certain sentences whenever any questions come up, as though they contain the answer to everything: "The main thing is to get permission from a medical officer," he says. "I know – I was a medical monitor." Although he seems lost, he speaks in an authoritative voice that makes it hard to feel sympathy for him. "I prefer the English method," he often says. "The German approach is too brutal for me." He can't sit still for more than a moment or two, walking around the camp in his long black coat with his hands clasped behind his back. People learn to avoid getting into long conversations with him, but that doesn't prevent them from speculating about where he was before he was brought here. Some are convinced that he is working as a spy; others believe he is a madman who was used to watch over other patients in a mental asylum; still others are convinced that he escaped from a hospital where he was the victim of Nazi experiments. The question of his identity is never solved and eventually everyone stops thinking about it.

One day an officer comes up to Peter and says, "You'd better come along with me." The grimness of the officer's tone makes Peter think that he's about to be accused of a crime. Has someone set him up? He has no idea of who it could possibly be. A few minutes later, he's standing in the officers' tent where a middle-aged man in a tweed suit is waiting for him.

"I'm an associate of your father's," the man says, shaking Peter's hand. Should he trust him or not? The man's manner is so annoyingly solicitous that he decides he's telling the truth.

"Do they allow you to write letters?" he asks him.

"Yes, of course."

"Ah, that's good, very good, as a matter of fact. And how is your health?"

"I haven't been sick ..."

"Good job! Your constitution must be very strong." An awkward silence follows, which he doesn't try to fill. "Are they feeding you properly?" the man says at last.

"I suppose it could be worse."

"Well then, everything is in order," the man says cheerily. Peter turns away, as a sign that the visit is over.

After he's left the tent, it occurs to him that this man was sent by Hans, which means that Hans hasn't been interned. This thought is a source of relief, but he still resents the man for showering him with pity.

He dreams of Mem so vividly that he wakes up feeling as though she's still near to him. He tries to hold onto this sensation for as long as he can. When it fades away, he struggles to put it into words: "Last night I was with my mother again. We sat in a little boat on a dark green lake. She was a stranger to me. I cried, as I hadn't cried for a long time. How good I felt then! And how sad! Complete, consoling reconciliation. O my mother! How beautiful her dark voice sounds! How expressively she moves her delicate hands! If you had a mother like mine, you wouldn't be able to follow the advice of the Old and the Wise!"

He is almost never without his journal now. People often ask him what he is writing down. "There's nothing happening here," they say to him. "What can be so interesting?" But the camp provides him with so many different types, from Lindau, a "whirlwind on crooked legs," to Joseph, hysterical servant of the people. The pettiest conflict seems worthy of writing down, like the incident that he refers to in his diary as "The Drama of the 400 Shoes."

The long-suffering Joseph finally quits his post as cook and joins the Welfare Office, which has just been formed. His first assignment is to distribute 400 pairs of shoes to the internees who need them most, which requires drawing up a list that will be submitted to the Quartermaster. Joseph is about to throw all his energy into this task, but Lindau suddenly tries to block him, saying that the Welfare Office isn't properly set up for a task of this magnitude and that he, Lindau, should organize it instead. Asch criticizes Lindau for trying to usurp Joseph's place; Lindau claims that Asch is out of line and that Joseph is in agreement with him. But it turns out that Joseph has been conspiring with Asch behind Lindau's back, and that both of them are determined to cut Lindau out, since Lindau, aggressive and calculating, wants to have a hand in everything. A meeting is called: Lindau is voted down. A young intellectual by the name of Wald is voted in instead. But Wald, a strikingly handsome man, with silky brown hair and dreamy blue eyes, is far less effective than the energetic Lindau, who constantly goads and criticizes him, until Wald finally breaks down and begs him to leave him alone. Through sheer force of personality, Lindau prevails over Wald, forcing him to withdraw his list, which includes 20 kitchen people who need new shoes – Joseph's idea. Lindau's list is submitted to the Quartermaster, which is hailed by Lindau and his supporters as a victory.

The final installment of "The Drama of the 400 Shoes" wipes out everything that has come before. The Quartermaster distributes only 40 pairs of shoes. No one knows what happens to the rest.

The news comes that the Germans have taken Paris, and the entire camp is devastated. No one can manage to hold onto hope; everyone is exhausted by this tremendous blow. The only person in the camp who seems completely untouched is the boy in the black rubber coat, who continues to march around the grounds with his hands clasped behind his back, muttering the same authoritative, nonsensical remarks.

Writing is a place of freedom for him, although he struggles with it constantly. "Doesn't each line impose itself on me? Doesn't the weight of the smallest word lie heavy on my brow?"

He rejects the idea that writing is a form of escape, a criticism that Hans has sometimes made: "As if it wasn't a difficult compulsion and duty: a necessity, a compulsion, until the hot hand, cramped by the pen, can't go on, and the brain struggles breathlessly after it."

Even as he dramatizes the struggle that writing entails, he is conscious of how difficult it is to be honest on the page: "Yes, I would like to write: good and round, never false, not interesting, not 'naïve,' not 'frivolous,' not as though I only dreamt, not as though I had always merely stuck my nose into dirt. This is what I want to be: eye and ear, understanding and heart – I want to master the crazy, cheap, expensive, wretched, incomparable mixture that has been forced on me, that makes up my fate."

But a moment later, he strikes a romantic pose, picturing writing as his mistress-mother: "I want to master and serve it, in order to elevate it and cast it down, like a fruit, like a beautiful woman, and to belong to it because it belongs to me – with great immeasurable trust, as if she were as good as a good mother."

He receives a package in the mail and tears it open immediately, without waiting to get back to his room. It contains a pound of chocolate, 200 cigarettes, round biscuits, strawberry marmalade. Who sent it to him? There is no address on the box. It must have been Hans because it couldn't be from Mem, who doesn't even know where he is. He runs down the street with his box in his arms, whistling to himself. This is the first package he has gotten since he was interned. He doesn't even know what to feel. Absurd that it means so much to him! Should he hide the chocolate in the crack in the wall or share it with Tommi and Vicki and anyone else who seems worthy to him?

As he is entering his building he hears someone say, "Have you heard the news? Tomorrow we're being sent to the Isle of Man!"

11.

The Isle of Man

1940

STANDING at the railing of the ship, he feels absurdly happy. The sun is dancing across the surface of the sea. Crescents of white foam are racing to the horizon. Moments after they've left Liverpool behind, they see three gigantic forms rising out of the water. One of them is the belly of a ship, with rusty red pipes poking out of it. The other is a steamer that has been cut into two parts that are standing upright, facing each other. Everyone calls out and waves, as though they are on a sightseeing tour. Despite his high spirits, he can't help pointing out that these boats must have been bombed and that the same thing could happen to them, but no one pays attention to him.

A trail of seagulls follows after them, swooping down and flying up again. "Look how they hover," the man next to him remarks. "It's as if they're standing in the air!"

"But they have such ugly wooden faces," he replies, suddenly irritated.

"Why did I say that?" he writes later in his diary. "Because my mother said it at some point. How often I've taken her vague, moody opinions as commands!" He foresees the tearing of these invisible threads as he moves forward into his own life. But toward what? An alien land? How sad it is to leave Mem behind!

By now the shore has disappeared and there is nothing but the sea. He reaches into his suitcase and takes out his chocolate and his cigarettes, sharing them with some men who are sitting on a pile of rope. "Is this a party?" a soldier remarks. "You aren't on a pleasure trip, you know."

"I know that," he says with a shrug, "but what's the use of crying?" The officer squints at him disapprovingly, then moves away.

The wind is increasingly cold and damp but Peter and his companions remain on deck, smoking too many cigarettes and watching the prow of the ship cut through the foaming waves. At last, they decide to investigate their sleeping quarters, climbing down a metal ladder into a chamber that is crowded and hot. His little celebration has come to an end; the friends he has made withdraw into themselves. "They were much more friendly when they were gobbling up my chocolates," he notes in his diary. Covering his eyes to block out the flickering yellow light, he falls into a heavy sleep

The next morning they see a brownish-green hill rising up from a rounded bay. As they get closer, they see a row of cream-colored façades that look orange where the sun is touching them. The sea is so still that they can see all the way down to the green-flecked blocks of stone underneath the pier. Couples in pastel clothes are strolling on the promenade. It's hard to believe that this idyllic resort is going to serve as their next holding place.

They come down the gangplank in a series of groups, forming into rows on the dock. A narrow-shouldered intellectual by the name of Weiss asks a tough-looking Viennese boy to carry his bags for him. "Why should I?" the boy asks defiantly.

"Because if you don't, you'll see what happens to you."

"What do I care about your suitcase?" the boy says, spitting into the water. "Am I your servant? I don't owe you anything."

"You'll see," Weiss says, shaking his fist at him. "In the last war, people like you – people with asocial behavior – were held longer than anyone else."

"If you didn't want to carry your own suitcase, you should have given it up," an internee by the name of Laufer says.

"This doesn't concern you!" Weiss shouts angrily.

"Enough is enough!" Laufer says. "Stop pestering the boy and get in line."

"What I'm saying to him is a matter of principle. Maybe that's something you don't understand!"

"Stand in the rows, you buggers!" the bobbies shout. But Weiss refuses to take his place, convinced that everyone in the group is on Laufer's side. A bobby comes and shoves him into place, which elicits curses and screams from him. A crowd of vacationers gathers to watch "the nasty scene" that has been caused by a group of dirty foreigners. Peter describes these spectators in his journal in contemptuous terms: dried-out spinsters, insipid, heavily rouged girls, young men in stiff collars and greasy coats, a pale-faced mama who stares at them in horror and whispers into the ear of her fat little boy.

At last, his group is taken to the Hotel Shaftsbury, a faded establishment that has been stripped of all furniture except for beds. The wallpaper is peeling and the rugs smell of mold, but a hint of luxury still clings to the brightly colored drapes. Marking off their area are the usual fences of barbed wire. Three steps away is the culture of the beach resort – the laughing, ice-cream-licking "free" people who peer at them curiously.

And so they settle into a life that makes even less sense than the life they led before. During the day, they have nothing to do. During the night, they watch the moon reflected on the sea. Rumors breed in their overcrowded hotels and rooming houses. What will happen to them if Ireland is attacked? Some predict that the British government will evacuate the Isle of Man, just as they evacuated the Channel Islands once the German troops reached the French coast, and that they will have no one to protect them when the Nazis come to round them up.

But hunger is harder to live with than anything else and it's sharpened by being near to the carefree spirit of the resort. For the vacationers, food is plentiful; for them, there is no fruit, no sugar, no butter, no eggs – only cabbage, potatoes, and herrings in rations that barely amount to 700 calories a day.

They still hold classes, ignoring the constant growling of their stomachs. The postal system frustrates them: few letters arrive, and they're not convinced that the letters they send are ever delivered. Whatever news they receive comes from conversations someone has overheard, or from a smuggled newspaper that is passed from hand to hand. Rumors circulate about where they will be taken next: some say Canada, others Australia, others New Zealand. Men with families are anguished at the prospect of being sent even farther away, while the younger ones like himself are open to adventure.

But what about the civilization that he holds so dear? What about Goethe, Schiller, Schopenhauer, Nietzsche? On the continent of Europe, that civilization is in the process of being destroyed. What will any of it mean in a wild, faraway place like Australia?

He gathers his courage and visits the philosopher Strich, who has a room at the top of a different hotel with a window that faces the sea. The sun is just beginning to go down: he stares out at the pale-yellow beach, the dark, glossy waves, the rose-colored clouds in the turquoise sky, desperately searching for something intelligent to say. The kindly Strich does his best to put him at his ease, but he finds himself slipping into the part of the talented but naïve young man. He can't stand the idea of being a cliché and delivers a stuttering train of overstated certainties that make him appear ridiculous. Why is he artificial in the presence of this pensive old man, who tells him so simply that he hasn't been able to work, and that this is the first time in his life that he's had a view of barbed wire and sea? He botches this meeting entirely, so that after it's over, it's painful to think of it.

He can never be alone, he's always surrounded by men. He has become part of a malformed organism that is barely managing to adapt. Punishing rumors stir up furious arguments; hunger has a way of making the gloomiest predictions seem the most true.

"Would you consider giving me a piano lesson?" one of his roommates says to him, a man with Aryan features who says he's a Jew. "Not now, but maybe next week," Peter puts him off. His roommate takes this as an opening. "The internment reminds me of my school years, "he confides, suddenly becoming expansive. "That's where all my worst instincts were developed." Peter decides not to give him piano lessons; he reminds him too much of Andreas, who became a Nazi and turned on him.

One day they are taken out for a walk by soldiers armed with bayonets. The Douglas Promenade on the free side looks shabbier than he expected it to; the posters on the kiosks are torn and the cakes in the windows look stale. At last they come to a meadow. He plucks a white flower and then a yellow one, wishing that he had someone to give them to. After the meadow comes a forest that is rich and green, with deep shadows and hazy pools of light.

"It's as beautiful as northern Italy here," says Herr Schoops to Herr Rogosivsky, a fellow scientist. Herr Rogosivsky notes that he saw a palm tree in one of the gardens and speaks of the gulf stream and tropical vegetation. The bored faces of the soldiers dissolve into broad grins as they pass a group of teenage girls in sunhats and summer dresses. They come to a promontory with a magnificent view of the bay, looking out over the tree tops all the way to the horizon. For a moment, they don't have a care in the world, but as soon as they go down into the valley, they feel trapped again.

The rumor on the food line is that they are going to be classified as prisoners of war. If that's the case, he notes in his diary, then officialdom is officially demented. "But there may be certain advantages," one of the camp experts points out. "For one thing, they'll have to feed us better under the terms of the Geneva Convention."

In Peter's opinion, everyone is missing the point, the larger point, that is. The truth is that they are struggling to embrace the New, which has nothing nourishing or real to offer them. Meanwhile, they are losing touch with the Old, which is, after all, where their spirits used to live. What are these new lands that they are constantly contemplating? What do they have to do with him? Home is where his mother lives, or used to live, in graceful ease. Everything else is foreign to him.

As he huddles under his woolen blanket, he thinks to himself that writing is his one way of opening himself to the world. But maybe he is sensitive only when he is creating a second identity for himself on the page; maybe in reality, he is living in a sack, oblivious to the reality that is actually shaping his fate.

Bitter accusations are made against the cook. He is stealing coffee, gulping down extra cups. Fury mounts against him and, when someone confronts him, he flies into a rage. A wrinkled old attorney speaks eloquently in the cook's defense, saying that it's outrageous that this hardworking member of the community should be treated so ungratefully. This expert speaker who has saved men from the death sentence uses every rhetorical device in the book to defend his "client." Hitler himself couldn't have found more pathos-filled words! Here on this "Man Island" they are losing all sense of proportion.

In the midst of their bickering, an officer says sarcastically, "I can give you some news that will make you all happy. "

"What is it?" they ask suspiciously.

"Paris has fallen."

The word is that they're going to Canada, even though they still don't know for sure. The married men draft letters to the authorities, begging not to be taken even farther from their families. A letter is written by Herr Gross, the man appointed as their "Camp Father" – they refuse to call him their "Captain" because it seems too militaristic to them – complaining over the lack of news and the fact that they are being treated like criminals. If this treatment continues, Herr Gross will no longer feel compelled to make any effort to maintain order in the camp.

Some refuse to believe that England will leave them in the lurch. Churchill will do the right thing, they're convinced of it. But then again maybe England will be conquered in a matter of weeks and they will be turned over to the Nazis, like the French refugees, or simply lined up on the beach and shot. "Yes, my dears, anything is possible," Vicki says, with one of his most satirical smiles. Laufer bangs out popular tunes on the piano, Braunbart explains the Miracle of the Marne, Rosenburg reads his Pascal out loud to anyone who cares to listen. How shapeless their reality is!

Writing is his only defense, his only way of reordering his life. And yet writing authentically is always a struggle. "How much trembles in me as intuition," he notes. "How little binds the pencil to the page." People tap him on the shoulder and say to him, "Don't write anymore. You'll ruin your eyes." "I write without looking at the paper," he answers them. "Then it will probably be illegible when you try to read it someday," they point out. But the more illegible his handwriting, the less afraid he is of what will happen to him if his journal falls into the wrong hands.

He is constantly gathering types, assembling a cast of characters for a novel that he may or may not write. There is Fabian, who reminds him of a carp, with his shiny black eyes and pouting lips. Filling in his portrait, he makes note of "the pushed together lower portion of his face. The scant red-blonde hair on the round skull. No eyebrows. The snuffling-hoarse voice. An unbelievably stupid face." And together with this, "his stupid optimism: the non-acceptance of bad news. Self-important empty petitions (congratulatory speeches to the cook, votes of confidence for x, votes for z) ... the second-most greedy eater at the table. This is Fabian. And he laughs a lot. Despite his shabbiness, he is bearable, because he can't be taken seriously."

He tries to see his fellow internees in universal terms, as actors in a philosophical drama. In Heichelheim and Weiss, the hypocritical scientists, "the animal, stupid, gluttonous, shrewd, appears as the true spirit; whitewashed intellectuals." Weiss, with his astonished, intellectual, bespectacled eyes and his thin, vulnerable chest is mixed up and irrational, even though he is trained as a mathematician. "How senselessly he steps out of line, confused, stupefied, and then again terrified in the face of power, a confusionist and weakling who doesn't know himself, with his intelligence hanging in the empty air and his colorless aestheticism: all so weak." Summing up his impressions, he writes, somewhat grandly, with a tragic flourish, "Yes, in the animal and the weakling, European culture comes to an end!"

There is a special roll call. They are divided into groups: all unmarried people between the ages of 20 and 30 are placed on a separate list. There are categories for Orthodox and Liberal Jews, as well as for Catholics and Protestants.

"Are they doing this for the army?" someone asks.

"It must be for Canada," someone else says.

"I ask you, Herr Heller, what will become of us?" one of the older men complains. Peter remembers Herr Hausig, and how he clung to his arm on that first day in Liverpool. Somehow the old ones always come to him.

"Why are we being divided into religious groupings?" everyone wants to know.

"We just have to wait," Herr Gross, the Camp Father says, spreading out his arms as though he's trying to hold back a flood.

At breakfast they receive word that everyone between 20 and 30 must come for a walk. There's no reason to get excited, they're assured; the authorities simply want to talk to them in the field.

A rich young man with a heart condition hurries up to Peter and walks by his side. He lent him his swimming trunks yesterday in exchange for cigarettes, which the young man – his name is Eitelstein – has interpreted as a sign of friendship. He has thinning hair and intelligent gray–blue eyes, but he doesn't have anything interesting to say. Peter lets his side of the conversation lag and eventually Eitelstein gets the message and moves away. He should probably have been more polite to him – after all, Eitelstein is immensely rich and regularly receives packages that contain all kinds of delicacies, like butterscotch candies and sardines. If he were to help him in some significant way – for example, save him from drowning – Eitelstein might express his gratitude by setting him up for life. But what a shabby speculation, after all. He would never have thought this way a couple of years ago, when he was still the son of a rich house.

They march up the hill in four straight lines, coming to a meadow marked off with barbed wire. The pot-bellied officer that they have dubbed "Colonel Blimp" is standing at the top of the hill, looking down on them with imperturbable calm. They lie in the grass, tired from the walk. The Colonel calls out, "My gentlemen, again an historical moment!" But instead of going on, he raises his stick and strolls around the meadow, moving among them without saying anything. A little troupe of prisoners starts trailing after him. He waves them away with his stick, as though they're a cloud of flies.

At last, the Colonel stops, lies down in the grass and closes his eyes. After all this build-up, he is taking a nap! An airplane circles above their heads. Is someone keeping watch over them? First circle, second circle, third. Someone says, in an expressionless voice, "Why doesn't he throw some bombs? That would settle everything." After the sixth circle they are called to the opposite end of the field. The Adjutant, a small, energetic man with a curly beard, speaks to them in a confiding tone, as though he genuinely cares about them. He tells them they will soon be transported to a place where they will have the opportunity to do useful work. He is sure they will all appreciate that. No one is allowed to take more than 40 pounds in their luggage, and he would advise them to pack immediately. (Still no word about where it is that they are going.)

He thinks about his father as he is packing his things and suddenly he feels terribly sorry for him. Whatever money he's managed to salvage will probably be taken away and he'll be living out of cardboard boxes, like everyone else.

After the packing is done, nothing happens, which puts everyone into a foul mood.

"I've lost my respect for the British," he hears one man say to the other. "How idiotic they are!"

"What do you want them to do?" the other replies. "If the Nazis come down in parachutes the way they did in Holland, they can't have Nazi sympathizers on the ground."

"But 90 per cent of us are Jews!"

"So? They don't have time to interrogate all of us."

"But look at all the talent they're wasting!" the other man remarks. "There are people among us – scientists, engineers, mathematicians – who could help them fight the Nazis."

"What if England hadn't taken us in?" the first man cuts him off. "Do you ever think about that?"

If the Germans succeed in taking over the civilized world, German will be spoken everywhere, and he won't have to be separated from his mother tongue: "… this rich, hard, powerful, objective, not easily understood language would be in every mouth," he reflects. "Here and there misused and often defiled. But also enriched, sharpened, hurled into large movement, thrown into the melting pot and fruitfully mixed." But then he draws back from this fantasy, recognizing it as a product of his homesickness for a culture that has already been ripped apart. "Because what is language when the spirit who knows how to use and to develop it is dead?"

Herr Levin, a nerve doctor by profession but now recast as their House Father, calls them together excitedly. As usual, he is overstrained and overworked, but he doesn't care, he is committed, as always, to working for the common good, and he will do his best to address the various concerns that must necessarily arise under the present circumstances, which could surely be much worse, but are highly stressful, to say the least. For 45 minutes he regales them with a blend of popular philosophy, anecdotes, Jewish jokes, presumably to soothe their jangled nerves. Finally he divulges that he has received some news that will affect all of them: a new list is about to be made up, separating the 16–20 year olds and 30–40 year olds into two separate groups. "Is this your big news?" someone cries. "We've been sitting here for almost an hour!"

"I can't tell you much more," he admits. "The officers themselves don't know what's going to be done with us."

"Then why did you call us here?"

"What I've just told you will affect everyone," Herr Levin says, delivering this empty sentence with emphasis. But when he sees that others are equally dissatisfied, he becomes irritated. "I'm surprised that you don't find these matters of interest," he says huffily. "I must say, it seems rather short-sighted. If you want my personal opinion, I'll give it to you – I believe that we're going to Canada, and that we'll be put to work there as peat cutters."

"Peat. What is that?" the man in front of him mutters. "A kind of dirt or sod that is dug up out of swampy bogs," the man next to him replies.

Peter has never seen it with his own eyes, but they had to learn all about it in Geography. He dimly remembers learning how peat is cut; there was a diagram of it in one of his books. He tries to summon up that diagram, but all he can remember is the boredom of those long afternoons. Peat cutting. Huh.

While he waits, he continues to write, fretting over the limitations of his style. He dreams of arriving at a style that is flowing and clear, a style that will allow him to uncover the fragile human reality that lies underneath the masks everyone feels compelled to wear. "So many faces are prefabricated," he writes, comparing them to generic, mass-produced suits. This is especially true of the young, who are so eager to "put on the affectations of the adults." And yet, if one really looks into a person's eyes, "how often the helpless, astonished child looks out." He doesn't underestimate the need for borrowed forms; in fact, it is the young who need what he describes as a "stenciled shape" the most. "It makes their lives simpler," he writes. "Armor, mechanization of reaction." But this mechanization of reaction is deadening in the end, which is why he seeks out the hiding places of the child in others and even in himself: "It is the child, it seems to me, who stirs up my immediate sympathy, and my sympathetic joy. Perhaps there is also such a thing as sympathy through recognition (compassion for a confused place, sufferings that are analogues to our own) – but we are moved immediately if a child looks sad or smiling out of its constrained flesh."

In his writing, he alternates between exposing clichés and attempting to arrive at a rendering of the real. For the rest, he is waiting, like everyone else, but perhaps, unlike some of the others, who are less accustomed to analyzing themselves, he is conscious of the fact that this time of waiting is opening up a new region inside of him:

> He who has seen the blue–gray fog, the damp, blue–gray asphalt, the double-row of one-armed stakes, the lonely black soldier who goes back and forth in silence – behind him, however, the blue–gray fog – whoever has seen the finely blurred line of the sea, the shimmer of the white foam on the little leaping waves, and the distant strips of sand, disappearing into the blue–gray fog … Whoever looks at the damp salty sorrow of the silence – oh, he has experienced more than someone who has travelled around the world – No excited talker, like Herr Fabian – will be able to disturb him. In the face of all petty noise, he only needs to think of the blue gray of the sky and sea, the double row of barbed wire stakes, the lonely soldier and the silence over the eternally crashing, white-tongued waves.

But his sense of isolation is shot through with the consciousness that there are others who have been stripped of the luxury of reflection:

> "Lights out there!" shouts the soldier. I collapse, as though from a blow … no longer "at home" – in the war, in the war! How can you presume to sit here and say "in the war"? Aren't the others dying over there? Aren't our friends being shot over there at this very moment? And I, scoundrel, dumb animal, can't see it, am too cowardly to look. They die, you coward! They are afraid, smile one time more, they strain their tired faces one more time and die. But you enjoy yourself with the comfortable consolation of writing and self-reflection.

Maybe he really is a burden, a parasite, after all, and maybe his writing is nothing more than a kind of therapy. But no, he doesn't write in order to analyze himself; he writes in order to feel that he is alive. He wants to live more than anything else, even if high-minded men like Erich would say that that desire is crude, and even if others are dying in the war while he sits here and reflects. What's the point of pretending to be nobler and purer than he is? "God forgive me!" he writes.

On July 2, at 2:00, they are told that in half an hour, they must appear on the Douglas Promenade with no more than 40 pounds worth of luggage. From there, they are led to the salon of the Palace Hotel, where blue-tinted portraits of Beethoven and Sullivan stare down at them from behind cheap gold frames and a swaying chandelier sprinkles dust onto their heads. They pace around the gaudy room, reciting schoolboy verses about the boorish Canadian who didn't understand the refined manners of the European. The soldiers watch over them from the corners of the salon with less interest than ever, as though they are already looking forward to being rid of them.

Tables have been set up for inspection, which will no doubt include the giving up of money. He has tucked a pound note under his collar and he can't stop thinking about whether anyone will see it or not. He whispers to the others, "Can you tell it's here, or does the collar lie naturally?" One reassurance isn't enough; he asks everyone he comes into contact with. He makes the mistake of staring at the guards, which is a sure way of raising suspicion, but nothing comes of it. At last, he decides to transfer the pound note from his collar to his sock – still no one notices – and now he feels confident, almost exuberant. He remembers the raisins in his pocket and starts to munch on them, only to discover that they have fallen out of their little packet, mingling with the bar of soap that he has put there in case he needs it for the trip. To calm his nerves, he eats the raisins anyway, with the result that he can't fully concentrate on anything that's going on, distracted by the process of extracting the soapy nuggets of fruit from his glued-together pocket.

The inspection is over quickly, and now he regrets the fact that he held onto his pound note instead of using it to buy food or cigarettes. What use will he have for an English pound when he gets to wherever it is they're going?

After all this, they finally march off, passing the older internees, who wave at them from behind the barbed wire. He catches the eye of the philosopher Strich, who nods at him and smiles. If only he hadn't wasted the time he had with him! For all he knows, he'll never see him again.

His suitcase still has no handle, so he has to carry it on his back, but now he also has a cardboard box for his papers and books, which he tucks under one arm. Tilting at an angle, he makes his way along the quay, stopping every now and then to rebalance his things. At last they board a small gray mail ship with a shiny roof. Resting his head against his suitcase, with his box in his lap, he manages to take a nap, periodically waking up and hearing bits of conversation.

"When are we going to get moving?"

"Whenever they're ready. There's nothing we can do."

"It would be easy to jump off and swim to shore."

"What would be the point? I never want to see this place again."

At dawn, the ship finally sets forth for Liverpool, where they will be put on another vessel, a cruiser, as Herr Wilgemuth predicts, lecturing them on the difference between a cruiser and a ship with his squeaky voice. Too restless to listen, Peter wanders away, looking down into the machine room and trying to interest himself in what he sees. "You know full well how different life would be if these machines didn't exist," he tells himself. For an instant, he is able to find a certain elegance in the intersections of white struts and rhythmically clanking steel rods. Maybe the machine represents the "idea" of bestiality – yes, bestiality freed from the flesh, he reflects, resting his elbows on the rails. Absurd! No, he needn't try to extend his sympathies to the machines, but to the sweating men who are exerting themselves down below. The truth is that he hates and fears enslavement to machines and, if he had to work down there, who knows for how many hours a day, he would suffer a boredom worse than death. Hopefully he won't feel the same way about peat cutting.

They finally arrive in Liverpool, once again passing the sunken ships. (This time, no one waves at them.) They still haven't been told where they are going, but he decides that it doesn't matter to him. He's fed up with all this speculation and theorizing.

On the pier, he struggles with his suitcase and cardboard box, but fortunately Reinhard Parisier, a fellow internee, offers to carry the box for him, which makes keeping up much easier. As he walks along the pier with his suitcase on his back, he remembers that he walked here with a girl by the name of Cathy – or was it Carrie? – only four months ago. He can still remember kissing her on the lips and neck while she protested, "Don't! Oh don't! You naughty boy! When will you ever learn to behave!" She wasn't beautiful, but she had wonderfully soft skin. Was that really only four months ago?

A group of men from the Kitchener Camp boast that they were treated like kings – double rations in exchange for easy work, movies, etc. etc. They are crammed into a waiting area where there isn't room to turn around, and where some attempt to sleep by sitting on their suitcases with their heads in their arms. All of a sudden, there is a huge commotion in the room, and he stands on top of his cracking suitcase so that he can look out of the window along with everyone else. There he sees a rust-covered crane that someone identifies as a luggage hoist. After the crane, they see the enormous bulk of a gigantic ship with the word *Ettrick* painted on its side. Everyone starts shouting all at once and there is total chaos in the room. Sweat trickles down his face and into his eyes and yet he hasn't moved an inch. He wishes that he had seen his father one more time, but he tells himself that they won't be separated for long. When his thoughts turn to Mem, there is unbearable pain.

12.

Sea Legs

1940

THE deck of the ship is packed with men: knees, elbows, and shoulders are pressing in on him. "There must be at least a thousand of us here," someone says. "Don't forget the German POWs," someone else replies. "I heard that there are over 800 of them."

"Why are we being thrown together with that bunch?"

"Think about it for a minute. It might not be such a bad thing. Under the Geneva Convention, the Brits have to treat them like human beings."

"So what?"

"So maybe it will spill over to us."

But no one has bothered to tell them where they are going, even though this is one of their rights. One man says they're going to be taken to Germany to be exchanged for the British prisoners taken at Dunkirk. Another says they're bound for Scotland, to build roads and fortifications. A third man is convinced they're headed for Madagascar. Peter sticks to peat cutting in Canada.

"Why are they going to such trouble to get rid of us?" a Cambridger remarks. "Everyone I talk to is Category B and C."

"They probably ran out of Category A and they're filling some kind of quota," the other replies.

"Typical."

After hours of standing on the deck, they are herded into the hold of the ship. The walls are covered with barbed wire and so is the door. There are machine gun rests in the corners. "They're pretty afraid of us, aren't they," someone remarks. "Look at that sign!" someone else exclaims. "It says Maximum Capacity: 48 Troops."

The heavy smell of machine oil settles in Peter's throat. All they have for ventilation is a single fan. Hammocks are slung up between the columns; everyone scrambles for them. He crawls into a hammock underneath two others and throws his arm across his eyes.

More hours pass: still no food or water and still no access to the latrines. Peter curls up in his hammock and tries to sleep despite the gurgling of his stomach. In this half-state, he overhears Vicki and a man by the name of Bethany-Hollweg talking about the difference between sherry and cocktail parties. Absurd as it is, their conversation is comforting to him; they wouldn't be talking like this if the ship were going down.

At ten in the morning they are brought to the latrines in groups. And then they are finally given something to eat. "It's been 30 hours," the man next to him says. "I wonder if they made the POWs wait this long." They are seated at tables, about 20 men at each, and served generous portions of bacon, sweet porridge, Australian butter, and thick white bread. Real conversation becomes possible again, and even a bit of optimism. Returning to his hammock, Peter jots down a few impressions – unshaven faces frozen in sleep; the weave of the hammock that casts a criss-cross pattern over the scene; the stench of sweaty armpits and feet; the cradle of the hammock rocking back and forth …

He wakes up to hear a man saying in an excited voice, "But we *have* changed direction, there's no question of that."

"Why would we be going back to shore?"

"I'll tell you why – there are German U-boats out there!"

And now he becomes conscious that his hammock is swinging more wildly than before. There is a cold shivery feeling in the pit of his stomach. Men are jumping out of their hammocks and squatting down over buckets; the air is filled with the sound of coughing and spitting.

"The ship in front of us has been torpedoed," someone says. "That's why we've turned around."

"Are we going back to England?"

"How the hell should I know?"

The miraculous rations continue to come. They gobble down the food greedily and then throw it up. There are troughs of vomit underneath the tables and there is a slick of vomit on the floor. Vomiting is discussed over meals; some people demand that this be banned as a topic of conversation, since just thinking about it is enough to bring it on. But the topic is impossible to suppress, since vomiting takes up most of their day and the sour smell of vomit saturates the air.

They see the German soldiers when the food is being given out. They look just as crisp and alert as they did when they first boarded the ship. "We wouldn't look bad either if we were allowed on deck," someone remarks. "I would give anything for a breath of fresh air."

A 17-year-old soldier in an aviator's uniform is baited about the prospect of a Nazi victory. "Exactly how will the Nazis divide the world?"

"We'll leave that to the Führer," the boy says with a shrug.

"So you have no idea! And yet you're willing to sacrifice your life!"

The boy smiles proudly and puffs out his chest. His whole being radiates certainty.

More news: it's true that the ship before them was attacked. It was called the *Arandora Star* 1 and it was destroyed by a German U-boat commanded by Günther Prien, a famous U-boat captain. Thanks to this decorated war hero, hundreds of men have drowned, a mixture of Jewish refugees and German POWs. "Unbelievable!" Peter hears one man exclaim. "The Germans bungled and killed their own." "Apparently the German POWs aren't much protection to us after all," another man remarks.

They learn that the *Ettrick* was sent back to get a convoy, and now it's back on course. Convoy or not, the sinking of the *Arandora Star* proves that anything could happen to them. But there isn't time to panic or even to think in a world dominated by vomit and diarrhea.

"We're eating too much food!" the Cambridger Asch proclaims.

"What's wrong with him?" someone remarks. "Does he want us to eat less and save the Brits some money?"

"No you idiot, he's afraid that we're using up our rations too fast and that nothing will be left over for the rest of the trip."

The buckets and basins are full to overflowing. The men who can hold their food are in the minority. "How are you Cambridgers doing?" Peter hears someone say. "Not too bad under the circumstances."

"Is it true that Blau threw up?"

"What Blau? Oh, you mean Blau from King's College. Like a heron."

Someone runs to the bucket with his mouth full. Another runs after him. "Gentlemen please! Let's not make a relay race of this." There are no more rags to clean up the mess. The tables are damp; the floor is treacherous.

Laufer plays his harmonica, Parisier lies inert on a bench, Peter rests in his hammock, chewing carefully on a crust of bed, and Asch runs around with a rag, muttering to himself, "There has to be a way to clean up this mess."

Closing his eyes, Peter tries to summon up the crystal-clear air of Grundlsee. What he would give to breathe in the smell of the woods! And then a metal hand grips the inside of his stomach and gives it a sharp twist. Where has that damn bucket gone?

A hero steps forward to save the day. He calls himself Count Fritz von Lingen, but he is actually Prince Friedrich Georg Wilhelm Christoph von Preussen, youngest son of the Crown Prince of Germany, grandson of Kaiser Wilhelm. His brothers have sided with the Nazis, but Lingen has attached himself to the Jews, which explains why he is in the hold of the *Ettrick* with them. "He has the head of a grayhound," Peter writes. Vicki says that Lingen has the typical Hohenzollern face. Fine-boned, lean, muscular, very blond, he is aloof but unfailingly polite. His clothing and his person are immaculate, which is a marvel in this increasingly filthy place. Lingen takes it upon himself to clean out the latrines, wearing a pair of greatly admired Wellington boots. Before long, he has formed a "bucket brigade" of young men who lord it over the rest of them in the name of Cleanliness. Although their attitude is resented, they succeed in doing their job, which adds to the aura surrounding their leader-in-chief.

"What a superb human being," a man named Perutz declares. "He's one of a kind," Parisier agrees. "We should choose him as our representative."

Peter is annoyed by the fact that everyone worships von Lingen. If they were back on land, they would see that he's more than a little odd.

Von Lingen's friends say he has an obsession with washing and polishing and that cleanliness is a compulsion with him. "But it isn't only that he likes cleaning," Parisier says to Peter. "It's the fact that despite all his breeding he's able to adapt himself to a bunch of Jews."

"Do you remember what he did at Huyton?" Perutz chimes in. "There we were, eating the most wretched food, and he goes to the cook, slaps him on the shoulder, and tells him that he has never eaten so well in his life! I swear the food got better after that."

Parisier: "That's another thing. He knows how to draw everyone in."

Belfuss: "We need a representative. We should choose him."

Perutz: "His grandfather was an idiot, but he understands high politics."

Parisier, like a broken record: "You have to understand. From such high circles! Adapting himself to us!"

In Peter's opinion, everyone has gone mad. What fools they're making of themselves! Democracy is a fiction, he writes. The Jews are no better than anyone else when it comes to a plebian reverence for aristocracy, and the Cambridgers are the worst of all. As someone raised in a privileged world, he refuses to lose his head over a count, unless he happens to be brilliant, which he's not.

In spite of these misgivings, he has to admit that he is genuinely impressed when the Cambridgers succeed in improving ventilation in the hold. After endless negotiations, they actually get permission to open the door that leads up to the deck. But there is one condition: the door will remain open only as long as no one ventures into the stairwell. The open door is an experiment. Unfortunately the stairwell also leads to the latrines, which are in high demand. Soon after the agreement has been put into effect, a man with dysentery becomes desperate to use the john, trying to push his way up the steps. A circle of Cambridgers forms around him, and when they step away the man is on the ground, unconscious, foul-smelling, no longer a threat.

Swinging in his hammock, Peter overhears a conversation about the *Arandora Star*. "How many people were drowned?" one man says. "Over half," the other man replies.

Did anyone bother to unlock the heavy door that led down to the hold of that ship, or did the torpedo blow it open, releasing its cargo of Jews? Peter pictures a ship exploding into a thousand pieces and raining down onto the sea. If Hans reads about it in the newspaper, he will probably assume the worst. *My son! My son!* he hears him cry. *I shouldn't have been so critical of you.*

He has tried to be tolerant of the Cambridgers but he can't – every day they become more irritating to him. At first he admired their nonchalance, but now it seems weak and deluded to him. More English than the English, they have become grotesque in their ceremoniousness. Peter would rather swing in his hammock feeling utterly lost than enact some overblown ideal of the British gentleman. It's one thing to be ignorant and coarse, but it's another thing for highly cultivated men to "play the part of the sane in well-cut madmen's clothing," as he writes in his diary. They are bad comedians, locked into stereotypical parts, incapable of feeling anything, including their own misery. No doubt he envies their knowledge and education and resents them for not recognizing him. But their contortedness is impossible to deny; clinging to their manners in this stinking hole, they are twisted and unnatural.

He has several conversations with an Austrian law student by the name of Ephraim who has recently passed his exams. He likes this Ephraim quite a bit, despite the fact that he is a better pianist than Peter and has more virtuoso pieces under his belt. Ephraim tells him that he is hoping to gain forestry skills in Canada, a sentiment that seems strange to Peter, especially coming from him. His face, after all, is pale and soft, and his fingers are long and tapered, like a woman's.

"But you're a lawyer!" Peter points out. "Not to mention your gifts as a pianist …"

"It will be better than doing nothing," Ephraim replies. "Eating. Sleeping. For a while, it's fine, but then you feel lousy."

His face is drawn and tense, and he has a nervous twitch over his left eye. 'So high-strung and fragile,' Peter thinks. He can't imagine him with a tool in his hands – an axe or a saw or whatever it is they use. "Do you really think it will satisfy you?" he says to him.

"What else should I do?" Ephraim shrugs. "It's not as though I have my law books with me. If I learn a trade, I can earn my bread as a skilled laborer."

"Why is it that all you intellectuals gush about physical labor?" Peter laughs. "I'd much rather read than do boring, repetitive work."

"In Canada, my degree won't do me any good," Ephraim replies. "All I'll be able to do with it is stick it into my hat."

"Maybe you're right," Peter says. But won't chopping down trees destroy those sensitive hands? He looks down at his own hands, which are square and broad. He's probably more suited for physical work, but he has absolutely no interest in it.

It's only when he's writing that he has a sense of purpose, that his existence seems justified. But writing doesn't come easily to him; at any given point, there is an excess to say, and yet the pencil comes to a halt in the middle of the page. "It doesn't matter how much one experiences," he reflects. "Being able to write really has to do with your capacity to digest what you or the world has stuffed into your mouth." Those who hurry over the page are suffering from what he describes as a chronic condition of diarrhea. When such people say "I can't go on" they are merely trying to hold it in, with a huge effort, for a few seconds longer. The alternative to diarrhea is constipation – a killing dullness, accompanied by "the ill-temper of blockage." "With people who have a poor spiritual digestion like me," he writes, "constipation and diarrhea, hypersensitivity and dullness, are interchangeable."

What is the solution? He hears his grandfather Leopold saying to him, "Eat slowly, chew everything thoroughly, don't just gulp it down." One has to trust in a process that is larger than oneself; if you allow yourself to distrust this process, everything is lost.

On July 13 they are ordered to come up onto the deck. After nine days, they finally breathe in fresh air. At first, the sunlight hurts his eyes, but then he gets accustomed to it, losing himself in the sight of dark green forests and light green meadows streaked with yellow. The forests are tremendous, and behind them rise wide, broad mounds that remind him of the hills that lead up to the Alps.

"Real forest, like at home!" someone exclaims.

"They have nothing like this in England," someone else agrees.

"I would give anything to lie under that bush – I could lie there for hours, completely alone."

"I like it here!"

"Here I'll stay."

"Look over there," someone shouts. "A car! The first car of Canada!"

A police boat comes up alongside them. Someone spots some tents and says that is where they're going to stay. Desperate to get off the boat, they grow increasingly agitated. A commander panics and starts swinging his stick. "Bloody bastards! Settle down!" he shouts.

He singles out a Jewish boy, striking him on the head, then on the back. "Get back into your place!" he screams at him. The boy cowers, trying to shield his face. There is nowhere for him to move. "You dirty bastard! I'll teach you!" the officer screams, striking the boy again and again. "He's letting loose like a madman!" Parisier exclaims. "Make room!" everyone cries. "Let the boy in, or he'll get beaten to death!" The boy crawls into the crowd and disappears.

Peter stares out at the shore, overcome by the realization of how helpless they all are. What is this goal that they are all so anxious to reach? An enormous steamboat passes them.

"Look at that! They're waving at us. Yes, they're waving. Can you believe that?"

The river is calm. The wind cuts across it from time to time, creating a ripple that looks like folded silk billowing across the surface of the water. "This is a new world," Peter thinks, trying to take it in.

Off in the distance they see a gigantic steel bridge, and they argue about how long it is. "I just counted 76 supports …" "I tell you, it's two kilometers …" And now they see a peninsula dotted with picturesque little villas that look charming from the distance. But when they get closer, they see that the villas are crudely made, with nothing to distinguish them. "Don't criticize already!" someone says. "This looks like *Pertschwach*," someone else says in a trembling voice.

The commander who beat the boy struts around swinging his stick. He has recovered from his fit of hysteria, but he gives no sign of being sorry for losing control of himself.

They come to a port with high buildings and cranes. "That one has

20 floors!" "We had buildings that high in Berlin." "In Vienna, we had the *Hochhaus*." "But look how many there are!" The buildings are red and black, with laundry hanging in front of the windows. There are bilingual signs in English and French, but Peter can't make them out. Slowly the boat starts turning toward the shore. There are rows and rows of soldiers standing on the pier.

"This is the end of our journey!" someone exclaims. But they are sent down into the hold again where they are held endlessly. Naturally the German POWs are allowed to disembark first. What are they, after all, but pathetic Jews? "Always *benibbicht*, made fools of," as someone remarks.

By the time they are brought back onto deck, many men are desperate to use the latrines. A man pees into a lifeboat and a soldier screams. For the fun of it, he points his rifle at him, but then he points it at someone else. Finally two basins are put on the deck, "one for peeing, one for shitting," the soldier shouts. Men make use of the buckets without any shame while the soldiers watch them and laugh.

Peter overhears one man scolding another for imagining that once they land they will be free. "They won't let us work here or move forward," he says to him. "For them, we're prisoners of war. Do you think they're going to take the time to weed us out from the POWs?"

"We're always screwed," another remarks. "In Germany we're pig Jews and in Canada we're Nazis. What am I anyway? A German *Saujud*."

From 10:00 in the morning until 8:30 at night they are on deck, but time accelerates the instant they touch the land. Running along a long hallway, with their bags on their backs. Hurry! Hurry! It's the American tempo! You have to be quick! From the hallway, they are herded onto a bus that says "Tour of Quebec."

"Yes, forget about your cares!" someone cries out. "Join the Jews and see the world!"

13.

The New World

Canada, 1940–41

THEY are driven to a high plateau that looks out over the St. Lawrence River. The soldiers make them wait until the last bus has pulled away and then they herd them through yet another barbed wire gate. The sight of the river at the base of the cliffs gives him a feeling of vertigo. When he is an old man, this sensation will come back to him, and he will be flooded with memories of the limbo that was Camp L.

They end up in a hut that smells of cooking oil, with long metal tables pushed up against the wall. There seems to be a kitchen area in the back, but they aren't given anything to eat or drink.

Peter succeeds in finding Reinhard, but he can't find Hans Werner; the room is so packed that he can hardly turn around. Reinhard isn't in a mood to talk; instead he lies down on one of the tables, flings out his arms, and goes to sleep. Peter finds a spot on a bench and closes his eyes, but voices keep forcing their way into his consciousness.

"Canada is our last chance, gentlemen!"

"This is a farce."

"You shits! Can't someone give me a cigarette?"

At last, his head drops to his chest. The next thing he knows, someone is poking him in the ribs. "Wake up!" a voice hisses in his ear. A fat smiling man is standing in the middle of the room. He's wearing a white coat, and there's a stethoscope around his neck. All the men are peeling off their clothes. A few moments later they are naked, standing in a row. Reinhard is next to Peter, yawning, rubbing his eyes. The doctor stands in front of Reinhard and says in a jovial voice, "Pull your skin back. Any itching?" Reinhard stares at him sleepily. The doctor presses together his index finger and thumb and pulls his hand back in slow motion, repeating this gesture two or three times. Reinhard turns bright red and quickly does what the doctor says, diving back into his clothes the second the "test" is done.

Before long they have to strip again, but this time they are told to keep on their underwear. Their clothes go in one pile and their belongings go in another. After a brief interval, they get their clothes back again, but their pockets are now empty, and as for their bags and suitcases, they have been taken away. Impounding sheets are laid out on the tables and separate forms are provided for reporting money.

"So this is America!" an internee remarks.

"They're better at this than the British, I can tell you that."

Peter stands in front of a little sergeant who can barely write. He has to spell out "P-e-t-e-r" and "V-i-e-n-n-a" for him. "Can you see to it that I get back my notebook?" he thinks of saying, but then he remembers that he has nothing to offer him by way of a bribe.

At midnight they are finally taken to their designated huts. The blankets are thin but they have actual beds, with mattresses that aren't too freshly stained. An hour later, they are brought back to the cafeteria and given water, corned beef, and bread. "POW rations," a familiar voice says. Looking up, he sees Hans Werner sitting diagonally across from him. "Does that bother you?" he laughs, delighted to see his friend. "If it does, I'll take your plate."

"How do you like this dump?" Hans Werner says.

"Anything is better than that stinking ship."

They discover that they've been assigned to the same hut and that Reinhard is in their hut as well. They try to figure out how many men each hut holds and they come to the conclusion that it's about 50 men, a mixture of Zionists, "Assimilanten," Nazi sympathizers, political refugees, and religious Jews.

Back in his bunk, Peter has trouble falling sleep. The man below him is snoring like a machine. He hangs over the edge and looks down on him, taking in his big belly, puffy red eyelids, and thick, fluttering lips. "Shut your mouth, can't you!" he finally bursts out, hitting his fist against the frame of the bed. The man's lips close for a second, then open again. The snoring is even louder than before.

In the morning, they are fed remarkably well: eggs, butter, Canadian bacon, porridge, tea. Although there is more than enough food to go around, everyone shovels it down as fast as they can.

After breakfast, they get their bags and suitcases back. His journal is returned to him, but a few scraps of paper with notes on them have disappeared. There are others who are much less lucky than him, like the Danish musician who has been robbed of his silver flute and who is now sitting on the floor with his head in his hands.

The internees appoint a committee to take stock of what has been taken away. No one has any faith in the impounding sheets. They count up their losses: cash in the amount of 22 pounds; 10,000 cigarettes; gold watches; shaving kits; a typewriter. Commander Macintyre, a short-legged officer with misty blue eyes, is outraged on their behalf. "I'll see to it that you get everything back," he promises them. But no one believes him, due to the efficiency with which their things have been taken away.

In the late afternoon, Peter lies on his bed, copying out a passage from Nietzsche. *"From that which you want to know and assess you must depart, at least for a time. Only when you have left the town can you see how high its towers rise above the houses."*

He closes his eyes and for an instant he is back on his little balcony on the Gloriettagasse. The light coming through the leaves is the color of gold and the vine that twists around the railing is covered with purple flowers.

"What's going on?" a voice shouts, making him sit straight up.

"Someone is having an attack!"

He jumps out of his bed and rushes forward with everyone else, sticking his book into his back pocket. A throng of men has formed at the opposite end of the hut. "Don't crowd him!" "Stand back!" "Give him some space!"

A skinny teenager with a scruff of reddish-blond hair is thrashing back and forth in his bed. "Let me out of here!" he screams at the top of his lungs.

"I know him!" Peter exclaims. "I talked to him on the *Ettrick*. He's been through the camps ..."

The boy's bunkmate, paunchy and balding, seizes him by the arm, but the boy twists away and starts hitting his head against the wall. "What are you doing?" his bunkmate yells, crouching over him and pinning him down. The boy spits into his bunkmate's face, reaches up his hands, and closes them around his neck. Several men intervene, pulling them apart. Two soldiers appear and seize hold of the boy. Before anyone knows it, they are dragging him out the door.

"Where are you taking him?" Peter asks. "To Solitary," one of the soldiers shouts. But there is no real Solitary in the camp, there is only one room with a working lock, and that's a closet-sized bathroom near the gate.

"Why aren't you taking him to the infirmary?" Peter calls out after them.

"We're afraid that he's going to hurt someone."

"What a joke," mutters Thomas Budde, a professional wrestler. "He couldn't hurt a fly." "He's stronger than he looks," his bunkmate says, rubbing his neck.

Peter goes back to his bunk only to discover that his book is gone. After a frantic search, he retraces his steps and finds it under the boy's bed, next to a bundle of rags with a belt tied around it and a pair of moldy canvas shoes. How on earth did his Nietzsche end up here? He brushes it off with his sleeve.

Less than an hour later, he walks into the refectory, passing by two soldiers, who are whispering to each other. "What's up with those two?" he asks the man next to him.

"How should I know? I don't trust any of them."

The Quartermaster, a man with pink-rimmed eyes and long, slack lips, makes them stand at their places before they get their food, calling out the names of the internees who have requested shoes. He repeats one name several times, saying it louder and louder. "Wait, I know that name!" Peter exclaims. "That's the kid from this afternoon."

Commander Macintyre whispers something to the Quartermaster, who looks at him intensely and then makes a mark on his list. "Did you see that?" Thomas says. "The kid's name just got crossed out!"

They go up, get their food, and sit down again. A rumor passes from one man to another, and when it reaches Peter, he can't believe his ears. The word is that the boy tried to escape and was accidentally shot in the head. "He was trying to crawl out the bathroom window," the man next to him says under his breath, "and for that some idiot shot him dead."

Someone is making this up, Peter thinks. *It's totally absurd.* But when he looks over his shoulder and sees an extra unit of soldiers standing in the back of the room, his heart starts pounding in his chest.

A group of Orthodox Jews at the next table begins to pray, rocking back and forth and wringing their hands.

"Well, that's one more plate for us," Thomas remarks. But a moment later, he pushes his plate away.

Everyone is jumping into committee work except for Peter. In his opinion, committee work is a colossal waste of time. "All that Reinhard can talk about are his committees!" Peter complains to Hans Werner while they are washing their clothes. "I don't like talking to him anymore."

"Wring it out like this," says Hans Werner, lifting a pair of dripping trousers out of the bucket and twisting them into a knot. "Even harder ... now shake it out."

"All he ever talks about is the Popular University," Peter goes on, absentmindedly slapping his shirt against the side of the bucket. ""Why can't they just hold the classes and stop making such a fuss!"

"Look at that shirt!" Hans Werner exclaims. "It's just as dirty as it was before!"

"Are you even listening to me?" Peter demands.

"Committee work brings out the worst in people," Hans Werner says, taking the shirt from him and rubbing soap into the stains. "But it's service, and for you that would be a good thing."

"Why do you say that?"

"Because you're too self-involved. When's the last time you did something for someone else?"

"What a hypocrite you are!" Peter blurts out, grabbing back his shirt. "What committees are *you* signing up for?"

But Hans Werner's remarks make him conscious of the fact that he always takes the position of the outsider and that he's cutting himself off. Maybe he would learn more about the life around him if he actually took part in it. On an impulse, he puts his name on a list, and the next morning he finds himself loading bricks into a rusted wheelbarrow and carting them to the far side of the camp.

"What are these bricks for?" he asks the other workers in his group.

It's a hot summer day and the sun is already beating down on them.

"The Commander wants to create a garden for the officers, and after that he wants to build them a swimming pool."

"Just for the officers?"

"What do you think? They're not about to build a pool for us."

At first, he is clumsy at his work, tipping over the wheelbarrow and bumping into things. Then he starts watching another internee by the name of Joachim, who handles his wheelbarrow effortlessly. He takes Joachim as his standard, imitating everything he does, down to the methodical way in which he loads his cart. Joachim is the expert: he was raised on a farm. Of course, Joachim's chest and arms are much more muscular than his, but after a few days of this, his arms will be stronger too. He loads the bricks as quickly as he can and practically runs to the far side of the camp.

"Hey, Yid!" shouts their foreman, a tall, sneering officer with a scar on his cheek. "What's your hurry? This isn't a relay race."

"But I was just trying ..."

"You were trying too hard."

"I don't understand."

"Let me make it clearer to you. This job is scheduled to take a week. If you keep going at that pace, you and your friends here will be out of work."

So this is what's expected of them: to work as badly as they can! Instead of going back for another load of bricks, he abandons his wheelbarrow in disgust and walks over to Reinhard and Weiss, who are arguing under the shade of a tree.

"No separation can be reached between Nazis and Jews," Weiss declares. "This is simply a fact that we have to reckon with."

"What are you talking about?" Reinhard says incredulously.

"The Commandant told us very clearly that every group must be represented in the Popular University, no matter how we feel about them."

"This is unbelievable!" Reinhard exclaims.

"What a wonderful idea!" Peter puts in, jumping at the chance for a fight. "Perhaps the curriculum should include a section on race." By now, Weiss is trembling from head to foot, and he looks even more upset when Hans Werner shows up. "The Jews always want to play democracy," Hans Werner remarks. "And nowhere has democracy been seen in as pure a form as in Camp L."

Seeing that he is outnumbered, Weiss flails his arms and talks non-stop until no one can take it anymore. At last, Hans Werner shouts in his face, "The world has no use for us, don't you understand? That's why we've been dumped here, along with Nazis and POWs. It just so happens that in this case, we outnumber the Nazis by 85 per cent. We can't let them into our university! If this causes a fuss, I personally will be very glad. Maybe the Canadians will actually take notice and separate us from them."

Before Weiss can answer, the foreman comes over and says, "The workday is officially done. If you want your 20 cents, you'll have to line up with everyone else."

The question of their status is always on their minds. No Jew wants to be classified as a German POW, except maybe for Lasskey, with his chubby hands and his lisping voice, who calculates the advantage in terms of chocolate and cigarettes. The question becomes even more pressing when they are told that they will soon be allowed to write home but that they will have to use POW letterhead.

"They're really sticking it to us, aren't they?" Reinhard says.

"If we accept this, we're lost," Hans Werner remarks. "We have to refuse."

"But I need to contact my parents," Reinhard complains. "I know what they're going through. I have to let them know that I'm alright."

The arguments about their status never go anywhere, Peter writes in his journal. They raise all the most urgent questions, but in the most superficial form. He feels a great need to solve the riddle of who he is, but clearing up his status isn't even beginning. What will become of all his dreams and ambitions? He is 20 years old and he hasn't accomplished anything.

Just pray that England prevails, some people say. Who can argue with that? But in the meantime, life is going on and he needs to anchor himself. Who is he and what will he be?

The only way to address the riddle of his identity is to devote all his time to practicing piano and writing. He gets permission from the Commandant to practice at 5:45 in the morning, and he manages to get himself out of bed before anyone else is up and about. After he has practiced for an hour, he has his breakfast, and then he goes out to the meadow with Hans Werner and reads Rilke's *Duino Elegies* with him. As they pore over Hans Werner's dog-eared book, they forget everything else, arguing heatedly as though everything depends on the meaning of a few clusters of words. What a nuisance that they have to go in for lunch! The clamor of the cafeteria hurts his ears and the sounds made by the noisily eating men are disgusting to him.

The entire camp lines up to get shots; a special tent has been set up between the huts with a flap that doesn't conceal anything. A blond-haired man with craggy features and an athletic build taps Peter on the shoulder while they're standing on line. "Excuse me," he asks, with a radiant smile. "Are you the pianist?"

Peter looks up into a pair of bright blue eyes that seem to be burning into him. "Well, I play piano ..."

"I had a feeling you were the one. You practice in the morning, just as the sun is coming up. My name is Franz, by the way. What's yours?"

"Peter," he says, avoiding Franz's gaze.

"You have a great talent, Peter. Has anyone ever told you that?"

"I'm just learning."

"Don't be so modest. Your playing is first-class. Do you know any folk tunes by any chance? My friends and I would love to hear some German songs. After all, many of us are Germans here, and we're all a bit homesick. Do you sometimes feel homesick too?" He says these last words in a languid voice that doesn't go along with his blazing eyes. "You're a wonderful pianist," he goes on. "I wake up at sunrise just so I can hear you play." He puts his hand on the small of Peter's back, but Peter twists away. A second later, two men come out of the tent.

"Well, how was it?" Franz calls out boisterously.

"I almost fainted from the pain," the first man says, winking at the man next to him, who doesn't say anything, tentatively feeling his arm and keeping his eyes on the ground, as though he's afraid of losing his balance.

"Step up Jew boy," one of the orderlies shouts at Peter.

"Don't talk to my friend that way!" Franz says loudly, for everyone to hear. The orderly looks at Franz, then at Peter, then at Franz again. "My apologies," he says with a smirk.

Peter doesn't flinch when he gets the shot, but he feels dizzy when he stands up.

"Don't forget my little musical request," Franz calls out after him as he leaves the tent.

Hans Werner has a bad reaction to the vaccine; by the evening, his face is hot and flushed and he has to lie down. Peter brings him water from the canteen and stays with him. Shivering under his blanket, Hans Werner talks in a delirious rush. "We ran away from Poland in the summer," he says, looking off into the distance. "It was summertime and we were wearing summer clothes. We wore those same thin clothes all winter long. By the end, they were completely in rags. We were always hungry, always trying to find something to eat, but we kept our spirits up by fantasizing about England. In our minds, England was a magical place ..."

"How many of you were there?"

"Just my brother and me. My parents stayed behind ..."

"Did you have any documents?"

"We didn't have a thing, but we were completely convinced that we would get to England in the end."

"How *did* you get there?"

"Someone gave us passes at the last minute and we got on a boat. It really was a miracle. Those first days in England were like a dream. I remember walking in Kew Gardens with my brother and feeling like we were in Paradise. There was an apple tree covered with white blossoms behind a little stone church. We sat under it for hours, and no one made us go away. But we were completely alone wherever we went. We had to figure everything out for ourselves."

"How did you get by?" Peter asks.

"We had almost no money, but we managed to get ourselves some clothes, and we acted nonchalant, even a little arrogant, so that people wouldn't back away from us. If you had run into me then, you wouldn't have known how dirt poor I was. It's all a matter of how you carry yourself."

Hans Werner finally falls asleep and Peter studies his sleeping face, which looks like a death mask, pale and sharply defined. Underneath that mask is the face of a sensitive boy. Pain, hunger, and fear have hardened him without completely taking away his vulnerability.

Herr Taebricht stands before them with his hands clasped behind his back, looking more like a schoolmaster than a democratically elected House Father. "I want everyone's total attention," he calls out, glaring at Blum, who is sewing a button onto Grumbein's shirt.

"But we haven't even had breakfast," a voice is heard to complain.

"I think that you'll all be interested to know that Captain Barrass ..."

"Who's that?" Grumbein calls out.

"Don't interrupt!" says Blum. "Let him talk."

Captain Barrass," says Herr Taebricht, "is a member of the Intelligence Office. You really should know who these people are by now."

"So what about him?" comes a voice from the back.

"Captain Barrass recently met with the officials in Ottawa and brought up the problem of our status."

"It's about time," Reinhard remarks.

"But they didn't see it as a problem," Herr Taebricht goes on.

"What the hell does that mean?" says Reinhard indignantly.

"They told Captain Barrass that until they are told otherwise, we are German POWs," Taebricht says.

Groans and hisses can be heard throughout the hut. "We'll be stuck here forever!" Thomas cries.

"But one good thing came out of the meeting," Herr Taebricht goes on. "When Captain Barrass told them that many of us plan to refuse to use the POW letterhead, they were impressed. They said they would report that fact to London by telegram."

"What does all this crap mean?" Grumbein says.

"Watch your tongue," Blum reproaches him, without looking up from his sewing.

"It means that the Canadians feel that their hands are tied, but that if they were given half the chance, they would get rid of us," Reinhard puts in.

That night, as they are entering the cafeteria, they see four cardboard boxes on a table just inside the door. One of the boxes has been torn open; inside it are blank postcards with official stamps. "We should just throw them into the garbage," one man says, but instead they eat their dinner and leave the boxes sitting there. At last someone goes to the door and comes back with a few of the cards, which he passes around. On one side, the cards say PRISONER OF WAR MAIL FREE; on the side is a blank for the sender's name, followed by the words NO RANK CAMP L. Some peer at the cards for a moment or two; others give them a cursory glance and push them away.

"What will we do?" the conversation goes.

"What *can* we do? They have us over a barrel."

"Let's wait to see what comes of the telegram."

"If there really *is* a telegram."

Back in his bunk, Peter is too tired to read, and yet it's not even eight o'clock. He takes out his journal, but he has nothing to say. "What's wrong with me?" he thinks to himself, wishing he could throw off this awful feeling of inertia. He imagines writing a letter to Anna Freud and telling her *I am suffering from a general malaise.* No doubt she would tell him that there is no such thing, he thinks angrily, but she would be wrong.

As a kind of experiment, he draws up a chart that will enable him to keep a record of the emotional state of the men in his hut and to determine whether his own emotions are completely tied to it. He isolates the arrival of the cards as the cause of a downward spiral that has dragged his spirits down as well. But the next day, when Herr Taebricht releases another bit of news – namely, that Captain Barrass has reported that every man in the camp will soon have an opportunity to work – there is enough excitement in the hut to warrant an upward squiggle on the chart. But this time his own feelings run counter to the general reaction.

"Why do you all romanticize physical labor?" he asks, even though he knows the answer in advance. Physical labor is wholesome, invigorating, meaningful, everyone says. No one seems to realize that what's really in store for them is mindless, stingily parceled-out work overseen by soldiers with bayonets and a system that promotes mediocrity.

"Do you really want to sit over your books all day?" Reinhard says. "Wouldn't it make you feel better to go out and split logs?"

"You can't be serious," Peter says.

"Decadent Jew!" Vicki laughs.

"You sound like a Nazi," Weiss intervenes.

"But I'm not, and that's the difference," Vicki says. "As a Jew, I can take liberties."

Peter continues to chart the emotions of the hut, noting that the mood goes up when Herr Taebricht tells them that the Home Office is being cross-examined regarding their internment. But as the conversation regarding their POW status goes on and on, he starts getting fed up with it. Everyone seems so childish and naïve! Don't they see that the decision ultimately lies with London, and that it doesn't matter what they want because they are in the grips of a machine that is indifferent to them? He remembers the dream he had as a boy, and he has the strange feeling that it was preparing him for the moment that he finds himself in now.

On July 31, Herr Taebricht calls them together and reads them the latest statement from the Home Office: "*Alien internees whose status can be properly authorized should be sent back to England.*"

"Can you repeat that?" someone cries.

"I can't believe my ears!" someone else exclaims. And then everyone breaks into cheering and applause.

"England probably wants to make use of specialized people who could help them with the war effort," Reinhard says. "Or maybe the Canadians are taking a stand," Hans Werner shrugs. "They're probably quite eager to get rid of us."

There is a huge shift in the collective mood. Suddenly people are asking themselves what they really want. Would it be better to stay put in Canada as civilian refugees or to go back to England where they could be reunited with their families? After the sinking of the *Arandora Star*, the prospect of a journey by sea is frightening. But one thing is certain: everyone has suddenly emerged from a period of despair – and that "everyone" includes him.

A formal statement is drafted to the effect that the majority of prisoners have decided to reject the POW letterhead. Spirits reach their highest peak: when they get back from dinner, the men are as rowdy as drunks out on the town.

A new soldier comes in before curfew and turns out the lights, threatening to lock them in until the next day if they don't quiet down. Two or three of the men are so infuriated that they lock the door from the inside. Discovering that the door has been latched, the soldier rips it open, marches up and down the aisles, and shines his flashlight into every corner. "Whoever messed with that door is going to pay for it," he says. "What an idiot!" Peter's bunkmate snorts. "He's the one who kicked the door in."

The festive mood that prevailed in the hut evaporates; the invasion of one soldier was enough to bring them down. Peter makes one more squiggle in his chart, and then he abandons it.

One hot, muggy day after another: boredom, irritation, lethargy. White glaring sky above a river of lead: fights erupting over nothing.

Hans Werner and his brother decide to stage a night of classical music, theater, and poetry. "We have to do something," Hans Werner says to Peter as they're doing kitchen duty. "We can't let ourselves sink to the level of animals."

"Who's going to provide the entertainment?"

"How about this: we take care of the literary side and you supply the music."

"But the camp is full of musicians," Peter says.

"If we wanted them, we'd ask them. We want *you*." He's terribly flattered that Hans Werner and his brother have chosen him but he's also afraid of what the camp critics will say about his playing. For the next few days, he practices feverishly.

On August 7, they take over the Recreation Hut, doing everything they can to transform it into a concert hall. For curtains, they hang blankets from ropes; for stage lights, they put candles in jars; for atmosphere, they stick dandelions into cans and scatter them around the room. One of the windows is missing a pane; they cover it up with a piece of cardboard that bears the words "The Serious Hour." High culture will be offered here, instead of the poker, ping pong, and jazz that so many of the men are addicted to. But when the ping-pong players get wind of what's going on, they drag their table back to its usual place in the left corner of what is now "the stage. " After a failed negotiation, Hans Werner and his brother call in Thomas to help them move the piano farther to the right. He lifts the upright off the floor and carries it across the stage, leaving them gaping in astonishment.

As the word spreads, there are unusual doings in the camp. Weiss finds a brush and vigorously cleans his jacket. Lasskey digs out some cologne and douses himself with it. The tailors in the camp are busy sewing strips of dark cloth over the red stripes that go down the leg of their denim uniforms. A little bottle of oil donated by the cook is passed between several men, who can be seen slicking back their hair with forks.

Everyone gulps down their dinner even faster than usual, but even the fastest eaters discover that they have to stand in line. At last the door opens and there is a stampede. Within a few minutes, all the chairs are taken. Several officers walk in after everyone else, robbing a number of internees of their front-row seats, but it's worth it because three of the officers bring their girls, causing intense excitement in the second and third rows.

Lingen now enters, fashionably late, looking more aristocratic than ever. A chair is found for him in the front but he turns it down, standing in the back with the internees who just lost their seats to the officers. "Now that's quality," Hans Werner remarks to Peter, Reinhard, and his brother, who are watching the audience through rips and cigarette holes in the curtains. Ordinarily Peter would mock Hans Werner for worshipping the count, but today he nods absentmindedly, preoccupied with his performance.

At last, they pull back the blankets and he sits down at the piano and begins to play the Bach Prelude. But people still seem to be drifting in. Why are they coming so late? He started too soon! At last, the doors stop banging, but now the jazz people are scraping their chairs and the classical people are trying to silence them. The instant he is finished, one of the jazz players runs up and plays a wild, dissonant piece that knocks the lingering notes of his performance out of the air.

A one-act play by an internee comes next, with the good-natured Reinhard cast as a prodigal son, and Pollack, the pleasure-loving Viennese who is always boasting about his successes with women, cast as the stern father who has kicked him out. Both of them overact their parts outrageously, shouting out their lines. During a dramatic pause in the battle between father and son, the tapping of ping-pong balls is heard, drawing everyone's eyes to the left corner of the stage.

"Hey, have some respect!" Thomas yells, starting to get out of his seat.

"Since when do you own this space?" the ping-pong players shout.

Hans Werner's brother rushes over to Thomas and whispers something in his ear. Thomas slumps back into his chair and the game goes on as before.

When the play is over and the ping-pong game has stopped, Hans Werner steps forward, grave and dignified. He proceeds to read several poems in a subdued, monotone voice that is designed to focus his listeners on what he refers to as "the Poetic Word."

216

"Speak up! We can't hear you!" the audience cries. Hans Werner turns bright red but goes on doggedly. More scraping of chairs; loud, exaggerated yawns. "Bravo!" Lingen cries out when he's done, but not even the applause of the count cheers Hans Werner up. He is so disgusted by the crassness of the crowd that he swears he won't make any more appearances for the rest of the night.

"You're not going to be my page turner for the Beethoven?" Peter says in a panic.

"Get Reinhard to do it. I refuse to go out there again."

Reinhard turns the pages so awkwardly that his arm constantly blocks out the music. Peter compensates by playing as wildly as he can, summoning up whole phrases from memory. But when he comes to the middle of the piece and discovers that two pages of the music have disappeared, he breaks into a cold sweat. Where have those damned pages gone? There they are, lying on the floor! He reaches down with a fury and puts the missing sheets back on the stand. Nothing can defeat him now! As he strikes the last note, he hears thunderous applause, and he turns to face his audience. But suddenly there is a commotion at the door, and then Zahn, a bald-headed madman who resembles a mole, runs down the aisle and jumps onto the stage.

"The Germans are bombing London!" he cries at the top of his lungs. He is trembling from head to toe, and his round brown eyes are ringed with fear.

His friend Kleinmeier appears at the foot of the stage. "Get down from here Zahn. You're making a fool of yourself!" Kleinmeier's irritation makes people laugh. But then there is a round of cheering from the Aryan side.

"Germany rules!" the Nazis shout.

A commanding officer steps onto the stage and Peter quickly steps down. "This performance is officially over. Everyone get back to your huts."

"Why are they shutting us down?" Hans Werner says.

"It's true then!" Reinhard exclaims.

"What are you talking about?" Hans Werner says.

"What Zahn said. It wasn't just craziness ..."

"Of course it's true," someone says in a familiar voice. It's tall, blond Franz, from the immunization line.

"How do you know?" Peter asks.

"Because a nice young officer leaked the information to us."

"But my parents are in London!" Reinhard wails.

"Pull yourself together," Hans Werner says, gripping Reinhard's hand. A crush of men is pouring out the door, and they are being swept along.

"Did anyone remember to put out the candles in the Recreation Hut?" Hans Werner's brother suddenly exclaims.

"I'll do it," says Peter. "The three of you go ahead." Pushing against the crowd, he goes back into the Recreation Hut, where he finds that someone has already put the candles out and that the blankets have fallen off of their ropes. He stands in the middle of the empty hall and tries to summon back the exultation he felt at the sound of the applause. But what did it matter, this little performance of his, when entire cities are going up in flames? How foolish he was to take it so seriously. He shakes his head and starts folding up the chairs.

This is the kind of moment that he remembers when he looks back on this time, a time that seemed as though it would never end. If anyone had told him how soon everything would change, he wouldn't have believed them.

Hans Werner is in such a rotten mood that it's hard to be around him. "You're not yourself," Peter remarks as they're peeling potatoes for dinner. "What's gotten into you?"

"Am I really the only one who understands what's going on?" Hans Werner breaks out. "Our entire world is falling apart!"

"But we're lucky ..."

"I'm sick to death of hearing that! Why should we be grateful for anything that's going on? We've surrendered everything and it hasn't done us any good. We're trapped and helpless even now. Have you ever stopped to think of what will happen to us if England is defeated? We'll be sent back to Europe to be killed off along with everyone else. Oh, but wait ... there will probably be some 'lucky ones' who will be packed off to the far ends of the earth and given the chance to set up wretched little communities, cut off from everything that ever mattered to them."

"You're hysterical," Peter says. "You have to get a grip on yourself."

"It's my own fault. I actually thought there was hope. But every miserable shred of news we get shows me how deluded I was."

When the potatoes have been peeled, Peter stands up, but Hans Werner doesn't move, closing his eyes and leaning back in his chair. He reminds Peter of Inge when she was drunk, sprawled out on the couch and railing against the world.

He makes his way back to the hut, but it feels claustrophobic to him there. He goes outside and walks around aimlessly, finally sitting on a crate by the cafeteria door. A line of brown ants is moving across a bare spot in the grass. Several of them are pushing what look like tiny crumbs; they must be heading for some storage place. He remembers the ant mounds that he used to come upon in the forests around Grundlsee, but those ants were different: their bodies were red and brownish black.

A shadow falls across the ground. He looks up and sees Franz looking down at him.

"Studying nature?" Franz says with a smile.

"Just trying to clear my head."

"People are still talking about your playing at the 'Serious Hour.'"

"That wasn't my best performance."

"A real artist – never satisfied! But why don't we hear you practicing anymore?"

"I haven't been able to concentrate."

"But as a musician, you need to keep perfecting your technique ..."

"Maybe I'm not a musician," Peter snaps. "Maybe I'm just a dilettante."

"I seem to have touched a nerve," Franz laughs. "Are we having a little crisis of confidence?"

"I just want to get out of here," Peter says. "I'm sick to death of this place."

As they are talking, an Orthodox Jew walks by, so absorbed in prayer that he doesn't seem to notice them. "Maybe you should take a lesson from him," Franz says.

"You're annoying me," Peter remarks, getting up and starting to walk away.

"Listen to me," Franz says, grabbing him by the sleeve. "I like you, even though you're a Jew, and I can tell that you're in trouble, because I've been watching you. What you need is someone to set you straight. You don't have the vaguest idea of who or what you are."

"What are you talking about?" Peter says.

"Here," Franz tells him, crouching down. "I'll explain it to you. You see these ants? The reason they're alive is that they're part of a community.

Each one of them has a specific job, and if they get attacked, they know how to protect themselves. You see this? This is their ant mound, their equivalent of our hut." He takes a wooden match out of his pocket and points at a little pile of sand. Then he rubs the match against a flint until it bursts into flame and sticks it into the center of the mound. Several ants rush up to the match and are immediately destroyed. He lets the match burn out, then lights another one. A few more ants circle the match without getting too close. Before it's burned down, it goes out. "Did you see that?" Franz says, turning toward him, so that he becomes aware of the z-shaped scar above his upper lip.

"That second match must have been damp," Peter remarks.

"Ah, but you're wrong. It was perfectly dry. The reason the flame went out is that they put it out with a special fluid they have in their abdomens."

"I don't believe that for a minute."

"Go ask Schaefer, the biologist. He's the one who showed this to me. What amazes me is that we're exactly the same as these ants. Each of us belongs to a larger group, and each of us has to learn our appointed task."

"And what is your task?"

"What do you think?" Franz says, straightening up. "I'm a German. I fight for the Fatherland …"

"And my job?"

"Your job is to be a Jew, and to accept it, like your friend over there. You'll never be an Austrian, let alone a German, like me, no matter how much Beethoven or Mozart you play."

At that moment, Weiss runs up to them with a terrified expression on his face. "Have you heard the news? More bombings in London … England is going through a massive attack!"

Peter suddenly feels sick to his stomach. "Go fuck yourself," he says to Franz, turning on his heel and quickly walking away.

One afternoon, a limousine pulls up to the gate and a man in a uniform gets out. His back is bent and he walks with a cane, but there is a sense of purpose in his wobbling gait.

"Who's that guy?" Thomas asks. "He looks like he's 100 years old."

"His name is Lord Marley and he has ties with the people in Ottawa," says the head of the Refugee Committee.

"God help us," Thomas remarks.

Lord Marley taps a bit of mud off of the toe of his boot and proceeds to enter through the gate. His skin has the texture of parchment paper and his legs are as thin as sticks. He stops in front of a poster that bears the words REFUGEE COMMITTEE, staring at it incredulously. "What's this?" he rasps. "No posters in a military camp. This is a military camp, is it not?"

The head of the Refugee Committee steps forward to introduce himself, but Lord Marley ignores his outstretched hand. "As the appointed head of the Refugee Committee, I'd welcome the opportunity to speak with you ..."

"I don't have much time," says Lord Marley, "so make it quick."

"As I'm sure you're aware, most of us here are Jewish refugees. And yet we've been forced to share our quarters with supporters of the Nazi regime."

"I'll bear that in mind," Lord Marley says, "but I'm here to inspect this camp, and so far I don't like what I see."

As he says these words, he flicks away some cigarette butts that are lying on the path and whacks at a clump of weeds. Everywhere he goes, he finds a target for his cane, frowning and shaking his head. "This isn't acceptable, not acceptable at all," he says to the head of the Refugee Committee, who is tagging along at his side, and to the group of men who are trailing after them. "I can already tell from the grounds that things are sub-standard here. You must hoe your corner, if you follow me. Look at this wreck of a shed. Letting things go like this is very bad for morale."

He makes a thorough inspection of both of the sheds, making more comments here and there.

"What's that you're reading?" he says to Peter when he comes to his bunk. "*Human-All-Too-Human*? What kind of nonsense is that? You'd do better to read a fitness manual."

No one succeeds in catching Lord Marley's ear; anyone who tries to ask a question is brushed aside. But in the middle of his visit, Count Lingen appears and introduces himself. Lord Marley looks him up and down, taking in his aristocratic profile and his Wellington boots. Without saying a word, he takes him by the arm and the two of them enter into a conversation that doesn't include anyone else. As Lord Marley is leaving, Count Lingen is heard to say, "... but the men here are very enterprising, you know. They've set up what they call the Popular University ..."

"Too much brainwork!" Lord Marley says, tapping his head. "Let them weed, let them clean, let them plant. Look at this view of the St. Lawrence River. Magnificent! With a little work, this place could be a paradise."

Lord Marley's remarks are repeated over and over, to the accompaniment of bitter laughter, but a week later all the Nazis are moved to Hut 14. The change takes place in less than an hour – a quick gathering up of possessions and they are gone.

"Now they can sing their horrible songs to their heart's content," Vicki says, dealing out cards on one of the vacated beds. "And we can breathe a little more freely," Hans Werner's brother says, picking up his hand. "Let's hope that this is only the beginning," Reinhard remarks. "The ultimate goal is to get them out of the camp."

"Correction," puts in Peter, who isn't taking part in the game. "The goal is for us to get out of here altogether."

On August 16, they take their first real walk, an outing that includes the entire hut. Only one man, who has a bad ankle, stays behind, after going around and asking everyone whether he should risk it or not. It's a good thing that he decides not to come because as soon as they're outside the gate, they start moving more quickly than they've moved for weeks, practically trotting across the wide expanse of open land known as the Plains of Abraham.

"This is like a dream!" Peter says.

"A good one for a change," Reinhard pants.

"Get in line or you're going back," the guards shout. "This is a walk, not a free-for-all."

They take in the world with hungry eyes, absorbing villas, gardens, beggars, cars. They see a man in a white linen suit who looks like a movie star and a woman with a peacock feather in her hat who is sauntering up and down the street and twirling a tasseled purse. Standing on a street corner is a group of teenage girls: some stare at them boldly, while others look away. They spend the next few blocks arguing over which one was the prettiest, the leggy blonde or the little brunette. They pass a little cafe where a man is reading his newspaper with a bored expression on his face. A woman sits down next to him, and he takes her wrist and says something that makes her throw her head back and laugh.

They come to a bus stop and someone is pulled out of line by a weathered-looking soldier with gray hair. It's little Grünwald, with his protruding ears and his odd way of walking with his toes pointed out.

"What's with Grünwald?" Peter asks.

"He's being taken to the dentist's," Reinhard says. "His tooth has been bothering him for the past week."

Peter looks back over his shoulder and sees Grünwald standing on the curb, a small uncertain figure next to the impassive soldier.

They eventually come to the old part of the city, with its cobblestones, narrow streets, bright awnings, flowerboxes, and carved shop signs. "I feel as though I'm back in Europe," Reinhard exclaims. "Is that what you want?" Hans Werner remarks. "To go back to what no longer exists?" "Just enjoy yourself for once," Reinhard replies.

It's nearly 6:00 when they finally get back, just in time for dinner. They see the gray-haired soldier smoking a cigarette outside the officers' quarters, but they don't see Grünwald anywhere. "What happened to Grünwald?" Peter asks the Housefather as he sits down at the table.

"Didn't you hear? He's still down in the city somewhere."

"Little Grünwald ran away?" Peter asks in surprise.

"No, he and his escort got separated in the crowd, and now no one knows where he is."

They all start talking about what they would do if they were free to roam the city until someone points out that they wouldn't have any money. "I'd land a job by the next day," a tailor says. And now they all start talking about how they would keep afloat.

It's nearly 9:00 when Grünwald finally reappears, his cheek bulging with cotton wadding and a brown paper bag tucked under his arm.

"Where did you go?" everyone says, crowding around him.

"I don't even know," Grünwald says. "I was completely lost ..."

"You could have bolted for it," Thomas says.

"Where would I have gone?"

"You could have made friends, eventually found a job."

"What makes you think that anybody would take in a runaway Jew?"

"So how did you get back?" Peter asks.

"It wasn't easy. I asked all kinds of people, and when I finally made it back here, I had trouble at the gate."

"What kind of trouble?" Hans Werner asks.

"The guard on duty said that he had never seen me before. They had to call someone out to testify for me."

They sit there in silence, picturing Grünwald waiting on the other side of the barbed wire and pleading to be let back in.

"What's in that bag you have?" Laskey finally asks hopefully.

"Just some extra cotton wadding for my cheek."

"Grünwald, you're an idiot," Thomas says.

At dinner, Lingen stands up and taps his spoon against his cup. "I'm sorry to be the bearer of bad news," he says, "but we've just heard from a reliable source that 2500 German planes are flying over England."

There is a moment of silence and then everyone goes back to their meals, gobbling down their food even more greedily than usual.

Half an hour later, they are back in the hut, where a quarrel between Thomas and Lampner, a professional soccer player, turns into a physical fight. Thomas soon has Lampner pinned down on the floor, with a small crowd of men cheering him on and other men pushing up against them to see what's happening. Two soldiers squeeze into the narrow aisle between the bunks and drag Thomas and Lampner apart. Herr Taebricht stands on a chair and shouts, "I beg all of you to calm down. This kind of thing won't do at all. As I've told you many, many times, we must conduct ourselves like civilized human beings."

"That's a load of crap!" someone cries.

"If you're not a good boy, they'll call you a filthy Jew!" someone else shouts.

"Listen to me. All of you!" Herr Taebricht shouts. "It's very simple. If you don't behave, your privileges will be taken away."

"Behave yourselves!" someone echoes him.

"Children, behave!" another voice shouts.

"Stop that at once!" Herr Taebricht cries. But the echoes keep coming long after he's stepped down from the chair, and as soon as the lights go out, more sounds are added, animal sounds – asses, goats, sheep, wolves, bees – in raucous defiance of the Housefather. The sounds grow louder and louder, drowning everything out. Then there are thumps and the sound of running through the aisles. "Behave yourselves, behave yourselves!" comes the refrain, followed by laughter, commands, cries of pleasure.

Is this really happening, Peter thinks, lying on his bed, *or is this all part of some perverted dream? All of them know that this war is also theirs; all of them know that everything is at stake. Have they forgotten that their friends and relatives are "over there," and that if England falls, these irreplaceable connections will be broken forever? People are dying for them across the sea, and all they can do is hold this insane orgy!*

"Don't you understand?" he cries out at last. "This is about all of us."

"Don't you understand?" someone repeats in a hoarse, trembling voice. Pressing his face into his pillow, Peter mutters furiously, "They deserve to suffocate in this camp. They deserve to wallow in the dirt." And then the tears come in a flood that he can't hold back. He is afraid for his parents, afraid of the war, afraid of dying, afraid of living in a foreign land, afraid of the loneliness that he is just beginning to discover in himself.

On August 21 they receive a questionnaire that has been issued by a governmental office in England. "Have you any special reason why you should be released?" the form reads.

"What an idiotic question," Peter exclaims.

"But if you answer correctly, they'll set you free – whatever that means at this point," Vicki remarks.

Next they receive word that it has been determined that all B and C cases are going to be reviewed with the aim of releasing certain individuals and sending them back to England. Speculations fly around the camp.

"We refugees will all be going back."

"Perfect. Just when the bombs are being dropped."

"Would you rather stay here?"

"Of course not. My family is there."

Peter lies on his bunk and listens to everyone talk.

"What do *you* think?" his bunkmate calls up to him.

"That we don't belong anywhere," Peter shrugs.

A few days later, they learn that all Category C internees will be released. Despite all their worries, they are extremely excited, fantasizing about what they will do in England.

"Isn't all this premature?" Hans Werner asks.

"On the contrary, we have to think about this," his brother says. "It's not only possible, it's more and more likely …"

Reinhard tries very hard to be restrained. "It won't come for a long time. It could take as long as six weeks …"

"Where do you get six weeks from?" Hans Werner's brother asks. "The undersecretary has come out and said that we aren't German POWs. Do you know what that means? We've finally been cleared. He has publicly acknowledged that we are refugees from Nazi oppression."

Peter reacts to the good news defensively, writing in his journal, "*Beware of stupid optimism.* So far nothing – *nothing* – concrete has happened." And yet he can feel, he can taste, the return of hope. "It bubbles in the youth like the carbon dioxide in champagne," he writes, "or like what is known in America as 'soda pop.'"

In the midst of all this excitement, Hans Werner retreats to his bunk and barely talks to anyone. Peter tries to make eye contact with him at lunch, but he keeps his head down and eats mechanically. Toward the end of the day, Peter finds Hans Werner standing outside, looking over the shoulder of an engineer by the name of Salk, who is sketching the view on four pieces of POW letterhead.

"Where have you been hiding yourself?" Peter says to Hans Werner.

"I can't stand all of this mindless talk."

"Everyone is just excited," Peter says.

"That's because they can't see the hole that's opening under their feet."

They watch as Salk makes a series of notched lines to indicate where the landscape runs up against the barbed wire. After that he makes a half-circle in the center of the page and then fills in the cliff.

"What are you afraid of?" Peter asks at last.

"Emigration!" Hans Werner explodes. "Have they all really forgotten how wretched it is? You go to an office. You sit in a room. After seven hours, someone finally comes out and says, 'Go away and don't come back again.' A man who has a family and who has to go out begging to put food in their mouths is thrown a handful of shillings and told that he should be grateful for it."

"I'm trying to work here," Salk complains. "Can't you talk somewhere else?"

Hans Werner turns away and goes on in a lowered voice. "And then you have to go back to that same office and say that you haven't found work and submit to being scolded again. After months of this, you develop sicknesses and twitches and ticks and you become just as alien to

226

others as the world is alien to you."

Salk adds a second half-circle to create the bend of the river and a small vertical line to indicate the church. Hans Werner stares at the drawing and shakes his head. "No, you can't understand it, you've led a sheltered life. You don't know what it means to be thrown from one shelter to another, hungry, freezing, desperate to attach yourself somewhere. And when a person is sensitive, more sensitive than most, so that life would never have been easy for him, even under the best of circumstances – if someone sensitive is forced to go through this, it's likely that he will never feel at home in the world."

From out of nowhere, Kleinmeier runs up to him and peers into his face anxiously. Hans Werner ignores him, then pushes him away. "Get out of my way! I need to be alone, or as alone as I can be in this damned place."

By nighttime, he seems like himself again, but now he has a throbbing toothache.

On September 20, without fanfare of any kind, 32 people are taken away. Everyone in Hut 14 disappears. "The Nazis are gone!" everyone exclaims. "No more Jew-haters!" Kleinmeier cries. "Wouldn't that be a miracle," Hans Werner remarks.

After weeks of no mail, letters start coming in. Finally there is news, there is contact with the outside world. Markow, who is addicted to sweets, receives a love letter with a bit of chocolate from his new bride and now he can't stop talking about how much he wants to sleep with her. For the past few weeks, he's been miserable because he's losing his sight, but he could put up with it if she were here. Nothing would matter, not even living behind barbed wire, if he could just spend a night with her.

Poppert gets letters from various friends who tell him they still haven't heard anything from his parents. The last thing he knew, they were in France, but that was when he was in England, which feels like a lifetime ago. "Did you get mail?" he keeps asking everyone, as though he suspects that the letter he is waiting for has already arrived and has simply been delivered to the wrong man.

Reinhard finds out that his father has been sent to a labor camp and that his mother has decided to rent out the top floor of their house since she has no other way of bringing in money. "My poor mother," he says. "It should never have come to this."

"At least she still has a house," Peter points out.

"But we have rugs and pictures, some really lovely things. What will happen to it all when strangers start coming in?"

"I can't believe there is still someone in this world who cares about rugs and pictures," Peter exclaims.

Hans Werner gets a letter from his landlady that was sent two months ago but that has only come into his hands today. She reports that her little Paddy dog had a terrible chase of pneumonia, but that the little scamp has survived.

Everyone gets letters, except for Peter, and every letter is a little Pandora's Box. He watches them come out of the post office clutching their envelopes; he sees them open them with shaking hands. After they've read and reread every word, they stand there looking stirred up and lost. For some, the news is good; for others, it's bad. But after they get their long-anticipated mail, all of them are even more frustrated than before. Maybe it's just as well that no one has bothered to write to him.

On September 5, 1940, his world turns upside down. Three letters come for him on the same day.

The first letter is from Erich and it's full of optimism. He is certain that England will prevail. He's still in Cambridge, where he continues to pursue his work. Peter can just picture him in his sunlit study. How he envies him!

The second letter that he opens is from Hans: he's in New York, trying to set up a new life. He says, "I worry about you constantly. I'm afraid that you're suffering." Reading his letter, Peter feels as though Hans is addressing him as someone who is immature and weak, and he wishes that he could see him face to face, so that he could see how he has changed. He isn't the boy who was so busy showing off that he nearly missed his train out of Austria. Apart from the fact that his meals are cooked for him, he's become completely self-reliant. He knows when to speak his mind and when to keep his mouth shut. Maybe most importantly, he no longer thinks that the world revolves around him, or that he can count on anything to come easily.

Hans writes that he's been in contact with the Burlinghams to see if they can get him a visa to study in the U.S.A. since one can't go there directly from Canada. Reading these lines, he is suddenly overcome with feeling for this difficult man. He describes him in his journal with a string of epithets: "ever a sustainer or a tyrant," "the boyishly nervous aging one," " the worthy in life and deed," "the all-too-intellectual," "the sniveling," "the raw," "the helpful," "the man full of buried tenderness, who is neither a businessman nor a poet" but "a man, a man …" And yet no matter how many phrases he finds for Hans, an uneasy question remains. If he were to see Hans tomorrow, would Hans acknowledge the changes in him, or would he still try to bend him to his will?

The third letter – he saves this one for last, almost afraid to open it – is from Tinky, written in her light, sloping hand. He can see her writing it – how many times has he watched her bend her face over a page, going back to when they were nine or was it ten years old? She's in New York too: in her letter she writes about visiting Coney Island, which she found to be "dreadfully coarse." Why does she bother to tell all this to him? Doesn't she have any idea of where *he* is? What would she say to his big-bellied bunkmate, who is snoring under him, or about Laskey over there, using a matchstick to clean the wax out of his ears?

"It must be strange to hear from me," she writes. Strange! It catapults him out of his world without providing any escape. "It would be wonderful to hear from you. Even if you hate me, please write." What is he to make of this? Is she so indifferent to him that she can strike this carelessly confessional tone, or does she actually have feelings for him? For the next few days, he is boiling with a mixture of desire, rage, despair, and hope. He takes every line of her letter and picks it apart, dramatizing his reactions in pages of writing that are at once confessions and literary exercises performed in front of an imaginary audience. Once he has taken the letter completely apart, he writes back to her, adopting a tone that is cool, affectionate, dispassionate. The point is to be manly without closing any doors.

After he has finally answered Tinky and put her letter away, he thinks about the one letter that he didn't receive. Where is Mem? What has become of her? Now more than ever, her silence frightens him.

At the end of September, they are ordered to fill out a registration form that involves checking off one of three categories:

1. Orthodox Jew
2. Regular Jew
3. Half-Aryan.

Some of them complain as they fill out the forms, saying they feel as though they are back in Nazi Germany. Others fill out the form and then become angry after they've handed it in. The majority simply fill out the forms without thinking about them.

After all the forms have been turned in, it comes out that all of the Aryans are being sent to a certain Camp A, where other Aryans will be waiting for them. The rest of them will go to a Camp N, which has just been completed, whatever that means.

"We were told that the questionnaire was just a formality," the cry goes up. "Now it turns out that it's going to decide our fates."

Letters of protest are quickly written up by every one of the camp's many organizations. For once all of the groups – the political refugees, the rabbis, the Popular University, the camp fathers – are in complete agreement. They will accept only one principle of separation: Nazi vs. Anti-Nazi. A division based on race is unacceptable.

The non-Jewish refugees who left Germany on moral grounds are particularly upset. Why should they be thrown in with their mortal enemies? But their protests stir up resentment in other quarters – if they suddenly change sides, everything will go smoothly for them, and who's to say that they won't adapt? This sentiment is met with bitter reproach – after all, the political refugees put their lives at risk in the name of their convictions. How can one speak of their situation so cynically? Some even go so far as to say that they prefer the political refugees to the Jews who have become so pro-Jewish that they have lost all sense of principle. Still, despite the increasing infighting and squabbling, there is consensus on one point. The great majority will accept only one criterion of separation: Nazi vs. Anti-Nazi.

The Director of Operations in Ottawa wants another list: occupations, Jewish and Gentile. They are unified in refusing to specify race, saying they will provide only the list of occupations. A letter is sent to Ottawa, signed by Lingen as Camp Supervisor, and Abrahamson, as head of the Refugee Committee:

"This camp consists of 89 per cent refugees from Nazi Oppression," the letter points out. "We, as the representatives of these refugees, have urged again and again since our arrival here for a separation from the minority in this camp who support or tolerate the Nazi Regime. We should like to take this opportunity of repeating this request. But at the same time we would like to express our most earnest wish that the majority of the refugees should not be torn apart. They have now lived together in internment for several months and would consider separation from their friends a severe hardship.

Above all, however, we should like to protest with all emphasis against a separation based on racial grounds. It is true that the majority among the refugees are Jews. But by no means all. Many of the others are persons who, though no longer of Jewish faith, are Jewish or partially Jewish by descent and had to leave Germany because of racial persecution. What is still more important, many others are refugees from Nazi Germany on political grounds. They are men who had to leave Nazi Germany ... because of their belief in principles for which this war is being fought ... It would be intolerable if these political refugees were now transferred to camps containing Nazi prisoners and were forced to live with their Nazi opponents. Both racial and political refugees have in common the enmity against Nazism and the loyalty to the British cause."

Ottawa continues to hold its ground, and the internees refuse to cooperate, doing everything they can to baffle any attempts to separate them along racial lines.

In preparation for departure, two piles of luggage begin to form, one for Camp A, the other for Camp N. Although the presence of these two separate piles seems ominous, the truth is that they are a jumble of the belongings of Aryans and Jews.

On the night before their departure, they hear shouting outside. There are soldiers in the alleys and they have their flashlights on. A few seconds later, the hut is bathed in an eerie glow. "They've turned on the floodlights," someone says. "What the hell is going on?"

"Has anyone here seen Lampner?" a soldier demands, throwing open their door.

"No!"

"He isn't here."

"I haven't seen Lampner all day."

After a thorough search – where should he be? Hiding under their beds? – the soldier goes away, but two hours later, he's back again. "If you know anything about Lampner, you'd better come forward," he says to them. "Holding back information will result in punishment."

Evidently Lampner, a superb soccer player who was bound for the "A" camp, has disappeared. After the soldier goes away, conversations flare up in the dark. "This will make trouble for all of us," Reinhard says. "The timing couldn't be worse. This was very selfish of him."

"I think he's bulletproof," Kleinmeier says with a crazy grin. "I hope he makes it to America."

"He's really done it," Thomas the wrestler says. "We used to talk about escaping together when we first got here, but in the end it just seemed like a fantasy."

"He can barely speak English," a friend of his points out. "How is he going to make his way? He'll have nowhere to turn."

"He's a political refugee," someone else remarks. "He couldn't stand the thought of spending who knows how long with a bunch of Nazi sympathizers."

Peter pictures Lampner, lithe and lean, with a long, narrow face that resembles a grayhound's, loping across the Plains of Abraham.

A soldier stands at their window and shouts, "You can all go back to sleep. He's been found. He jumped from the roof of the refugee committee hut."

"Is he badly hurt?" Thomas says. But the soldier has already moved on. Five minutes later, he comes back. "He's alright. He's going to jail."

"Thank God," Thomas says. "How long will he get?"

"I don't know – outside he would get two years, but for a POW it would be 28 days."

After the soldier leaves, there is more analysis. Someone comes up with the theory that Lampner probably chose this day because he thought they would skip roll call altogether since everyone was leaving that morning. As it turns out, his punishment is 28 days in jail. Whether he will be placed in Camp A with the Aryans or Camp N is anybody's guess.

14.

Camp N

Canada, 1941

THE train rattles along its tracks, carrying him deeper and deeper into the land. He doesn't have a ticket or a map or a schedule, only a journal for catching random impressions. The colors of the leaves are amazing to him: lemon-yellow, burgundy, acid-green, and now this meadow that looks so unbelievably soft that he wants to roll around in it like a dog. In the middle of the meadow is a tree that looks as though it's on fire, and under the tree is a velvety bed of moss. How he wishes that he could bring a woman there! He closes his eyes and conjures her up: her thighs, her lips, the smell of her hair …

"I say, do you have a cigarette?" someone shouts in his ear. It's Goldmann, the most British of the Cambridgers.

"Damn it, Goldmann. Can't you go bother someone else?"

"Sorry old man, but you owe me one."

"You're a pain in the ass."

Peter hands him a cigarette and takes one for himself. By way of thanks, Goldmann gives him a light with an absurdly stylized turn of his wrist. "What does the 'N' of Camp N stand for, do you think?" Goldmann drawls, gazing at his own reflection in the window of the train.

"Nothing. Nobody. Nowhere," Peter snaps.

"Aren't we in a cheery mood!" Goldmann remarks, strolling away in a veil of smoke.

Peter looks out the window again but the meadow is gone and the sun is buried in a mass of clouds. "Where the hell are we?" someone in the seat behind him says.

After what seems like an endless amount of time, the train slows down, rumbling along grass-covered tracks that lead into a gigantic shed with a corrugated metal roof. "Is this a station?" Peter asks the man next to him. For the past four hours, the man hasn't said a word, calmly staring out the window and picking at his teeth.

"Judging from the barbed wire over there, this is our stop ..."

"But there's nothing here."

"Didn't you see the watchtower as we were coming in?"

"I didn't notice ..."

"Looks like they threw it together in a rush."

"How can you tell something like that?"

"I used to be a carpenter."

They get off the train, stepping onto a cement floor that is covered with broken glass. Running through the middle of the floor is a gigantic trough filled with oily black water. Peter goes up to the edge to see how deep it is and sees a dead rat floating there.

"What's this ditch for?" he says to the carpenter, quickly stepping back.

"This must have been a repair shed at some point. They probably used it to fix the trains from below."

A pimple-faced soldier pokes at them with a leather-covered stick. "What are you two gawking at? Get into a group."

Peter gets separated from the carpenter, but he ends up in the same group as Reinhard and Hans Werner. The three of them huddle together, stamping their feet and slapping their arms. After another medical examination and another search, they stand in line to use the john.

"Only six latrines for 800 men," Reinhard remarks.

"Maybe they figure that Jews don't need privacy," Hans Werner remarks.

"If we did, we'd be shitting in our pants," says Rothstein, a butcher from Düsseldorf.

No beds, only metal tables, and not enough. Somehow they manage to find a table with some space left on it.

"Hey, this table is taken," says a bull-necked man with a missing tooth. "My friends and I like to stretch out."

"But there are only three of you," Reinhard says indignantly.

"That's right. Do you want to make something of it?"

The man's two friends are now sitting up and staring at Reinhard out of heavy-lidded, bloodshot eyes. One of them starts rolling up his sleeves and muttering something under his breath, but just in the nick of time,

Levy, their new self-appointed representative, jumps up on a table and claps his hands. "I know you're all hungry," he shouts, "so let me take the roll call so we can get some food."

"We don't want to eat their slop!" someone cries.

"We want out!" someone else chimes in.

"They told us there would be a camp here. This place is a dump!"

"There's only one way to show them where we stand. I say we mount a hunger strike!"

"To hell with all this crap. I want to eat," shouts the bull-necked man, but no one except for his two cronies listens to him.

"Not a crust of their bread!" goes up the cry. "They told us there was a camp here. That was a lie!"

The crowd becomes more and more heated up. Levy tries to reason with them, but his voice is drowned out. As the tension rises, Peter forgets how hungry he is, charged with the energy that is flying around the room.

A new intelligence officer appears before them. Strikingly handsome, he carries himself like a movie star. "I've come here to listen," he says to them in German, stroking his chin while one man after another starts speaking up.

"How can it be that we were locked up for five whole months only to end up in a place that isn't fit for animals?"

"We were promised that things were going to improve!"

"There are 800 of us here, and most of us are Jews. Whoever is in charge of this shithole can't use the POW excuse anymore!"

The intelligence officer listens sympathetically, turning his head in a way that offsets his impressive profile.

"That guy is from Cambridge!" Reinhard suddenly exclaims. "He was a student at King's College. He spent £5000 in a single year!"

"How did he end up here?" Peter asks.

"His papa must have bought him this post."

The Cambridgers come forward and greet the intelligence officer, who tells them that he is shocked to find such distinguished colleagues here.

"For Polish Jews, he thinks this place is good enough, but not for Cambridgers," Hans Werner remarks.

The intelligence officer listens to everyone for nearly an hour, but in the end he shows his hand. "If you don't get into line for roll call there will be no evening meal," he says, twisting his cherry-red lips into a frown.

"What a phony!" Peter says disgustedly to Hans Werner.

They put the idea of food out of their minds, hunting for boards and crates that can be used to make beds. Their tiredness and hunger make them feel drunk; they lie on their boards and talk deep into the night.

At last, everyone starts to fall sleep, but when he closes his eyes, Peter can feel the chill on his eyelids, nose, and cheeks. He rubs his palms together and places them over his eyes and mouth, breathing warm air into the palms of his hands, but now the backs of his hands start getting cold, so he thrusts them under his coat. He hears a voice saying, *You haven't lost your gloves. Nurse has tucked them into your pockets. Go ahead, put them on.* He bends down and scoops up a handful of snow. He can see every angle of every crystal in the bright cold air. He throws the snow into the air and watches it disappear into the glittering mound that has risen under his feet. He points his skis down the slope and pushes off, gliding across mammoth bodies of snow. He passes houses that are buried so deep in snow that they look like meringues topped with turrets of whipped cream. And then there are no more houses, only doors set into the sides of hills, with chimneys poking out of them. In front of one such cave-house, he sees a woman with a braid of jet-black hair and the broad cheekbones of an Eskimo. She's wearing a coat of white leather and fur, but her boots are black, with bright red tassels. A girl of 11 or 12 comes out of the door and the older woman lays a bright yellow cape around her shoulders. He recognizes the girl as Tinky right away, but he knows better than to call out her name.

The girl crouches down and goes flying down the hill. Are those skis she's wearing? Why isn't she using poles? Although she's moving over the ground, she's flying like a bird. He follows her down a slope of blue–gray ice, trying desperately to keep up with her. At one point, it looks as though he's heading straight for a chasm, but when he reaches the brink, he sees a series of glittering white hills stretching out before him all the way to the horizon. The slopes are covered with tracks, and the tracks form a series of letters, but he can't make out what they're saying. In the effort to read them, he loses sight of her, and he becomes frantic to find her again. But just when he's beginning to give up hope, he sees her all the way down in the hollow of a valley. How smart she looks in her yellow cape! She seems to be warming herself in front of a little fire.

He skis in her direction, but slopes keep getting in the way, stretching out the distance that divides him from her. He takes a wrong turn and finds himself speeding toward a gray mountain topped by a half-circle of jagged stone teeth. At the foot of the mountain lies a gaping chasm that goes all the way down to the center of the earth. He twists his body away with all his might and ends up on a cold stone floor. What is that board above his head? he wonders, rubbing his eyes. And this wooden box with the word "TOILET" stamped on it?

"She must have been quite something," someone says.

"What are you talking about?"

"You kept calling out somebody's name, and then you rolled off that board and fell flat on your face ..."

"I'm glad I provided some entertainment," he replies.

And now he's waiting for the toilet again, light-headed, hungry, tired. A sergeant major walks up and down the line, trying to recruit 100 men to help set up the camp. Some men turn their backs on the sergeant major; others stare at him expressionlessly. "We need workers!" the sergeant major shouts at the top of his lungs, doing a pantomime of digging, lifting, etc., as though he assumes they don't understand what he's saying.

"As you can see, we're busy," Goldmann quips.

"To hell with all of you!" the sergeant major says, his face turning bright red. "If you Jews want to live like pigs, go ahead."

At around 1:00, the Sergeant Major conveys an ultimatum from the Commandant. If the camp continues to refuse to cooperate, the commandant will lock the doors, turn off all heat and water, and send out a request to have them moved to the Nazi camp.

"Let it come to that!" everyone cries. Peter shakes his fist along with everyone else. A balding official with a sly, pudgy face pushes his way through the crowd and gets up onto a crate. "I want to speak with you man to man," he says. "I'm talking to you because I sympathize with you. I have a full understanding of your problems."

Right away, the men begin to jeer; he puts out his hands as though he's imploring them to stop. "I am a representative of the Montreal Refugee Committee," he goes on, "and I know Saul Hayes, your representative in the Jewish Congress, personally."

"Let's at least give him a hearing," Levy cries. "Saul Hayes is someone who could do something for us."

"We've heard that before," various people cry.

"Just listen to what he has to say and then decide."

"I'm here to tell you that you're making a big mistake," the official goes on. "If you continue on this course of action, it will be ruinous for you.

Let me explain something about Canada. This isn't a land of grand hotels. We have 30,000 newly enlisted soldiers, and we don't have anywhere to put all of them. The winters in these parts are long and cold, but right now it looks like many of our soldiers will be sleeping in tents. We aren't holding anything back from you. There are no other camps in Canada for you at this time. I wish things were different, but they're not, so let's try to make the best of what we have. If you give us your cooperation, we'll provide whatever materials are needed to make this camp habitable. Are you really going to let your sick and your old live in this filth? What about the spread of disease? I don't think any of you have really thought things through. The truth is that if you fail to cooperate, you'll not only hurt your own case, you'll deal a blow to the Jewish cause in Canada."

"But we've been cheated," various people say. "We were promised that our living conditions would improve …"

"And they will improve, I promise you, but only if you work with us."

After the lawyer leaves, there is intense debate, culminating in what they call the Three-day Compromise. Within this next three days, Saul Hayes must visit the camp; Ottawa must be informed and send a commission; the British intelligence officer must be informed. If these conditions aren't met in 72 hours, the strike will be resumed. In the meantime, they'll work hard to show that they're not lazy or irresponsible.

"Even in this dump, we have to prove ourselves," Peter remarks to Hans Werner.

"That's what it means to be a Jew," Hans Werner shrugs. "Haven't you figured that out by now?"

Thanks to the Three-day Compromise, they have their first meal: shining red apples, thick slices of bread with slabs of corned beef, butter, maple syrup, tea, milk.

"I'll bet you anything that those three were eating before the hunger strike ended," Reinhard remarks, nodding in the direction of the bull-necked man and his two cronies, who are shoveling down food at the next table. "What does it say about the Canadians when apes like that …"

"Let it go," Hans Werner interrupts.

Almost immediately, shipments begin to arrive: beds, toilets, kitchen sinks. Efforts are made to recruit as many men as possible for heavy work. The most ridiculous of these efforts is the speech delivered to them by an enormous man with a straggling moustache and drooping jowls who introduces himself as Major O'Donahoe. "Listen to me," he says in a heavy Scottish accent. "I'm here to tell you how things work. No monkey business, do you hear? You play ball with me and I'll play ball with you. If you don't play ball, bad things will happen to you. Now I'm not threatening you, understand? What I'm telling you are just the facts. Don't try any funny stuff with me. You know what I'm talking about!"

"What does he mean about 'funny stuff'?" Peter whispers to Hans Werner.

"I have a feeling he's drunk. He's just saying whatever comes into his head."

"We're going to treat you fair," Major O'Donahoe goes on. "This," he sweeps his hands to take in both sheds " is your new home. It's no palace, I admit, but let's be honest – it could be a hell of a lot worse."

"Maybe he's just stupid," Peter whispers to Hans Werner.

"That too," Hans Werner agrees.

"You're all Jews, aren't you?" Major O'Donahoe goes on. "Well, that doesn't mean that you don't have to keep clean. A little soap and water is all it takes. And after you've washed, behave yourselves and do as you're told and you'll get all kinds of privileges. Do you all want us to win the war? Of course you do, because you don't want to stay here in Canada, you want to go home. Well, if you want to go home, give us a hand. We need business managers, carpenters, woodcutters …"

Soon after Major O'Donahoe invites them to "play ball," army personnel appear in the camp and the building effort begins in earnest. A huge kitchen is installed; toilets are set up; bunk beds are assembled; showers are put in. By the end of two or three weeks, everyone agrees that Camp N is habitable. The Popular University is set up, and various clubs, initiatives, and organizations that began at Camp N start functioning again.

Life at Camp N starts to resemble life at Camp L, but for some reason it's harder for Peter to adapt. There is a work requirement here, but it's minimal: after spending a couple of hours "helping the war effort," he has more than enough time to read and write. Why is it so hard for him to concentrate? In Camp L, he spent hours lost in his own world, but here he finds it hard to sit still.

"You seem a little under the weather," Reinhard remarks while they're assembling crates.

"I can't stand it here. This place isn't for me."

"Do you think it's right for any of us?" Reinhard says incredulously.

"Of course not. That's not what I mean."

"Why don't you join an organization?" Reinhard says. "You could help me with the university ..."

"No, I can't," Peter says, suddenly distraught. "The problem is I'm struggling."

"What do you mean?"

"I don't know how to explain it, not even to myself. I want to say something on the page, and I search and search, but I can't find the right words ... And in the middle of this struggle, which takes all my strength, I want to say, 'What do I care about you people! I wish you all the best. I hope that all goes well with you. If you can't stand each other and have to beat each other up, or even kill each other, I'm sorry, but there's nothing I can do. Whatever happens, I have to go my own way. I'm searching for my whole life, and if I don't find it, I might as well be dead.'"

"But what about the people around you?" Reinhard asks.

"Until I find myself, they don't matter to me."

"You spend too much time in your own head," Reinhard says. "Maybe your great struggle would be resolved if you learned to care about someone other than yourself."

"You don't approve of me, do you?" Peter says, looking Reinhard straight in the eye.

"Does it even matter to you? The way you talk I wonder if you care about anyone."

"Maybe it does and maybe it doesn't," Peter says, picking up his hammer and driving in a nail. If only he could talk to Mem! He wishes that he could tell her how hard things are for him now. More than anyone else, she would understand.

He ends up on a work detail in the boiler room with Steinhart, a bow-legged plumber with squinting eyes, and Feinberg, an engineer with greasy black hair. Since he doesn't understand the first thing about what they're doing, they have him hold the lantern while they crouch on the floor and tinker with various pipes and dials.

"I can't wait to get out of here," Steinhart says, sitting back on his heels and wiping sweat off his face. "I know exactly what I'd do. I'd go to the movies and find a girl and take her to my place …"

"And what place would that be?" Feinberg laughs.

"Okay, her place then," Steinhart says, annoyed.

"The first thing that I'd do is get myself a good shave," Feinberg says, "and after that, I'd go out to a bar and order the best whiskey in the house."

"What if the bar doesn't serve Jews?" Feinberg says spitefully.

"Shine the light here," Steinhart says to Peter, ignoring Feinberg's attempt to get even with him. "No, not there. Right here. You see this section of the wall? It's only about one-and-a-half meters away from the barbed wire."

"I know what you're going to say next," Feinberg says.

"Don't act so superior! You think about it too."

"What are you two talking about?" Peter asks.

"That it wouldn't be all that hard to build a tunnel under this shed," Steinhart says.

"Is that really true?" Peter asks.

"Don't encourage him," Feinberg warns.

"Do you want to hear how it could be done or not?" Steinhart says.

"Here we go," Feinberg sighs. "This is all he ever talks about."

"We'd have to extend the ditch," Steinhart says, "which would take some time, since we could only work on it at night. After that was done, we'd have to start the tunnel …" He's suddenly become very serious. "Once we got through the tunnel, we'd have to get up the embankment without anybody seeing us in the watchtower, but we'd be safe once we made it to the tall grass."

They're all standing up now and Peter's still holding the lamp, which casts a bright glow over their faces. Feinberg is quiet as Steinhart talks, and then he suddenly jumps into the conversation. "After the grass there is a stream," Feinberg says. "If we waded through the stream, any dogs they sent after us would lose the scent. After that, we'd have to cross a fairly big street and make our way over the hills, preferably through the forest."

"How do you know all this?" Peter says.

"One of the soldiers told me. He was raised on a farm around here."

"How long would it take to get to the border?" Peter asks.

"Not all that long," Steinhart says. "We're only 28 miles away. We'd have to travel at night, of course. We'd need money and a map and some food to keep us going."

"I wouldn't want to try it in the dead of winter," Feinberg puts in.

"No, it would have to happen now or in the spring," Steinhart agrees.

"But by spring we might be out of here," Peter says.

"Don't hold your breath," Steinhart says.

They add detail after detail to the plan, growing more and more excited, as if they're setting out tomorrow. When they finally take leave of each other, they swear to keep this chat to themselves, like boys who have stumbled into a forbidden game. But this isn't a game that simply plays itself out, it's more like a seed that takes root in Peter's mind, growing a little more every day until he can barely think of anything else.

One afternoon – it's unusually warm and almost everyone has gone outside – he finds Hans Werner sitting cross-legged on his bunk and reading from his tattered copy of the *Duino Elegies*. His long, equine face is paler than ever, and the grey blanket that he has thrown over his shoulders makes him look like a monk. How still and silent he is, as though he is superior to everything around him. Seeing him like this, Peter is seized with an impulse to subvert his equanimity.

"Do you ever fantasize about running away?" he says to him.

"Not really," Hans Werner replies.

"Don't you want to get out of here?"

"Of course I do, but I'm not interested in doing anything stupid before I'm officially released."

"I wish I were as disciplined as you."

"It's not a matter of discipline. It's just that I know how hard things will be when we get out."

"You always come back to that," Peter says, "but there's really no way of knowing how things will be."

"Listen to me," Hans Werner cuts him off. "But really listen for a change. For most of your life, you've had everything handed to you. Once you get over that border and give your Papa a call, your charmed life will probably start all over again. But I don't have anything or anyone here, and I have no reason to believe that things will be easy for me. So for as long as I can, I intend to focus on my work – in fact, that's what I'd like to do now."

With this, Hans Werner returns to his book, but Peter won't let the matter drop.

"But what's the point of steeping yourself in German literature when you know as well as I do that our entire culture is being destroyed?"

"What would you prefer for me to do?" Hans Werner says angrily. "Read political tracts? I'm no more political than you."

"So poetry is your religion ..."

"No, it's more than that."

"What do you mean?"

"Religion tells us what we should be. Poetry shows us that we can only come to ourselves by constantly struggling to understand who or what we are."

"I see that you don't go in for dogma," Peter says. "but in your resistance to dogma, you're quite absolute ..."

"Don't resort to clever paradoxes," Hans Werner exclaims. "Have the courage to be tougher on yourself."

But the truth is that Peter agrees with Hans Werner, and over the next few months he makes an effort to be more like him, retreating into his writing for several hours a day. He writes essays, short stories, plays, but above all he writes poetry, secretly hoping to replace Hans Werner as the Poet of Camp N.

Time passes, measured out in small events that seem strangely cut off from the catastrophe that brought them here. Although they talk constantly about the war, there are moments when nothing that is said seems real to him. He has no idea of what has become of Mem, but he holds on fiercely to the belief that she is alive. (And he is right: not only is she alive, she is working on a film about a tormented woman who abandons her little boy in order to be with her lover.)

As soon as letters start coming through, he hears from Hans, who is trying to figure out how to get a U.S. visa for him. Hans is now convinced that the Burlingham–Tiffany connection is the best chance they have, and that they would be fools not to make use of it. Although he is still angry at Tinky for breaking off their relationship back in Liverpool, Peter knows that what Hans is saying is right. Hans gets in touch with Tinky and she writes to Peter, telling him she'll do anything she can to get him out. In fact, she'll gladly marry him if it means that he can come to the United States.

Tinky's letters are confusing to him. Is she bringing up marriage because she loves him or because she wants to secure his release? He writes letter after letter to her, only to tear them up. At last, he confesses that he is in love with her, but that he doesn't know if the woman he loves is real or based on the past. And as for the love that she has rediscovered in herself, what if she finds him so changed that she doesn't feel an affinity with him anymore? (The truth is that he feels tougher and more self-reliant now, and his hope is that this will make him more compelling to her.)

In a letter to Hans, he says he wishes that he and Tinky could have more time before leaping into a decision that will determine the course of their lives. If only he could get a visa to Mexico or Argentina and meet her there so that they could see if they could really get along. But in another letter he writes that he thinks their marriage will hold …

And then one spring afternoon, while he is weaving nets, a soldier comes and escorts him to the medical tent. But instead of the doctor, he sees a girl who is standing with her back to him. She is wearing a bright yellow jacket over a flowered skirt and her hands are thrust into her pockets. Her shoulders are narrow and slightly hunched, and her feet are placed stubbornly apart. Where has he seen that stance before?

The soldier directs him into the tent and the girl turns toward him. Could he be losing his mind? Or could it be that there is someone in the world who is an exact replica of Tinky? But before he has time to make sense of what he sees, she comes toward him and takes his hand. Her hand in his is cool and soft. It pains him that she has hands like this, since she's sure to take them away again. She says something to him and he says something in return but afterwards he can't remember what he said. She takes a step back and looks him up and down.

"I must look like a monster," he says, suddenly conscious of the fact that he is unshaven and unwashed.

"No, you look perfect. You look exactly like yourself."

"Even in this ridiculous uniform?" he laughs.

"It looks very sturdy," she says, touching his sleeve. "But why do they make you wear that red circle on your back?"

"So that they can shoot at me if I try to escape."

"How terrible!" she bursts out.

"You don't have to pity me," he says almost angrily.

"I don't," she says, lowering her voice. "I just want to get you out of here."

He turns away from her for a moment to slow things down. Everything is happening much too fast. His eyes fall on the top of the soldier's boots, which are visible below the flap of the tent.

"I believe he's trying to give us a little privacy," he says, turning back to her. She comes up very close to him and puts her arms around his neck. It's only when he closes his eyes and breathes in her scent that he really understands that she's here. He remembers that day in the snow in Breitenstein, when he wrote their initials in the snow, and then L for Love and H for Hate, and how he was burning with a fever that made him laugh and cry. And now Tinky, his Tinky, is in his arms, with her soft, boyish body and her gray–blue eyes. She's come all this way to see him, to help him get out, crossing distances that he knows nothing about. What a fool he would be to question her! The only answer is to hand himself over to her, to allow her and her family to rescue him.

EPILOGUE

It was a year before Peter was released from Camp N, a year that he later described as a "minor chapter in the history of the Holocaust." If his time in Camp N saved his life, it also taught him what it means to live in a foreign country without any rights. And then through the magic of American (Burlingham–Tiffany) connections and money, he was released. With the help of a Canadian sponsor found by Hans, he was granted permission to study at McGill University, where he earned a Licentiate of Music. (His transition to freedom, however, wasn't smooth: during his three years at McGill, he was required to report to the police once a month, and when he eventually told the authorities that he planned to emigrate to the United States, they accused him of exploiting the generosity of Canada.)

Peter and Tinky married and had a daughter, naming her after Anna Freud. In their small Toronto apartment, Peter finally began to receive letters from Mem. He learned of how she was managing to survive the war, at first living and working in Italy, where she was a script advisor to Rossellini and De Sica, and then, when Italy became too dangerous, moving to Switzerland with her new husband, Jean Pierre, a young Swiss architect. Every letter that Peter received from Mem was wrenching to him and it often took him a long time to answer her. When he finally did, he usually sent his writing to her, asking for her artistic judgment, which held great authority for him.

In her letters to Peter, Mem tried desperately to reestablish her connection to him. The truth is that when she left Hans, she had assumed she would be able to see him whenever she liked, never dreaming that a war would drive a wedge between their lives. She wanted so badly to come and visit him and to see her little grandchild, begging him to describe her in more detail. She hoped that when Peter saw her, she wouldn't be a disappointment to him; she was now a middle-aged woman after all.

But Mem's greatly anticipated union with Peter's new family was never to come. Peter and Tinky soon realized that they had made a mistake in trying to hold onto the emotions of childhood and their marriage broke apart.

Alone once again, Peter thought about what living in exile really meant. It meant being an outsider, never belonging, never sinking down roots. Hadn't he been living in exile all his life? As a boy, he was cut off from his mother, the center of his universe. His analysis hoped to lead him to a more grounded condition, but reality didn't cooperate. As a Jew, he was never fully accepted by society, with the result that he was driven out of the land of his birth. As a refugee, he was expelled from the country that he had fled to as a sanctuary. But all of this must have happened for a reason, a reason that he wanted and needed to understand. His confinement in Canada had exposed him to a different way of life; there he became less isolated, more connected to the sufferings of others. But there was more, he was certain of it, even though he didn't know exactly what it was. Maybe living in exile was part of what it meant to be a Jew. Assimilated as he was, this would never have occurred to him before the war, but it seemed undeniable now that he had lived with his fellow refugees behind barbed war. And maybe the constant uprooting experienced by Jews over time was key to understanding the modern condition.

He moved to New York and plunged himself into a Ph.D. program at Columbia, becoming one of the first Jewish Germanists to come up through the ranks. But it was often hard for him to concentrate, due to what he later summed up as a "defensive excitability, a sexualization of anxiety, a vacillation between self-contempt and megalomania" – feelings that no longer seemed tolerable in his free life. Suffering from an almost physical sense of rootlessness, he sought out psychoanalysis in New York, having sessions with Ernst Kris, a member of the newly transplanted Freud circle and a friend of his father's.

Eventually he married my mother, an exchange student from Germany, and had four children with her, three daughters – I am the second – and a son. Thanks to his early psychoanalysis, he was always conscious of the fact that the ambivalence that he had felt as a boy was inscribed into his life as a man. The contradictions of his identity as an assimilated Jew, a Jewish Germanist, a writer carrying the rhythms of German into English, a newly minted American constantly homesick for Austria but refusing, for many years, to return to it – the contradictions went on and on, and because he had been taught to be relentlessly honest with himself, he was never able to forget that they were there. And there were difficulties in his life as a father as well – loving, compassionate, insightful, generous, he was also prone to fits of rage that were most acute when he felt vulnerable to humiliation, and that were visited on his children, especially his son.

He stayed away from Austria for many years, but then he began making regular trips back to Vienna and Grundlsee. On one of his last trips, he took me along with him, and we visited his stately old house on the Karolinengasse, eventually making our way to the Belvedere Gardens.

"Do you remember that dream I told you about the other day?" he said to me. "The one that took place by this fountain here?"

"Of course I remember," I said to him. But he told it to me again, with a new urgency, as if he was telling it to me for the first time.

"Strange, isn't it?" he laughed when he was done, walking to the edge of the gravel path and stepping up onto the curb. "This is all I had to do!" For an instant, he became a little boy, innocent of the burden that he was carrying.

AUTHOR'S NOTE

On November 7, 1972, my father received a letter from Anna Freud. He was 52 years old and well established in life, but the letter reactivated a childhood encounter that had been formative yet never fully resolved. Anna Freud's words were simple and direct, which made her gesture towards him all the more mysterious:

> Here is the collection of your poems from the year 1930. You will be interested to see them, and I think they are really quite remarkable.

A folder of short stories and poems was included. He had given them to her during his childhood analysis. She had promised him that she would type up these works and keep them in a special file and, to his amazement, she had remained true to her word, holding on to them for 40 years. By sending him his childhood productions, she was confirming the role that she had played when he was under her care: keeper of secrets, archivist of his accomplishments, and, above all, powerful surrogate for the artist mother who had abandoned him.

As if the return of his earliest writings wasn't surprising enough, she went on to say:

> There is another question I have to ask you. When I looked for the poems I naturally found the whole file which represents your analysis in childhood, and I wonder what you would like me to do with it. Should I leave it with a covering note to be sent over to you after my death, or would you rather have me destroy it now, or leave it to be destroyed? I cannot judge whether it would

be upsetting for you to see the content, or whether you would find it merely very interesting.

Do let me know.

Yours sincerely,

Anna Freud

On December 21, after a month of debating with himself, my father finally wrote back to her:

It was a joy to get your letter with the poems (which arrived two days prior to the first public reading of my – adult – poetry to a small audience). Above all, I am deeply grateful for your offer to leave the record of my early analysis to me.

He told her that he was in the midst of studying the writings of Sigmund Freud, after which he planned to study her writings in depth. He explained that this was part of an attempt to come to terms with his own "relationship to psychoanalysis which has been dominated for too long by positive and negative sentiments."

All of this was a build-up to a demand couched in the form of a slightly apologetic request. He wanted Anna Freud's notes, and he didn't want to wait until she died: he wanted her to send them to him now.

The delayed response of Anna Freud – her reply is dated March 27, 1973 – reveals very little of what she thought about his wish. It merely outlines the action that she had decided to take:

Dear Peter,

It took me a long time to answer your letter, but I suppose this was due to my hesitation over whether it is really all right to send you the records of your childhood treatment. But by now I have resolved my doubts and am preparing the parcel for you, which will be quite a big one and which will therefore go off by surface mail. I wonder very much how you will feel about it, and whether you remember any of the details I have recorded.

And then, as if anticipating that reading through the case history will stir up old feelings of guilt or shame, she adds:

> I do not know whether the records will make it very clear, therefore I want to add that you were a very nice child, very engaging, very intelligent and very companionable.

The large parcel took its time to travel from London to Buffalo. Finally, on February 4, he announced:

> Your package arrived between Christmas and the new year, and I was so happy about it that I meant to write you immediately a long and significant letter – which, in turn, caused me to delay my answer and my thanks.

After months of fearing that the package would never come, he was able to thank her for "the most precious and most unexpected present that I have ever had the good, if undeserved, fortune to receive." He told her that he would have to work through her notes in a completely novel way because his situation was unprecedented. "I will not treat them the way one might treat some snapshots from childhood," he wrote, wanting to assure her of his seriousness. Then he embarked on a journey of memory.

I was away at college while this exchange was taking place, wrapped up in my own life. Eventually my father's search resulted in a book that contained his case history and, in addition, his own notes. It was impressionistic and scholarly at the same time. It included the drawings that he had made during his sessions and his childhood literary productions.

It was only after my father had died that I felt free to open his book. The boy that I met in its pages was very much like the father I knew – combative, affectionate, confiding, self-doubting, disarming, ambitious. Reading his book and, later, listening to the interviews he had conducted with his fellow schoolmates at the Hietzing School, I kept wondering: what had become of that boy when his analysis with Anna Freud was done and the Hietzing School was closed? How had he carried his childhood experiences and the knowledge that he had gained into a treacherous and difficult world?

Luckily, I also had access to his internment diary. When I translated this diary from German into English, it gave me insight into his adolescence and early adulthood.

"There are no facts, only interpretations," Nietzsche said. The book I have written about my father is one of many possible interpretations of his life. It's an attempt to create a cohesive narrative that's true to the inner shape of his story. All along the way, he has inspired me – his struggles, his doubts, his dreams, his fears, in an increasingly fragmented reality.

EXPLANATORY NOTES

Part I

Early Sorrow

Page 4   *"left-wing liberal, capitalist, avant-garde style"*: Peter Heller, *A Child Analysis with Anna Freud*. Trans. Salome Burkhardt and Mary Weigand. Connecticut: International Universities Press, 1990. p. xxi.

Page 4   *Red Vienna*: A term used to describe the flowering of progressive ideas that occurred in Vienna during the 1920s. Under Social Democrat mayors Jakob Reumann [1919–23] and Karl Seitz [1923–34], attempts were made to reform almost every realm of public life: education, public health, social welfare, public housing, taxation – the list goes on and on. A spirit of experimentation also manifested itself in literature, music, art, design, and architecture. Enlightened theories of human development and associated therapeutic practices, including psychoanalysis, flourished at this time. But this period that witnessed so many breakthroughs was far from tranquil. In his foreword to *Red Vienna and the Golden Age of Psychology, 1918–1938*, Rudolf Ekstein notes that "Red Vienna is an example of not merely a political party, a program of promises, but was a movement. I still have the songs of that time in my mind, which were the background of a new ethics. It was an ethics of sharing, of caring and to use the words of Adolf Adler, growing 'Gemeinschaftsgefühl.' It was in this atmosphere that psychologists were to think, and to go beyond theory to practical application and therefore, after the First World War, also came 'Schulreform,' later to be destroyed by the Fascists while they sang 'We shall go on marching until all is falling to pieces, Germany belongs to us today, and tomorrow the whole world.' In the growing political and social turmoil, unemployment, demonstrations, and the beginning of concentration camps, psychology grew. Turmoil stimulated creative thinking, a new way out, a new education. What would the conditions need to be in order for the struggles of freedom and their results not to be destroyed moving toward World War II? ... This was the Golden Age, but at the same time it seemed as if we all lived on a volcano, a human volcano ready to explode at any moment." For a detailed description of the forces at play in Vienna at this time, see Sheldon Gardner and Gwendolyn Steven, *Red Vienna and the Golden Age of Psychology, 1918–1938*. Praeger, 1992.

Page 5   *Ein Mann Sucht Seine Heimat* was published under the pseudonym
          Martin Haller. Zurich: Europa Verlag, 1936. It was one of the first novels
          about interwar Jewish exile.

Page 6   *In his memoirs: Memoirs of a Reluctant Capitalist* was published by
          Hans Heller under his adopted American name, John Heller. New York:
          Abaris Books, 1983, p. 45.

Page 8   *"She had the same eyes..."*: Käthe Leichter memoir in *Käthe Leichter:*
          Leben, Werk und Sterben Einer Österreichischen Sozialdemokratin, ed.
          Herbert Steiner. Vienna: Ibera Verlag, 1997, p. 377–9 [my translation].

Page 9   *"In Käthe Leichter's life..."*: Gerda Lerner. *Why History Matters: Life and*
          Thought. New York: Oxford University Press, 1997, p. 50–1.

Page 12   *...in a thinly fictionalized story...*: Peter Heller. "Georg. Eine Jugend
          im Wien der Zwischenkriegzeit" in *Der Junge Kanitz und Andere*
          Geschichten. Vienna: Theodor Kramer Gesellschaft, 1998 [my
          translation].

Page 18   *"I admired, worshipped, and loved..."*: *A Child Analysis with Anna Freud*,
          p. xxiii.

Visitations, Habitats

Page 23   Franz Singer (1896–1954) was an Austrian architect and designer. He
          studied at the Weimar Bauhaus and founded the Atelier Singer-Dicker
          with artist and educator Friedl Dicker.

Page 24   Adolf Loos (1870–1933) was a ground-breaking Austrian architect and
          the author of several influential works of architectural theory, including
          Ornament and Crime, his manifesto of modern architecture.

Page 29   Karl Boromäus Frank (1893–1969), also known by the pseudonyms Paul
          Hagen and Willi Mueller, was a member of the German underground
          movement against Hitler, a socialist and the author of *Will Germany*
          Crack? (1942) and *Germany After Hitler* (1944). After the war, he settled
          in the United States and became a psychoanalyst.

Page 30   Liesel Viertel, the Austrian actress Elisabeth Neumann-Viertel
          (1900–94). She appeared in numerous German films in the 1920s
          and 1930s. During the Nazi period, she worked in the United States,
          appearing as a character actor on Broadway and in Hollywood films.
          After the war, she returned to Berlin, performing in theaters there.
          She was the second wife of Berthold Viertel, director, screenwriter,
          and producer.

The Hietzing School

Page 35   *loveable* Peter Blos, "The Dolphin Keeper: Recollections." March, 1980. Erik H. and Joan Erikson Papers, Houghton Library.

Page 35   *Erik Erikson puts Mabbie first...*: Erikson's reflections on his students at the Hietzing School can be found in "The Fate of the Drives in School Compositions (1931)" in *A Way of Looking at Things*. New York: W.W. Norton & Co., 1987.

Page 38   *"I would like Anna Freud..."*: Letters quoted by Michael Burlingham, *The Last Tiffany*. New York: Atheneum, 1989, pp. 214, 215.

Page 38   *"ambassador of psychoanalysis"*: *The Last Tiffany*, p. 213.

Page 39   "Authentic Proofs of the True Kinship Between the Two Old and Honorable Families of Freud and Burlingham" by Mabbie Burlingham. Private collection.

Page 40   *Rassenkunde* or racial science, the racist pseudo-science that became part of the school curriculum during the Third Reich. One of the foundational texts was *Rassenkunde des Deutschen Volkes*, or *Racial Science of the German People*, by Hans Günther, published in 1922. In this work Günther argued for a hierarchy of races, with the "Aryan race" at its pinnacle. Hitler used the work of Günther, a Nazi Party member, to back up his program of genocide.

Page 43   August Aichorn (1878–1949), psychoanalyst, teacher, and educational reformer, who worked with children and neglected youth in Vienna. A close colleague and friend of Anna Freud's and a major figure at the Hietzing School.

Page 48   *Gymnasium*: In the Austrian school system, the term "Gymnasium" refers to the schooling that follows the mandatory nine years of elementary education. The Gymnasium years culminate in the *Matura* exam.

Page 50   *In his comments on Erikson's analysis*: Peter Heller, *The Burlingham-Rosenfeld School (Vienna 1927–1933. A Documentation)*. Unpublished manuscript with introductory essays by Erik Erikson, Günther Bittner and Rolf Goppel, Oskar Ochs, and Ernest W. Freud, and the following sections: "Teachers," "Pupils," "Founding Mothers," "Christmas Papers 1928, 1929," "Questionnaires." Private collection, p. 520.

Page 51   *Ernstl Freud, who considered Bob his best friend, remembered how he had scaled the walls...*: Ernest W. Freud, "Bob Burlingham." On the occasion of Robert Burlingham's funeral, January 30, 1970.

Page 51   *"...radiant and blossoming..."*: Quoted in *The Last Tiffany*, p. 211.

Page 51   *To her mind, he had been diverted from the path of homosexuality*: Reflecting the prejudices of her time, Anna Freud worked to steer young boys away from homosexuality, which she considered to be a misstep in their Oedipal development, a misstep that, in her opinion, could be avoided.

Lessons in Self-defense

Page 55   *...Anna Freud tells the story of a ten year-old boy who made a thrilling discovery*: for Anna Freud's discussion of her ten-year-old patient, see *The Ego and the Mechanisms of Defense* in *The Writings of Anna Freud* (Volume II). New York: International Universities Press Inc., 1966, pp. 98–100.

Page 57   *"My entire library"*: *Memoirs of a Reluctant Capitalist*, p. 61.

Page 57   *"The cable car from Grigno..."*: Quoted in *Memoirs of a Reluctant Capitalist*, p. 34.

Page 60   *"What Anna Freud describes..."*: *A Child Analysis with Anna Freud*, p. 331.

Page 62   *"There is a war"*: *A Child Analysis with Anna Freud*, p. 11.

Page 66   *He takes a train with Margot*: Margot Goldschmidt, governess to the Burlinghams.

Page 66   *"On a trip to Cannes..."*: *A Child Analysis with Anna Freud*, p. 87.

Page 67   *"Another memory comes to mind"*: *A Child Analysis with Anna Freud*, p. 323.

Page 67   *He doesn't want to admit...*: *A Child Analysis with Anna Freud*, p. 211.

The Real Berlin

Page 71   Conrad Veidt, 1893–1943, a star of early German film. Best known for his roles in *The Cabinet of Dr. Caligari*, *Different from the Others*, *Waxworks*, and *The Man Who Laughs*. Blacklisted in Germany after fleeing with his third wife, Ilona, who was Jewish. Continued to work in England and Hollywood.

Page 71   Elizabeth Bergner, 1897–1986. Highly successful Austrian Jewish actress who played in Max Reinhardt productions in Berlin and fled to London during the Nazi times, appearing in Broadway productions as well. A story drawn from her acting career (1950) eventually became the basis for *All About Eve*.

Page 71   Pola Negri, 1897–1987. Polish stage and film star who worked closely with Ernst Lubitsch and achieved worldwide fame. She signed with Paramount in 1922, becoming the first European actress to be contracted with Hollywood.

Page 71   Friedrich Wilhelm Murnau (1888–1931) was an acclaimed German director. His films included *Nosferatu* (1922) and *The Last Laugh* (1924), which introduced the prototype for the figure of the Joker.

Page 71   UFA, Universum Film Aktien Gesellschaft, a major German film company from 1917 to 1945, located in Babelsberg, outside Berlin. Before the Nazi period, UFA was home to some of the greatest filmmakers in Europe.

Page 72   Joe May, 1880–1954. Austrian director and film producer, renowned in German cinema.

Page 75 Gustav Frohlich, 1902–87. German film director and actor.

Page 75 Dita Parlo, 1908–71. German film actress who made her first appearance in *Heimkehr* (1928) and appeared in *L'Atlante* (1934) and *La Grande Illusion* (1938).

Page 78 Betty Amman, 1905–90. A German–American film actress who was best known for her role in *Asphalt* (1929).

Page 83 Albert Steinrück, 1872–1929. German stage and silent film actor who appeared in 88 films.

The Zobeltitz Plan

Page 89 *Hanns Zobeltitz was a bad novelist:* Hanns von Zobeltitz, a prolific German novelist who published under a variety of names.

Page 90 *In his case history: A Child Analysis with Anna Freud*, p. 83.

Page 90 *Engelbert Dollfuss:* Dollfuss (1892–1934), of the Christian Social Party, was promoted from Minister of Agriculture to Chancellor in 1932. On September 11, 1933, Dollfuss dissolved the Austrian Parliament and formed the Vaterlandische Front (Fatherland Front), soldifying the rule of AustroFascism. He was assassinated in the Chancellery by Nazi agents in a failed coup attempt on July 25, 1934.

Page 90 *...a patchwork of conflicting ideologies:* Looking back on this moment, Hans Heller wrote: "In the years prior to the Nazi take-over the radicalization of European, and also of Austrian life, proceeded at a rapid pace. The distinctions were as simple as the colors which stood for them: Brown for Nazism, red for Eastern Communism, pink for Western Socialism, and green for conservative home-bodies. They were all militant and aggressive." *Memoirs of a Reluctant Capitalist*, p. 64.

Page 90 *"The grotesque idea...":* A Child Analysis with Anna Freud, p. 320.

Page 91 *Wouldn't it be wonderful...:* Bob was touched by the fact that Dorothy turned to him; he reported in his diary that his conversation with Mother was "sweet." See *The Last Tiffany*, p. 218.

Page 91 *he couldn't eat his dinner:* Three years later, this same Herr Wimmer betrayed Eva Rosenfeld's husband to the Austrian police for participating in a workers' revolution and was dismissed.

Page 92 *"I really don't quite know what to say."* Anna Freud's Letters to Eva Rosenfeld, ed. Peter Heller. Madison: International Universities Press Inc., 1992, p. 152.

Page 97 *They keep trying to uncover the meaning of his dreams, like detectives tracking clues.* It's only when he comes back to the dream of the bulls as an old man that he surmises that the tangled entrails of the bull are the beginnings of a dream that is looking into itself.

Page 97 *Ostjude:* Eastern Jew. There was cultural tension between the highly assimilated Jewish population of Vienna and the unassimilated Jews who had immigrated to Vienna in large numbers from the East.

Page 106   *"Honored Ticket-holders, and Patrons!": A Child Analysis with Anna Freud*, p. 274.

Page 109   Arthur Schnitzler (1862–1931), Austrian novelist, short story writer, and dramatist.

Page 109   *"The two directions": A Child Analysis with Anna Freud*, p. 233.

Sex and Politics

Page 113   *The Tiller Girls:* a popular dance troupe established in Manchester, England, by John Tiller in 1889 that came to have branches all around the world.

Page 116   *"...prostitute and mother": A Child Analysis with Anna Freud*, p. 239.

Page 116   *"Hours, long hours, must I wait":* "A Life" in *A Child Analysis with Anna Freud*, p. 275.

Page 117   *Schwarzwaldschule:* Founded by Eugenie Schwarzwald, educational reformer and philanthropist, in 1911. The first school in Vienna to prepare female students for university entrance. Mem had attended this school, which had an array of highly talented and renowned teachers. Robert Musil based the character of Diotima in *A Man Without Qualities* on Eugenie Schwarzwald.

Page 117   *"We Must Study": A Child Analysis with Anna Freud*, pp. 261–4.

Page 118   *"...the white knee-socks of the Nazi party...":* In the introduction to his internment diary, Peter Heller notes that the school body of the Realgymnasium was highly politicized. While his parents were Social Democrats, he remembers that others "came into class under the banner of the Heimwehr and the Christian Socialists; and one ever more powerful group came with the swastika, or, if this was forbidden, wearing the recognized clothing style of white knee socks" (my translation).

Page 120   *Nazi posters and pamphlets:* American psychoanalyst Esther Menaker writes about the way in which Nazism was already making its presence felt in Vienna in 1930: "Within the first week after our arrival in Vienna, we witnessed a torchlight parade of Nazi youths, militantly chanting their nationalistic party songs as they goose-stepped along the Ringstrasse. The next morning the streets were littered with small paper swastikas like the confetti that is used to celebrate happy occasions. The halls of the university were filled with Nazi announcements with their inflammatory propaganda. There were frequent student riots at the university – especially in the medical school – in which Jewish students were beaten up and sometimes seriously injured. The atmosphere at the university was tense and potentially explosive. As we gradually grew accustomed to this scene, we were generally able to detect the increase of tension that invariably preceded a riot, and on those days we did not attend classes. In the light of the Nazi rise to power in Germany, and subsequently in

Austria, the murder of six million Jews and the horror of the concentration camps, and the destruction of almost all of Europe in the Second
World War, these events seem trivial. Yet they were among the signs that
foreshadowed the coming catastrophe, the portent of which no one in
1930 could fully believe." Esther Menaker, *Appointment in Vienna*. New
York: St. Martin's Press, 1989, p. 45.

Page 123   *The Social Democrats are fighting out of the Karl-Marx-Hof:* built
between 1927 and 1929, the Karl-Marx-Hof was the largest of a series
of Höfe (courts) designed to provide low-income housing for workers.
During the civil war of 1934, the Karl-Marx-Hof became the center of
Social Democratic opposition to government forces and rightist militias
in Vienna. According to official reports of the times, 102 government
casualties and 193 Social Democrat casualties resulted from the civil war
of 1934; however, the Social Democrats claimed a loss of 1500. Dollfuss
banned the Social Democrats in the wake of this conflict, eliminating
what one historian has described as "the last mass movement capable of
saving the land from the Nazis."

Page 133   *What about what's happening here?* The Austro-Fascism of the 1930s
was fundamentally different from German National Socialism insofar as
the former was based on the Catholic idea of a corporative state and the
latter was predicated on the sacredness of the German race. However,
Hitler's determination to absorb Austria into Germany was no secret to
anyone; in fact, it was stated openly in *Mein Kampf*. Nazi sabotage and
interference in Austrian affairs were unrelenting.

Graduation

Page 136   *...the plebiscite that's happening on Sunday:* On March 9, 1938,
Schuschnigg called a plebiscite to decide whether Austria wanted to
be annexed to Germany, throwing Hitler into a fury. Pressured by
Hitler into calling off the plebiscite, Schuschnigg resigned. On March
12, German troops marched into Austria. On April 10, a propaganda
referendum was called on the Anschluss [annexation] with Germany.
By official accounts, 99.73 percent of Austrians voted in favor. The
voting was not confidential but public. The ranks of those who were not
allowed to vote included communists, socialists, and citizens of Jewish
or Gypsy origins, roughly 8 percent of the Austrian population.

Page 137   *The Chancellor!* Kurt Alois Josef Johann Schuschnigg (1897–1977).

Page 140   *The Gymnasium on the Kleine Sperlgasse:* Between 1941 and 1943, this
same school was used as a collection place for 45,000 Jews who were
subsequently deported to the camps.

Part 2

Experiments in Living

Page 160   Erich Heller (1911–1990) was born in then Bohemia (later
Czechoslovakia) and emigrated to England in 1939. He became a British
subject in 1947 and eventually emigrated to the United States. An eminent
figure in the field of German literature and philosophy, his best-known
work was *The Disinherited Mind*.

Kindly Come Along with Me

Page 169   *"...B category..."*: According to historian Ronald Stent, "the government
had decided on supplementing the information which they already had
in Home Office files and police and M15 records, by individual examinations of every German and Austrian, male and female, over the age
of 16. The work was to be undertaken by local tribunals under legally
experienced chairmen. These tribunals were asked to grade aliens into
three categories. 'Security' was the decisive criterion:
Class 'A': Aliens about whose loyalty and reliability the tribunals had
doubts and who might constitute a potential security risk. They were to
be arrested on the spot for immediate internment.
Class 'B': Aliens about whose loyalty the tribunals were not absolutely
certain and who for one reason or the other should be kept under a form
of supervision. They were left at liberty but subject to certain restrictions. They were not allowed to move further than five miles from their
place of residence without prior police permission nor to be in possession of such articles as cameras, maps, field glasses, arms, etc.
Class 'C': All those about whom the tribunals were satisfied. They were
free from restrictions other than those which had been applied to them in
peacetime."
Ronald Stent, *A Bespattered Page? The Internment of 'His Majesty's most
Loyal Aliens.'* London: Andre Deutsch Limited, 1980, pp. 35–6.

The Isle of Man

Page 190   Arthur Sullivan (1842–1900), British composer best known for his 14
operatic collaborations with dramatist W.S. Gilbert.

Sea Legs

Page 195   *The Arandora Star:* "The *S.S. Arandora Star* was a luxury cruise ship converted for troops. It was destined for Canada when, on July 2, 1940, it was torpedoed by a German submarine. Of the 805 drowned, 452 were Italian civilians and 151 were 'Category A' and 'Category B' internees, including Jewish refugees. The victims included many prominent anti-fascists who had escaped from Germany, Austria, and Italy. Horrifying stories of ineptitude on the part of the British crew and panic among the internees shocked the public. One survivor recalled, 'The stern of the ship was high in the air, the men were fighting over lifeboats, of which not all could be put afloat. I found a beam, sprang after it into the sea and held fast ... Many lifeboats were lost. Bodies were washed away by the waves. Old people drowned almost without exception." *"Enemy Aliens:" The Internment of Jewish Refugees in Canada, 1940–1943* (Vancouver Holocaust Education Centre, 2012).

The New World

Page 203   *Camp L* was located outside Quebec City.

Page 212   Captain Godfrey Barrass, a British officer who had accompanied the refugees from England and who then served as an intelligence officer in Canada.

Page 220   Lord Marley, Vice Chairman of the Refugee Committee of the British Parliament.

Page 221   *Human-All-Too-Human?: Human, All Too Human,* by Friedrich Nietzsche.

Page 231   *"This camp consists..."* Quoted by Erich Koch, *Deemed Suspect.* Toronto, Methuen, 1980, pp. 124, 125.

Page 231   *Camp N* was located in Sherbrooke, Quebec.

Camp N

Page 237   *Saul Hayes* (1906–80). National Executive Director of the United Jewish Refugee War Relief Association in Montreal. Executive Vice President of the Jewish Congress until his retirement in 1974.

SOURCES

Blos, Peter. "The Dolphin Keeper: Recollections." March, 1980. Erik H. and Joan Erikson Papers, Houghton Library.

Blos, Peter. Transcript of tape-recorded interview with Robert Stewart, New York City, May 22, 1966. Private collection.

Burlingham, Dorothy to Peter Heller. Letter about the Hietzing School. May 9, 1974. Private collection.

Burlingham, Elizabeth to Peter Heller. Letter containing description of experiences at Hietzing School. September 24, 1982. Private collection.

Burlingham, Michael John. *The Last Tiffany: A Biography of Dorothy Tiffany Burlingham*. New York: Atheneum, 1989.

Danto, Elizabeth Ann and Alexandra Steiner Strauss, ed. *Freud/Tiffany: Anna Freud, Dorothy Tiffany Burlingham and 'The Best Possible School.'* New York: Routledge, 2019.

Erikson, Erik. "The Fate of the Drives in School Compositions (1931)" in *A Way of Looking at Things*. New York: W.W. Norton & Co., 1987.

Freud, Anna. *The Ego and the Mechanisms of Defense. Writings of Anna Freud,* Volume II. New York: International Universities Press, 1966.

Freud, Ernest W. "Bob Burlingham." On the occasion of Robert Burlingham's funeral, January 30, 1970. Private collection.

Freud, Ernest W. "Die Freuds und die Burlinghams in der Berggasse: Persönliche Erringerungen." Sigmund Freud House Bulletin. Vol. 11/No. 1. Summer 1987.

Friedman, Lawrence. *Identity's Architect: A Biography of Erik H. Erikson*. New York: Scribner, 1999.

Gillman, Peter. *Collar the Lot: How Britain Expelled its Wartime Refugees*. London: Quartet Books Ltd, 1981.

Heller, Hans. *Zwischen Zwei Welten: Errinerungen, Dokumente, Prosa, Bilder*. 1 Auflage 1985. Verlag: Olivara – Libri, A-4600 Wels. Druck: Karinthia, Klagenfurt.

Heller, John. *Memoirs of a Reluctant Capitalist*. New York: Abaris Books, Inc., 1983. (Note: Hans Heller took the name John when he went to the U.S.)

Heller, Peter. *Eine Kinderanalyse bei Anna Freud (1929–1932)*, with a commentary by Günther Bittner. Wurzburg: Königshausen & Neuman, 1983.

Sources

Heller, Peter. "Ambivalence and Nostalgia." A lecture given at the Austrian Literary Society, 1988.

Heller, Peter. *A Child Analysis with Anna Freud*. Trans. by Salome Burkhardt and Mary Weigand. Madison, CT: International Universities Press, Inc., 1990.

Heller, Peter, ed. *Anna Freud's Letters to Eva Rosenfeld*. International Universities Press Inc., 1992.

Heller, Peter. *The Burlingham-Rosenfeld School (Vienna 1927–1933). A Documentation*. Unpublished manuscript with introductory essays by Erik Erikson, Günther Bittner and Rolf Goppel, Oskar Ochs, and Ernest W. Freud, and the following sections: "Teachers," "Pupils," "Founding Mothers," "Christmas Papers 1928, 1929," "Questionnaires." Private collection.

Heller, Peter. "Der Kopf des Bandwurms: Anna Freud's 'Nachtrag zu Peter's Analyse.'" *Weiss und Lang. Psychoanalyse Heute und vor 70 Jahre*. 1996.

Heller, Peter. *Die Internierung der Emigranten 1940. (Berichte und Tagebucher am britischen und kanadischen Gefangenlagern.)* Unpublished diary of Canadian internment, with reflections and postscript. Peter Heller Archive, Leo Beck Institute, New York

Heller, Peter. Transcript of unpublished interview with Frau Mag. Ingrid Scholz-Strasser, 1992. Private collection.

Heller, Peter. "Reflections on a Child Analysis with Anna Freud and an Adult Analysis with Ernst Kris." *Journal of the American Academy of Psychoanalysis* 1992; 20(1), 48–74.

Heller, Peter. "Georg. Ein Jugend im Wien der Zwischenkriegzeit" in *Der Junge Kanitz und Andere Geschichten*. Wien: Theodor Kramer Gesellschaft, 1998.

Heller, Peter. Letter to Elizabeth Young-Bruehl with thoughts on her biography of Anna Freud. December 11, 1987. Private collection.

Heller, Peter with Hans Heller. Taped interview on life in Vienna in the 1920s and early 1930s, 1974. Private collection.

Heller, Peter with Hans Heller. Taped interview on life in Grundlsee, 1974. Private collection.

Heller, Peter with Elizabeth Jonas. Taped interview, June 16, 1975. Private collection.

Heller, Peter with Dorothy Burlingham. Transcript of taped interview at Maresfield Gardens, June 13, 1975. Private collection.

Heller, Peter. Letter to Thesi Bergman. January 1971. Private collection.

Heller, Peter with Thesi Bergman. Taped interview, 1976. Private collection.

Heller, Peter with Liesel Viertel. Taped interview, 1980. Private collection.

Heller, Peter with Paul Kay. Taped interview titled "Reminiscences of an Analysis with Anna Freud 1929–32," 1984. Private collection.

Heller, Peter with Ernest Freud. Taped interview on the Hietzing School at the Freud Museum, London, 1997. Private collection.

Heller, Peter with Ernest Freud. Taped interview, 1998. Private collection.

Heller, Peter. Taped interview with Victor Ross on internment (undated). Private collection.

Sources

Heller, Peter. Taped reading of unpublished 1940–1 journals of Margarete Steiner, undated. Private collection.

Heller, Peter. Taped reading of unpublished 1960 journal of Margarete Steiner, undated. Private collection.

Heller, Peter. Correspondence with Margarete Steiner (Mem), dating from mid-1940s to her death in 1961. Private collection.

Heller, Vivian. Taped interview with Erich Koch, fellow internee of Peter Heller. Private collection.

Koch, Eric. *I Remember the Location Exactly.* Ontario: Mosaic Press, 2006.

Koch Eric. *Deemed Suspect: A Wartime Blunder.* Toronto: Methuen, 1980.

Leichter, Käthe. "Universität" in *Leben, Werk und Sterben Einer Österreichischen Sozialdemokratin.* Ed. Herbert Steiner. Vienna: Ibera & Molden Verlag, 1997. Account of her association with Margarete Steiner (Mem) on pp. 377–9.

Midgley, Nick. "The 'Matchbox School' (1927–1932): Anna Freud and the Idea of a 'Psychoanalytically Informed Education.'" *Journal of Child Psychotherapy* 2008; 34(1), 23–42.

Midgley, Nick. "Peter Heller's *A Child Analysis with Anna Freud:* The Significance of the Case for the History of Child Analysis." *Journal of the American Psychoanalytic Association* (JAPA), March 16, 2012.

Midgley, Nick. *Reading Anna Freud.* London: Routledge, 2013.

Rosenfeld, Eva. *Recollected in Tranquility.* Unpublished memoir. Private collection.

Steiner, Margarete (Mem). "Resumé of My Activities as a Film-Writer." Undated. Private collection.

Stent, Ronald. *A Bespattered Page? The Internment of 'His Majesty's most Loyal Enemy Aliens.'* London: André Deutsch Limited, 1980.

Traven, B. *The Death Ship: The Story of an American Sailor.* New York: Lawrence Hill Books, 1991. (Originally published in German as *Das Totenschiff,* 1926.)

Die Matura: Jährliche Erschiende Satyrische Kampfschrift der Arbiturientenschaft. Wien 1938. Public school publication that refers to Matura Year in Vienna, 1938. Private collection.

"Enemy Aliens:" The Internment of Jewish Refugees in Canada, 1940–1943. Vancouver Holocaust Education Centre, 2012. Includes video recordings of Erich Koch's descriptions of camp life.

INDEX

antisemitism 16, 17, 23, 48, 64, 83, 86–7, 110,
    118, 119, 127, 133, 135–6, 145
    see also Nazis
Arandora Star 195, 197–8, 214, 262n
Aryans
    Aryanization of factory 141
    division of internees by race 230–2
    Mabbie Burlingham's treatise 39, 40
    see also Nazis
Austria
    economic collapse 63, 90
    fleeing 67, 68, 145–9
    German occupation 137–49
    political ideology 90, 259n, 261n
    revisited after the war 249
    rise of Fascism 23, 63, 90, 110, 118, 120, 133,
        260–1n
    rivalry with Germany 61
Baer, Basti 22–3, 44–5
Baer, Sigurd 44–8, 55–6, 60, 61–2
Bergman, Thesi (nursemaid) 11, 32, 67, 89, 94–5,
    104–6, 117, 141–2
Blos, Peter 22, 23, 35, 93
books
    burning 110, 138
    censored 148
    in childhood 10, 11, 67–8, 108, 109
    importance to Hans 57, 109, 138, 158
    in internment 164, 173, 191, 205, 206,
        209–10, 242
Burlingham, Dorothy 18, 23, 39, 40, 49, 92, 93, 157
Burlingham family 18, 24–5, 35, 38, 39–40, 43,
    91, 93, 100, 101, 156
Burlingham, Mabbie 18, 35–41, 43, 44, 93
Burlingham, Robert ("Bob") 18, 35, 38, 49–52,
    93, 101
Burlingham, Tinky 18, 24–6, 93, 100–1, 118,
    155–7, 229, 236, 243–5

Cambridge 160–5
Cambridgers in internment 165–6, 167, 170, 171,
    197, 198, 235
Camp Father of internees 172, 184, 185
Canada 203–45
    anticipation of 181, 184, 185, 188, 198–9
    Camp A 230–2
    Camp L 203–32
    Camp N 233–49
categorization of "enemy aliens" 169, 185, 193,
    225, 230, 262n
committees
    of internees 167, 205, 207
    Refugee Committees 220–1, 230, 237–8
communists/communism 29, 77, 80–1, 84, 138
The Death Ship (book by B. Traven) 67–8, 148, 149
democracy 197, 208
Dollfuss, Engelbert 90, 122, 123, 259n, 261n
dreams
    Anna Freud's analysis 3–4, 11, 55–6, 60, 63,
        65–6, 67–8, 94, 96–7, 109–10, 115–16
    Belvedere Gardens 3, 13, 249
    Peter's understanding 60–1, 63, 259n
    prophetic 67, 68, 149
    Sigurd throwing a ball 55–6, 60–1
    two directions 109–10
The Ego and the Mechanisms of Defense 55
England 153–78
Erikson, Erik (Homburger) 21–3, 35–7, 38, 40,
    41–2, 45–53, 93
escape attempts from internment 206, 232, 241–2
Ettrick 192–201
Fascism *see* Nazis
Fellerer, Max 6, 27, 28, 31, 105–6
Frank, Karl 29–31, 79–82, 95–6, 106, 108–9, 256n
Freud, Anna
    analyzing dreams 3–4, 11, 55–6, 60, 63, 65–6,
        67–8, 94, 96–7, 109–10, 115–16

Index

attitude to Mem 12, 14
Hietzing School 16–17, 18–19
meeting Peter in London 156
questioned by Gestapo 142
relationships with Dorothy and Eva 18–19
sending files to Peter 251–3
Freud, Ernstl (previously E. Halberstadt) 17, 21, 35, 51, 100
Freud family 39–40
Freud, Sigmund 10, 64, 108, 142
German POWs 193, 194, 195, 201, 209, 212–14
"The Great Relapse" 94
Grundlsee vacations 27–32, 93, 134
gymnasium education 117–18, 121–2, 135–6, 139, 140, 148–9
Halsman case 63–4
Hayes, Saul 237, 238, 263n
Heller Candy factory 4, 107–8, 140–1
Heller, Erich 160, 161, 162, 228, 261n
Heller, Hans 4–7, 14–15
    end of marriage to Mem 6–7, 15, 69–70
    in England 154, 155, 156–7
    relationship with Inge 16, 23, 106, 141, 143, 144, 154, 158
    relationship with Peter 23, 32, 57–8, 97–8, 108, 133, 134, 136, 143, 155, 228–9
    writing 57–8
Heller, Inge Schön 16, 23, 94, 106, 111, 133, 141, 143–4, 154, 158
Heller, Margaret (Mem) see Steiner, Margaret
Hietzing School 16–19, 21–3, 32–3, 35–54, 86, 91–4, 117
homosexuality 51, 53, 65, 66, 89, 257n
House Father of internees 187–8, 212, 213, 214, 224
internee status versus POW 201, 209, 212–14, 226
internment
    Canada 201–45
    England 163–78
    Isle of Man 179–92
    voyage to Canada 193–201
Iona, Elizabeth 40–4, 47
Isle of Man 179–92
Italian trip 123–4
Kohn, Hans Werner (internee) 170, 203, 204, 207, 208–10, 211, 214, 215–19, 223, 226–7, 234, 235, 238–9, 242–3
Leichter, Käthe 7–9, 69, 82
letters to internees 181, 227–9, 243–4
Lingen, Count von (internee) 196–7, 216, 217, 221, 224, 230

Liverpool 158–60, 170–2, 192
London 153–7
Marley, Lord 220–2
"Matura" exam 117, 133, 135, 139, 145, 149
'Mem' see Steiner, Margaret
"missing sexual scene" 95, 98–100
Muschi see Rosenfeld, Eva
Nazis
    German occupied Austria 138–41, 145, 148–9
    internees 201, 208–9, 221–2, 227, 230–1
    rise of Fascism in Austria 23, 63, 90, 110, 118, 120, 133, 260–1n
    rise in Germany 72, 77, 84, 110
    schoolboys 118, 119, 135–6, 260n
Nietzsche, Friedrich 10, 129–30, 205, 253
Oedipal interpretations 26, 37, 42, 46, 50, 63, 64
Opalski, Victor 143–5
Paris 129, 131, 145–6, 147, 153
Parisier, Reinhard 192, 196–7, 200, 203–4, 207, 208, 209, 212, 214, 216–18, 222–3, 225, 228, 232, 234–5, 238, 239–40
parties 24, 119–21
pedagogy on psychoanalytic principles 17, 23, 50
physical labor, attitudes to 198–9, 213
piano playing 32, 101, 154–5, 156–7, 158, 159, 161, 162, 209, 210, 215, 216
poetry/poetic imagination 25, 68, 102, 116–17, 159, 160, 243, 251, 252
"Popular University" in camps 207, 208, 221, 239
prophecy 161–2
psychoanalytic childhood environment
    Hietzing School 16–19, 21–3, 32–3, 35–54, 86, 91–4, 117
    ideals 17, 23
    legacy for Peter 61
racial issues 39, 40, 208–9, 230–1
    see also antisemitism
Red Vienna 4, 23, 255n
Refugee Committees 220–1, 230, 237–8
refugee status 155, 159, 160, 163, 164, 169, 225, 231
Rosenfeld, Eva ("Muschi") 16, 17–18, 23, 91–2
Rosenfeld, Victor ("Vicki" later V. Ross) 17, 21, 24, 35, 91–2, 162, 166–8, 170, 184, 213, 222
schools
    Evangelical Elementary School 16
    gymnasium for Jewish boys 139, 140, 145, 148–9
    Hietzing School 16–19, 21–3, 32–3, 35–54, 86, 91–4, 117
    Realgymnasium 117–18, 121–2, 135–6, 139, 145

Index

statelessness 67–8
Steiner, Margaret ("Mem") 5–9, 12–14
    Anna's disapproval 12, 14
    attitude to Anna 14, 61
    desire to bring Peter to Berlin 85–7
    Grundlsee house vacation 27–32
    illness 94–5
    influence over Peter 179
    life in Berlin 69–87
    life in the war 243, 247
    miscarriage 6, 69
    relationship with Hans 5–7, 15, 69–70
    relationship with Käthe Leichter 7–9
    relationship with Peter 7, 9, 14, 27–8, 31,
        58–60, 70, 94, 102–3, 111–15, 131–3, 247–8
stories
    Hietzing School children's writing 36–7, 41–2,
        45–7, 49–50
    Mem telling to Peter 29, 58–60, 102
    Peter fictionalizing his relationship with Tinky
        156–7
    Peter remembering childhood/youth 12–14,
        119–21
    Peter writing in childhood 12, 52–3, 97
    telling versus writing 58, 60
    see also writing
Sylvia (early girlfriend) 119, 120, 121, 124–32,
    140

Taebricht (House Father) 212, 213, 214, 224
Thesi *see* Bergman, Thesi
trains and stations 13, 66–7, 111, 112, 129–30,
    132–3, 146–9, 154–5, 233–4
UFA (Universum Film Aktien Gesellschaft)
    71–86
Vienna 3–68, 89–149
war
    influence on Peter's childhood 62–3
    see also internment
Werner *see* Kohn, Hans Werner
Wolf, Tommi 68, 145–9, 153, 173
workers' strike 122–3
writing
    analysis of children's compositions 36–7,
        41–2, 45–7, 49–51, 52–3
    digestion comparison 199
    Hans 57–8, 59
    importance to Peter 54, 166–7, 176, 177–8,
        183, 184–5, 188–90, 199, 243
    literature versus sport 56
    Peter's early ambitions 56, 60
    versus oral storytelling 58, 60
    see also stories
Zobeltitz plan 89–91, 259n